INFORMATION TECHNOLOGY
A Revolutionary Change

INFORMATION TECHNOLOGY
A Revolutionary Change
(In 9 Volumes)

Volume 6
(Network Revolution: Challenges and Opportunities)

Editor
RAMESH CHANDRA
Vice-Chancellor, Bundelkhand University, Jhansi (U.P.)

KALPAZ PUBLICATIONS
DELHI–110052

INFORMATION TECHNOLOGY: A REVOLUTIONARY CHANGE

(Information Technology)

Rs. 8000 (Set)
Rs. 900 (Each Volume)

ISBN: 81-7835-201-X (Set)
ISBN: 81-7835-225-7 (Vol. 6)

Published in 2003 in India by
Kalpaz Publications
C–30, Satyawati Nagar
Delhi–110052
E-mail: kalpaz@hotmail.com

Laser Typesetting at: Varsha Graphics, Delhi
Printed at: Mehra Offset Printers, New Delhi

Contents

Preface

The network technologies allow remote, virtual collaboration in ways that were not possible just a few years ago. They offer unique opportunity to streamline the delivery of government services, enhance communication with its citizenry, and serve as a catalyst for empowering citizens to interact with government. Internet, the network of networks, is uniquely decentralized, global, abundant, inexpensive, interactive and user-controlled. It provides immediate access to information from around the world. With simple e-mail, it is as easy and inexpensive to send a message to another continent as to the building across the street. Search engines on the World Wide Web list local and foreign sites without distinction.

The networks provide individuals and informal organizations the ability to communicate inexpensively. From their virtual platforms, individuals and organizations are publishing newsletters, advertisements, voters guides and other election-related materials; creating dynamic forums that support issue-based organizing, interactive discussions, and political advocacy; and registering voters. A connection to the net can increase access to information in less-developed countries by putting within easy reach one of the world's great repositories of information, much of it free and continuously updated, and by making that information more easily manageable and transferable. Such benefits do not depend on a large number of persons having the means to purchase their own equipment and Internet accounts.

In light of the networks vast potential for empowering people to exercise the right to free expression, some have argued that governments have an affirmative obligation to facilitate Internet access for all segments of the population on terms of nondiscrimination. On-line communications are particularly susceptible to unauthorized scrutiny. Encryption technology is needed to ensure that individuals and groups may communicate without fear of eavesdropping.

The net has the potential to be a tremendous force for development by providing quick and inexpensive information, by encouraging discussion rather than violence, and by empowering citizens, to cite but a few examples. But this potential can be realized only if it becomes a truly global effort. Policy makers must make every effort to ensure that internationally guaranteed rights to free expression are extended to on-line communication and call for the repeal of censorship legislation. Without such commitments, individuals face the danger of seeing their rights eroded by the very technologies they are embracing.

Editor

Chapter 1
Global Information Development Strategies

The first phase of an emerging country's economic growth is typically based on providing low-cost labour to developed countries. Asian Less Developed Countries (LDCs) have in this way provided international companies with the opportunity to cut the costs of labour-intensive products, which has particularly appealed to the highly competitive electronics industry. Many electronics companies from the United States, Europe, and Japan relocated their labour-intensive electronics assembly operations to the LDCs of Asia starting in the late 1960s. Korea, Taiwan, Hong Kong, Singapore, and Malaysia were early beneficiaries of such labour strategies. For example, in the late 1960s, Sylvania moved low-end stereo production to Hong Kong and Singapore; in the 1970s, Intel and Motorola set up low-cost semiconductor assembly facilities in Malaysia; in the 1980s, Philips began production of colour TVs in Taiwan, and Apple began producing its computers in Singapore. Most major electronics companies have multiple operations in Asia, and most of them already have operations in China.

On the basis of the success and rapid expansion of their labour-intensive industries, in the past 20 to 30 years Korea, Taiwan, Hong Kong, Singapore, and Malaysia have all experienced significant increases in wages, living standards, and numbers of citizens who can be termed "middle class." Their successes in turn have made them less competitive in the low-cost labour market. Today, many of the companies formerly involved in labour-intensive activities in these countries are moving these operations to LDCs such as Indonesia, Thailand, Vietnam, and the Philippines to keep labour costs competitive and to gain access to new markets and revenues.

China has been the biggest beneficiary of this migration of lower-wage jobs within Asia. By June 1996, China had registered some 280,000 foreign firms with paid-in capital of approximately $155 billion that provided 17 million jobs. In 1997, some factory wages for computer assembly in China were as low as $65 a month for 72-hour work weeks.

Korea and Taiwan have located business subsidiaries in China or the countries of Southeast Asia; Hong Kong and Singapore have made a business of assisting foreign enterprises to set up new low-cost labour arrangements in neighbouring LDCs. Thus, while their own abilities to offer low-cost labour have declined, Asian NIEs are still involved in the low-cost labour market in ways that are attractive to Western companies. Summarized below are some of the means by which Asian NIEs have taken and are continuing to take advantage of low-cost labour to improve their economic status.

Korea: Building the Strength of the Chaebols

Korea is unique among the countries discussed in this report in that early on, several of its own industrial companies were the biggest corporate beneficiaries of the country's plentiful, inexpensive labour. Taking advantage of government-subsidized loans and tax breaks, Korea's chaebols (vertically integrated, family-owned industrial conglomerates) capitalized on the country's low wages (and licensing of foreign technologies, etc.) to mass-produce competitively priced light industrial and consumer exports; as a result, both the chaebols and the Korean economy grew very rapidly. Within the past decade or so, Korea's main chaebols have moved beyond their own labour markets to establish electronics and other assembly facilities in Hong Kong and China, Malaysia, Vietnam, and other parts of the world-not only to take advantage of cheaper labour and new market access, but also to establish a global presence.

Taiwan: Importing Labour and Investing Overseas

Following extraordinary successes in manufacturing and assembly endeavours, rising wages in Taiwan began to threaten the competitiveness of its electronics and other products. The government passed a law allowing firms to bring in workers from outside the country for up to two years, and by 1996, nearly 25 percent of Taiwan's manufacturing workforce was foreign. The majority of foreign labourers came from the Philippines, which offered a well-educated, hard-working, English-speaking workforce. In addition, Taiwanese firms began transferring labour-intensive production to such countries as the Philippines and China. Since so many of Taiwan's foreign workers came from the Philippines, building facilities in that country was ideal; the facilities could then hire repatriated workers who had already worked two years in Taiwanese factories.

Even though many Taiwanese firms have been eager to locate operations in China, government authorities have encouraged firms to balance political risks by investing elsewhere as well. The uncertainty created by the transfer of Hong Kong to China on July 1, 1997, caused the Taiwanese government to prohibit large-scale infrastructure investments in mainland China for dams, power plants, airports, roads, and ports. Such projects are typically capital-intensive and subject to political intervention. Electronics and related investments are less problematic; however, the government limits investments in any mainland Chinese project to a maximum of $50 million. With its proposed free-trade area, Okinawa may soon become a beneficiary of Taiwanese investment.

Hong Kong: Partnering with China

Although its economy was once synonymous with low-cost assembly, Hong Kong began responding in the late 1980s to the pressures of escalating wages, limited resources, and global competition by establishing manufacturing partnerships with Chinese companies. Both the real and the nominal growth of Hong Kong's industrial base declined 8 to 10 percent annually between 1988 and 1991 as operations moved across the border to take advantage of cheaper labour and land costs in China's Guangdong province. The Shenzhen special economic zone there allowed Hong Kong-based companies to supply parts and materials duty-free to Chinese companies, use their factories and workers to make products, then ship finished products duty-free back to Hong Kong for re-export to world markets. Between 1982 and 1994, Hong Kong's manufacturing workforce nearly halved its contribution to the GDP, from 20 percent to under 12 percent. In spite of Hong Kong's decline in manufacturing, total employment increased during this period from 2.4 to 2.9 million, and per capita GDP increased 21 percent as displaced workers continued to provide highly valued services such as product design, parts procurement, production coordination, and product marketing and shipping.

Singapore: Promoting Regional Cooperation

In 1960, Singapore's GDP was S$2.1 billion; in 1995, it was S$34.5 billion. In the same period, manufacturing's share of GDP rose from 18 percent to 27 percent, while the contribution of electronics to manufacturing output rose from under 10 percent to over 50 percent. Greater economic prosperity and full employment led to rising wages; in response to this situation as well as to its limited labour, land, and natural resources, Singapore has been aggressive in moving labour-intensive operations offshore. The government encourages both domestic and foreign companies to shift production and marketing operations to neighbouring countries where costs are lower while maintaining high-level management and administrative functions in Singapore.

Singapore's experience with Japanese audio equipment maker Aiwa exemplifies the country's movement away from simple, low-cost assembly work to higher-value-added phases of production. Aiwa, which by March 1997 had moved 90 percent of its production outside Japan, relocated its largest Asian production facility from Singapore to Indonesia, but at the same time established its regional centre for planning and research in Singapore.

Singapore links its domestic economy to regional outreach activity primarily in the form of trade "triangles" and industrial parks. Goh Chok Tong, Singapore's first deputy prime minister, created the first economic triangle for regional development in Southeast Asia in 1989. Under the original "SIJORI" triangle plan, the Malaysian State of Johor (next to Singapore) and the Indonesian province of Riau were to provide the land and low-cost labour for industry while Singapore provided technology and capital. Results have been mixed. While Singapore did expand its low-cost labour pool, Riau has become a tourist resort, and the State of Johor is now trying to improve its economic base by attracting technology, capital, and labour-intensive business away from Singapore. To facilitate exporting labour-intensive operations while keeping the administrative functions of multinational companies (MNCs), Singapore has built Southeast Asia's most complex and advanced infrastructure (airports, ports, transportation, power, telecommunications, human resources, finance, living conditions, tax system, etc.). Despite this effort, ongoing cost pressures have continued to erode Singapore's image as an attractive business centre. Singapore is now helping firms develop overall low-cost strategies by building high-tech industrial parks in China, Vietnam, and India, with varying degrees of success. Increasing the number of low-wage jobs provided the initial stimulus for Asian economic growth, but expansion in manufacturing output tended to occur primarily as a result of increasing capital input or numbers of workers. As capital inputs became less cost-effective and employment levels topped out (despite labour imports to fill shortfalls in unskilled workers), productivity rates began to level off and even decline. To ensure their continued economic competitiveness, the Asian NIEs have committed to further improving their civil and transportation infrastructures, legislative and tax structures, and educational institutions, and especially their advanced technology and research capabilities as part of long-range plans to achieve first-world economic status.

Upgrading Technology and Related Capabilities and Infrastructures Most of the emerging economies of Asia have based the second phase of their economic development strategies on upgrading their technology capabilities and related infrastructures. The addition of technology allows industries to increase the value added to products and services and increase their contribution to society. While Asian NIEs are moving away from low-skill, low-cost jobs, they are simultaneously working intently to develop domestic technology capabilities, building on their earlier successes in contract labour businesses. Three common aspects of Asia's technology-building strategy are building research and education infrastructures focused on science and technology; targeting critical advanced technologies and products for development; and attracting (and keeping) foreign technology leaders and state-of-the-art technologies. One approach practiced by all the countries covered in this study combines all three of the above: building advanced science and technology (S&T) parks.

Another common approach in this stage is modernizing and improving national education levels, especially in science and technology. Education has a historically high social value in many Asian cultures, but it is also a developmental imperative. The goals are clearly to prepare the workforces of tomorrow and to support continued economic development, although the particulars vary greatly from country to country. Korea's literacy rate is now one of the world's highest, about 95 percent, and the country is building impressive advanced research capabilities within its public and private universities (many are industry-funded), with a new emphasis on improving critical thinking and interdisciplinary cooperation to better support innovative capabilities.

China's literacy rate, narrowly defined as only 4.5 years of education, still is only about 80 percent. The country is struggling with resource allocation trade-offs between educating the masses broadly or educating a more elite group to meet the country's advanced economic requirements. Malaysia is building up both basic and advanced literacy levels and also has a unique program within its "Vision 2020" plan to instill in workers a work ethic that supports greater productivity as well as to train personnel in specific high-tech skills industry requires.

Building National Research Infrastructures Korea Government-supported research institutes (GRIs) have been set up throughout Asia. Korea has used GRIs effectively to prime the pump for its technological developments. The Korea Institute of Science and Technology (KIST), organized in 1966, was that country's first multidisciplinary industrial research organization. It has focused on basic problems relating to technology transfer. In 1971, the Korea Advanced Institute for Science was established to provide postgraduate education in science and engineering. The Electronics and Telecommunication Research Institute, one of Korea's leading GRIs, has evolved since 1976 out of a series of research organizations associated with different government ministries and is now affiliated with the Ministry of Information and Communications. It is recognized as the top information technology research institute in Korea and is a world leader in such technologies.

Through the 1970s, various GRIs carried out high-risk research in low-profit areas and in areas where Korean universities lacked capabilities. Before Korea's fiscal crisis, the Ministry of Science and Technology, just one of the ministries supporting S&T, gave GRIs roughly $10 million of support annually. Since the mid-1990s, GRIs have struggled to respond appropriately to industry's rapidly changing needs. The rapid pace of technological change has given a competitive edge to researchers with close industry and market ties.

Meanwhile, between 1982 and 1989, the number of private industrial research institutes in Korea increased from 46 to 749 because of the government's cooperative R&D program. By 1992, the number had increased to 1,435 thanks to government support and tax incentives. During the 1970s, much of the private research focused on imitating foreign products and licensing foreign technology. In the 1980s and 1990s, the focus of private research has continued to be on products, but increasingly, these products are based on proprietary technologies, not imported ones. This shift was dramatically demonstrated when Samsung announced in December 1995 its 1Gbit DRAM (dynamic random access memory) breakthrough, ahead of all competition.

Information services, multimedia, computer systems, satellite communication systems, and new display technologies are among the subjects of Korea's current private R&D efforts.

In Taiwan, the Ministry of Economic Affairs (MOEA) and the National Science Council direct most strategic technology investments and programs. One of MOEA's best-known technology centers is the Industrial Technology Research Institute (ITRI), which has played a primary role in providing advanced technological support for a wide range of industries, about half of which are electronics related. These electronics technologies are addressed through the Electronics Research and Services Organization (ERSO) within ITRI.

ERSO focuses on semiconductor integrated circuit (IC) devices, display devices, microwave components, and electronic technologies packaging. It also provides technical services to industry. ITRI's R&D function is critical in Taiwan, since many Taiwanese companies are too small to afford R&D; for this reason ITRI has concentrated its efforts on applied research and product development, particularly for key components that are medium (three to five years) and long-term projects (over five years). After product development and initiation of pilot production, ITRI terminates its direct participation. Its \$260 million annual budget is about 80 percent government-funded. Indirect Taiwanese government sponsorship of favoured product development and commercialization includes initial tax holidays, 10 to 20 percent tax credits, 50 percent partial funding or loans, and up to 60 percent matching grants for training programs.

Extensive public involvement in high-tech R&D is relatively recent in Singapore. The National Science and Technology Board (NSTB) was established in 1991 to promote R&D activities required to enhance the electronics industry's core capabilities and to fund and coordinate R&D in universities, polytechnics, and industry, in accordance with Singapore's "E-2000" development plan. NSTB's mission is to make the city-state a centre of excellence in selected fields of science and technology to enhance its competitiveness in industrial and service sectors. NSTB's five programs are:

(1) partnering with industry,

(2) recruiting and training on R&D workforce,

(3) establishing and maintaining national research institutes and centers,

(4) providing an R&D infrastructure, and

(5) building international alliances and cooperative agreements.

NSTB undertakes precompetitive collaborative research with industry partners and has established the following national research institutes and technology competency centers:

1. The Institute of Microelectronics supports VLSI (very large scale integration) design, failure and reliability analysis, and advanced packaging and silicon processing.
2. The Center for Wireless Communications focuses on spectrum, wireless multimedia, modulation, and transmission.

3. The Data Storage Institute concentrates on magnetic computer-assisted design, magnetic recording, mechatronics, servo controls, laser processing, and optical technologies.
4. The GINTIC Institute of Manufacturing Technology provides computer-integrated manufacturing, automation, and process development support.
5. The Center for Signal Processing supports the computer, multimedia, consumer, and communications industries.
6. The Institute of System Science emphasizes applied research in natural language processing, neural networks, fuzzy logic, and broadband networks.
7. The Information Technology Institute emphasizes information management, multimedia, and artificial intelligence. NSTB's partnering programs include assessment of technology trends and industry needs, support of company-based research, and funding of consortia-type research.

Although Singapore's public research institutions are providing crucial support to the country's electronics and other modern industries, by far the largest amount of research expenditure in Singapore has been private. Since at least 1978, private sector R&D investment has generally equalled or exceeded the combined investment by the government, universities, and public research institutes. The overall R&D investment rate in Singapore has about tripled in the past decade.

Malaysia's GRIs include the Standards and Industrial Research Institute of Malaysia and the Malaysian Institute for Microelectronic Systems (MIMOS). MIMOS, started in 1985 within the prime minister's office and now a department of the Ministry of Science, Technology, and the Environment, is Malaysia's national center of excellence in microelectronics and information technology. MIMOS projects are product oriented and focused on boosting the competitive and innovative levels of the domestic electronics industry. Six research departments indicate the fields of interest: semiconductor technology, design methodology, computer technology, product development, industrial technology, and telecommunications technology. Large-scale MIMOS projects include a microelectronics center in the Kulim Hi-Tech Industrial Park and an operational microchip plant.

Targeting Technologies and Products

As Korea's private R&D activities have grown, the government has shifted its R&D activities to large-scale projects. By 1989, KIST had participated in 5,600 research projects valued at over $260 million and employing a staff of 592, including 459 in research. In 1992, the Korean government launched 11 Highly Advanced National (HAN) projects to address the development of next-generation products and technologies. These projects included development of the following:

- highly integrated semiconductors
- an integrated services digital network (ISDN)
- high-definition television (HDTV)
- new medicine and new agricultural medicines
- advanced production systems
- new advanced materials

— next-generation vehicles
— new functional biomaterials
— technology in environmental engineering
— new energy resources
— next-generation atomic reactors and verification

Product-oriented projects target future market opportunities. "Fundamental" projects develop technologies that focus on core technologies that will advance economic, social, and personal life. The HAN projects combine joint investment by the government and Korea's largest chaebols with interministerial cooperation and coordination. Universities, industries, and GRIs coordinate on each project. The results have been considered only moderately successful, since global competition intensifies the speed required for technology development. Aside from such government activities, Korean chaebols also have targeted certain technologies and markets-such as DRAMs-with great success.

Taiwan has targeted critical components and products to maximize the benefits of its research programs. MOEA has developed a systematic "program for the development of critical components and products." The program focuses resources of the government and the private sector on developing critical components and products, replacing imports with local suppliers, improving local capabilities, and supporting the development of emerging industries. Critical products included HDTV, digital audio tape recorders, electronic still cameras, a variety of computer peripherals, and automated manufacturing equipment.

Each item was classified into one of three groups: A, B, and C. In the A group, a GRI such as ITRI is entrusted to obtain licenses or to develop the technology, or both. In the B group, MOEA provides government financial assistance to develop prototypes of the targeted component or product. In the C group, the government supports production capacity by providing such incentives as tax credits, acquisition of industrial land, government participation in the investment, favourable loans, training of professional personnel, and special duties and import regulations.

In 1995, critical components in group A included fuzzy logic ICs, liquid crystal displays (LCDs), high-density static and dynamic RAM, a variety of radio frequency ICs for telecommunications, light-emitting diodes (LEDs) for displays, and charge-coupled devices for video. Most A components were also classified B and C. As A projects were completed, they moved into categories B or C: silicon wafer fabrication had only a C priority to ramp up output.

Display components. Taiwan is working hard to end its reliance on imported visual displays and related materials for high-end products, mostly from Japan. In 1995, Japanese firms provided all of the 10-inch LCD panels used in Taiwan-produced notebook personal computers (PCs); local vendors provided 90 percent of the LCD displays used in electronic dictionaries, although 90 percent of the materials used to produce them were imported, mostly from Japan. Japanese firms supplied 87 percent of the high-resolution cathode ray tube (CRT) monitors for computers and 30 percent of the mid-resolution monitors. To overcome this deficit, the government has designated displays as a critical component and has supported development of next-generation display products. In 1995, two firms produced high-technology active-matrix LCDs in Taiwan, and 13 firms produced lower-quality passive matrix displays. 10-inch colour passive-matrix and active-matrix LCDs have begun pilot production, and high-end active matrix LCDs over 10 inches are being developed. ICs for colour filter drivers are still imported.

Taiwan has become a close follower of the United States in high-luminance LEDs, and ITRI has developed blue LEDs, which allow full-colour displays to be developed with LED technology. In 1995, Taiwan firms produced 20 percent of the mid-resolution and 80 percent of the low-resolution CRT monitors for Taiwan-made computers, although 40 percent of the monitor materials had to be imported. Taiwan had already begun to mass-produce CRTs up to 21 inches, had pilot production of CRTs over 28 inches, and was developing a wide 16:9 ratio CRT for use in HD TVs.

Semiconductor components. Among the key components it has targeted, Taiwan has been successful in entering the semiconductor industry. In 1995, Taiwan had 12 firms producing ICs with total revenues of $4 billion. These firms supplied 19.1 percent of the domestic IC requirements and planned to provide 37.8 percent of domestic demand by 2000. By then, they planned to invest $16.5 billion in 20 semiconductor wafer fabrication facilities ("fabs") with a capacity of 4.8 million ICs per month. Taiwan's goal is to increase its global share of the semiconductor market from 2.5 percent in 1995 to 7.5 percent by 2000.

Taiwan's 12 IC firms are the result of strategic alliances and technology agreements with the world's leading semiconductor firms. United Microelectronics Corp. (UMC) was spun off from ITRI/ERSO in 1979. It has strategic alliances and technology agreements with SGS-Thomson, Thesys, Meridian, and Microstar (MSI). The Taiwan Semiconductor Manufacturing Company (TSMC), spun-off from ITRI/ERSO in 1982, has technical and strategic alliances with Advanced Micro Devices (AMD), Cirrus Logic, Amadent (AMAD), and Integrated Silicon Solution, Inc. (ISSI). TSMC, now the second largest foundry in Asia, supplies Fujitsu, Ltd., of Japan with 16-megabit DRAMs under Fujitsu's brand name.

TSMC planned to begin producing 64M DRAM chips for Fujitsu in 1997 using Fujitsu's technology. Acer has an IC joint venture with Texas Instruments. Taiwan's largest conglomerate, Nan Ya Plastics, has licensed the technology of Oki (Japan) for its new DRAM fab. In 1994, Vanguard International Semiconductor was spun off from ITRI/ERSO to produce submicron memory ICs in Taiwan. Most of the capital came from government and local banking sources. To further strengthen the IC industry's infrastructure, ERSO established the Electronics Testing Center in 1982. The first domestic mask manufacturer, Taiwan Mask Corporation, and EMMT System Corporation were spun off in 1988. In 1995, 26 companies in Taiwan were involved in IC design with total revenues of $593 million.

Attracting Foreign Technology Leaders

The example of Taiwan's targeted investment in ICs illustrates another ingredient of successful economic development in Asia: in order to enter and compete in markets for technologically advanced components and products, Asian NIEs have relied heavily on cooperation with foreign technology leaders, often by expanding on relationships begun in contract labour arrangements. For a newly industrializing economy, overcoming the financial and technical challenges of expanding into advanced fields may be feasible only with such cooperation. For this reason, Taiwan, Singapore, and Malaysia have been strongly committed to attracting and keeping the involvement of leading companies, especially in the 1990s. Once foreign corporations have a stake in local markets, they typically continue to upgrade technologies.

U.S., Japanese, and European firms are rapidly transferring technologies into Southeast Asia, reducing the time it takes to produce next-generation products locally. For example, because Intel's customers must be able to install new microprocessors in the latest products, it produces motherboards to facilitate the introduction of its latest microprocessors. It also transfers next-generation assembly technologies to Asian customers as quickly as possible to ensure market penetration. Orient Semiconductor Company in Taiwan licensed tape carrier production technology for making daughter boards for notebook computers. Singapore provides a full range of programs, while Malaysia and Taiwan offer much simpler and more focused incentives. Hong Kong has taken a more passive approach.

While many Asian NIEs are working hard to attract foreign firms, there is some hesitation about inviting too much foreign involvement. Most of them have used various import controls or regulations to place some restrictions on local operations of foreign firms. China, for example, is caught between its need to protect its weak state-owned enterprises (SOEs) from foreign competition and its need to increase their access to foreign technologies. To upgrade and modernize its SOEs, China is working to provide internal support while encouraging limited partnerships with foreign firms. The majority of PC exports from China are made by joint ventures of SOEs with foreign companies.

Malaysia has historically had a strong emphasis on national self-reliance—a theme that echoes throughout Asia-but in the past 10 years has decided that in the interest of accelerating its economic growth, it is willing to postpone this goal in the short term in order to achieve world-class economic status more quickly. Therefore, Malaysia has become more open to foreign direct investments since 1990, and has offered significant incentives to foreign companies willing to invest in enterprises that facilitate technology transfer. These incentives include generous "pioneer status" investment tax exemptions and allowances, financing of up to 100 percent of some costs if technology transfer is involved, infrastructure construction, relaxation of regulations governing employment of skilled expatriates and foreign workers, and specialized training of workers.

More than most other Asian countries, Singapore sees attracting MNCs as the centerpiece of its development strategy. Half the 4,000 MNCs located in Singapore have established regional headquarters there. Over 80 MNC offices, including Hewlett-Packard, Compaq, Motorola, Hitachi, Matsushita, Philips, Seagate, National Semiconductor, SGS-Thomson, Siemens, Murata, SCI, Sony, Thomson, Toshiba, IBM, and Texas Instruments each spend over $25 million per year in local expenses. Since MNCs are the driving force behind Singapore's industrial development, the Economic Development Board (EDB) plans to provide special incentives to attract another 120 regional headquarters, each spending over $25 million per year, by 2000. Companies awarded status as operational or business headquarters benefit from incentives that include tax concessions on offshore income. Responding to liberal incentives and excellent supporting infrastructures, MNCs continue to establish advanced technology centers in Singapore.

Motorola set up 120 engineers at its Asian Motorola Manufacturing Systems facility in Singapore to carry out manufacturing R&D and to transfer developments to other sites in the region. SGS-Thomson Microelectronics conducts semiconductor research on digital signal processing, BICMOS (bipolar complementary metal oxide semiconductor) silicon wafer processing, and advanced packaging technologies. Siemens Components has established an R&D IC design center, including testing, packaging, and manufacturing technologies for use in the region. In July 1997, Germany's Wacker Siltronic AG announced its plans to spend S$478.5 million (US$337 million) to build Singapore's first silicon wafer manufacturing plant, which will supply silicon wafers to wafer fabs in the Asia-Pacific region. With 400 companies from northern Europe, Singapore opened the North European center of trade and industry in 1998. It will house up to 100 midsize companies from Denmark, Finland, Norway, Sweden, and Iceland. The North European center will be 90 percent financed by Singaporean companies at a cost of $69.8 million. A German center opened in 1995.

Building Advanced Technology Parks

High-profile advanced S&T parks, like special economic

zones, are popular in Asia as a means of upgrading technology. They are designed to combine and concentrate the advantages of many of the kinds of strategies summarized above:

(1) support R&D, commercialization, and education activities;

(2) focus on key technical fields and products; and

(3) promote and facilitate international financial and technical participation.

They have the added advantages of bolstering national pride, fostering interdisciplinary synergies, and enhancing concentration and control of limited resources. Countries usually offer special incentives for both foreign and domestic investment in projects within the parks that further specific national development goals. For example, China offers foreign firms reduced tax rates of 15 percent and greater incentives at start-up time for qualifying projects in its industrial parks. Firms are exempt from taxes for two years once they begin to make profits; then they are exempt from 50 percent of their taxes between years three and five. Firms that export at least 70 percent of their output are taxed at a 10 percent rate.

Singapore, having successfully established science parks of its own, is making a business of helping other countries establish and run focused high-technology parks. The China-Singapore Suzhou Industrial Park, initiated in 1995, has attracted investment commitments of $2 billion from 62 international companies. About 20 companies are already in production, among them Selectron Corp., the world's second-largest producer of motherboards, which has established a $45 million facility. The Vietnam-Singapore Industrial Park was launched in May 1996 near Ho Chi Minh City. India and Singapore established the Information Technology (IT) Park in Bangalore in September 1995 specifically to take advantage of India's 140,000 low-cost computer programmers. With stiff competition from other IT parks in India and the region, such as Malaysia's Multimedia Super Corridor (MSC), the focus of the Bangalore park was expanded in early 1997, and it was renamed the International Technology Park.

In 1980, Taiwan established its Hsinchu industrial park, now home to a large share of the island's high-tech manufacturers, including, in 1995, 51 semiconductor firms, 39 PC/peripheral firms, 30 telecommunications firms, 25 optoelectronic firms, 16 precision machinery firms, and biotechnology firms; of these, 25 percent were foreign owned. The park provides one-stop permitting, five-year corporate income tax exemptions, low-interest loans, and tax credits for R&D investments, factory automation, and human resource development. Annual sales in 1994 were $6.4 billion. On the basis of the successes of the Hsinchu park, in 1997 the government opened a new science park at T'ai-nan in the south of Taiwan.

Thirty-eight wafer, computer, and other factories are being built there, including plants for United Microelectronics Corp., Texas Instruments-Acer, several Japanese electronics firms, IBM, Motorola, and new 8-inch- and 12-inch-wafer plants for TSMC, Taiwan's oldest electronics company. Mosel Vitelic is spending about $3.6 billion to build a 12-inch-wafer plant there. The new park fits into Taiwan's blueprint to become a "high-tech island" and its expectation that, by 2000, 40 percent of the island's manufacturing output will be in technology-intensive industries.

Malaysia operates several industrial parks under the premise that a group of industries working in a common environment can accomplish much more than in isolation. The government strategy is to include both public and private research institutions, promote hybrid technologies, upgrade local university laboratories, establish technology centers, and fund both joint and individual R&D projects. Two well-established Malaysian industrial parks are the Technology Park of Malaysia (TPM) near Kuala Lumpur and Kulim Hi-Tech Industrial Park near Penang.

TPM was started in 1988 "to be the best in providing the infrastructure, facilities, and services related to the development of knowledge-based industries." TPM's main thrust is support of industrial high-tech entrepreneurship. Over the next five years, TPM plans to focus on three broad technology fields: manufacturing and industrial engineering, information technology and multimedia, and biotechnology, emphasizing R&D, commercialization, and human resource development. As is common, general and customized financial and other incentives support foreign participation in the parks.

Developing Globally Competitive Businesses

With increasingly sophisticated technology capabilities, the third phase of an emerging country's successful economic development tends to be based on transforming local firms into first-class high-tech competitors in the global marketplace. While foreign-owned MNCs may aid in developing an economy, sustained development now requires establishing domestic industries' strength in emerging industries and technologies. Being able to upgrade imported basic technologies and develop higher value-added components and products is just the beginning. Domestic firms tend to contribute more to the local economy and are less likely to move out when costs of doing business rise. The success of local firms requires that they achieve economies of scale and size adequate to support state-of-the-art research and development of products for emerging industries. To reach adequate size, firms must expand into markets beyond their home bases, thereby competing with leading multinational firms. Like Japan, Korea has been especially successful in developing world-class competitors. Today, Singapore has the most dynamic strategy for building its own global players.

Korea's chaebols, large conglomerates, have been the major beneficiaries of government development policies and research support. Samsung, Daewoo, and LG have become leaders in the global electronics industry over the past 25 years. Despite current restructuring, these family-dominated companies established after World War II continue to rank among the largest companies in the world. Korean chaebols accounted for 8 of the 12 largest East Asian firms and 43 of the largest 100 East Asian firms in 1995 sales, excluding Japan and China. Korea's largest 8 chaebols are Samsung Electronics Co., Hyundai Motor Co., Korea Electric Power Corp., Pohang Iron & Steel Co., Yukong, Ltd., LG Electronics Co., Kia Motors Co., and Daewoo Heavy Industries Co. Chaebols produce almost 50 percent of Korea's gross national product (GNP) and account for 70 percent of the country's exports. The top 30 chaebols control 821 firms. In 1995, the Samsung Group, Korea's largest chaebol, had sales of $87 billion, 233,000 employees, and 340 facilities in 66 countries. The group's goal is to be ranked among the world's top 10 companies by 2000. Samsung has focused on four core industries: electronics, machinery, chemicals, and finance. Samsung's strategy of "globalization and localization" includes operations worldwide to access local markets. In 1995, Samsung had regional headquarters in Europe, North America, Japan, China, and Singapore. To compete globally, Samsung's strategy has been to produce the world's best products. The group invests more than 7 percent ($2 billion) of its total revenue in R&D in order to build technological leadership.

Daewoo Group revenues were $65 billion in 1996, with $13 billion in exports. Daewoo has 25 domestic companies, 277 overseas subsidiaries, and over 191,000 employees worldwide. In 1996, Daewoo ranked 34 in the Fortune Global 500. "Daewoo Globalization Through Daewoo Technology" is the theme of the company's Vision 2000. Daewoo had 12,000 R&D personnel in 1996 and invested $1 billion in R&D. It challenges member companies to become industry leaders by the year 2000. Goals include total group sales of $177 billion with a worldwide network of 650 facilities in over 150 nations. This network will include 430 sales subsidiaries, 130 manufacturing subsidiaries, 20 technical and design R&D centers, and 70 local branch offices engaged in trading and related activities.

The LG Group launched Leap 2005 in March 1996 with the goal of reaching annual revenues of $385 billion by 2005. LG intends to set the global standard for quality and service in emerging business sectors such as communications, multimedia, environmental technologies, bioengineering, broadcasting media, heavy industry, energy, and infrastructure development. LG's core industries include chemicals and energy, electronics, machinery and metals, trade and services, and finance businesses.

To help meet the ambitious goals mentioned above, Korean chaebols make significant investments overseas as they build global competitiveness. In 1995, foreign direct investment in Korea totalled $1.9 billion. In contrast, overseas direct investment by Korean firms reached $3.1 billion as the government reduced foreign investment restrictions and simplified procedures. The top five chaebols plan $70 billion in overseas direct investment in the coming decade. LG Group plans to build a home electronics and semiconductor plant in the United Kingdom at a cost of $2.6 billion. Hyundai Electronics Industries Company plans to set up a $1.4 billion semiconductor plant in Britain.

Korean chaebols are also buying foreign firms to gain instant access to foreign markets and to add brand names and new technologies. Daewoo purchased France's Thomson Multimedia and acquired a majority share of Zenith to become the world's biggest producer of televisions. Samsung bought a large stake in AST Research, a California PC maker. Hyundai acquired 40 percent of Maxtor in 1993 to build a position in the disk drive business.

Although for the most part the success of the chaebols has until recently impeded the growth of new, smaller companies in Korea's computer market, TriGem has become one of Korea's new success stories. This midsize firm held a 22 percent share of Korea's PC market in 1996. In 1995, TriGem manufactured over 600,000 PCs and recorded revenues of over $850 million. Foreign companies had only a 7 percent share of the

Korean PC market. Hewlett-Packard and IBM, the leading U.S. players in Korea, could garner only 2 percent and 1 percent of the market, respectively. The Korean government has been seeking ways to promote the growth of new businesses; TriGem's success indicates some progress on this front.

Taiwan's Global Market Position

Taiwan is concentrating on electronics, its top export; already it has become the world's fifth largest supplier of PCs. Taiwanese firms moved from assembling products such as transistor radios, TVs, and tape recorders in the 1960s, to manufacturing CRTs in the 1970s, to producing colour monitors, semiconductors, electronic watches, and IBM-compatible PCs in the 1980s, becoming larger and more successful in each stage. In the 1990s, Taiwan's strategy moved it into production of the microelectronic components needed for its leading suppliers of motherboards, monitors, scanners, and computer mouse devices. Taiwan's global market share in key electronics components. In 1995, computer monitors were a $7.2 billion business for Taiwan, which had a world market share of 57 percent. Taiwanese companies held 65 percent of the world motherboard and keyboard markets, 64 percent of the scanner market, 38 percent of network cards, 35 percent of power supplies, 32 percent of graphic cards, 27 percent of portable PCs, and 11 percent of CD-ROMs. Taiwan also held 72 percent of the worldwide computer mouse market in 1995.

Taiwan's computer-related output was valued at $19.7 billion in 1995. Information products rose from 22.8 percent to 33.8 percent of Taiwan's electronics output between 1986 and 1995. The shift into computers and related components has been highly successful. In 1995, Taiwan held 27 percent of the global notebook PC market and 10 percent of the desktop PC market. Taiwan supplies all computer components except hard disk drives. While Taiwan's share of notebook PCs was projected to exceed 38 percent in 1997, the production of desktop PCs was being moved to low-cost labour countries such as China and the Philippines. Taiwanese firms have excelled in introducing computers with the latest components.

Taiwanese vendors have become original design manufacturers that sell "ready to go" products to original equipment manufacturers. While it took three years for Taiwan to introduce the first IBM-compatible 286 computer in 1985, Taiwanese firms were only two months behind in introducing the first Pentium-based systems in 1993. By 1997, Taiwan was first to introduce the latest components and most advanced computer designs. With growing strength in product design and new product development, Taiwanese companies continue to strengthen their global market position.

The Taiwanese firms Inventec, GVC, Tatung, First International, Elite, Quanta, and Twin Head are the major suppliers to the world's top 10 PC companies, including Compaq, IBM, Apple, Packard Bell-NEC, AST, Toshiba, and Hewlett-Packard. They all aspire to stand-alone status like that of Acer, Inc., Taiwan's leading global player, which ranks as one of the five largest component makers in the world and has one of the top 10 PC brands in the world.

Singapore's Strategy for Local Enterprises

Singapore's EDB is working with over 250 local firms to help them become Asian MNCs with operations in at least three countries, with sales over $400 million, and with established brand names such as Creative Technology. EDB has identified promising local enterprises with strong core capabilities, clear vision, and high growth potential. Aztech Technology, which accounts for almost 90 percent of the world's sound card market, is one such company. Singapore's largest semiconductor foundry, Chartered Semiconductor Manufacturing (CSM), is 84 percent owned by the government and produces application-specific integrated circuits. Within the world's $6 billion semiconductor foundry market, CSM ranks second, with 5.3 percent of the market. (Taiwan Semiconductor Manufacturer Company is the leader, with about 20 percent.) Of CSM's $1 billion in revenues, about 60 percent comes from the United States, and another 30 percent comes from Taiwan. Toshiba Corporation and CSM have announced a five-year partnership to produce embedded DRAMs for multimedia applications. This leading-edge systems-on-silicon technology was to enter the market at the end of 1998. CSM plans two additional wafer fabs, including a joint venture with Hewlett-Packard and Singapore's EDB.

Singapore's strategy is to develop 100 promising local enterprises with revenues greater than $100 million each within 10 years. These firms are growing at an average of about 30 percent annually. By 2000, EDB expects that between 50 and 70 will exceed the $100 million goal and be capable of competing in the global marketplace. EDB manages a $1 billion fund for strengthening partnerships between MNCs and local enterprises, helping the local firms go regional. EDB shares start-up costs and business risks with key investor companies by co-investing in strategic projects both in and outside Singapore. It makes equity investments in projects that support its programs and fill critical gaps in industry technologies.

Future Developments

The rapid progress of the Asian NIEs through the three stages of development is due in large measure to careful planning, continuous re-evaluation, and long-range goals for product and component developments. With resources still limited, hard decisions must be made about what industries to support in order to continue planned development into the future. All the countries discussed here have detailed central plans for their development into the twenty-first century, and all of those plans include a renewed emphasis on targeting high-end electronics and information technologies, attracting multinational investment, providing a first-rate technology infrastructure, and fostering the growth of indigenous high-tech global players. The plans noted below offer a glimpse into the mind-set of Asian leaders.

Korea: Advanced Telecom and IT

Korea's national commitment to key technologies and products prominently features information technologies, including telecommunications, information systems and software. This country plans for this sector-6.9 percent of the national economy in 1996-to grow 19.6 percent a year to 2001 (double the average world growth) and to contribute a 10 percent share of the domestic economy by 2001. To achieve this goal, annual public and private sector investment-8.7 trillion won in 1996 (about $10.3 billion at 845 won/US$1)-is expected to almost triple by 2001. As an indication of the dedication to and progress in developing this sector, Korea's number of phone subscribers increased from 3 million in 1980 to 10 million in 1988 and to 20 million as of May 1997, in a country with a population of 46 million. In 1980, 10 percent of the switching systems were electronic (TDX); in 1988, 70 percent were electronic; and in 1997, 100 percent were electronic, 65 percent digital. The government's forecast is that by 2001, subscribers to wireless telecom services (cellular and PCS) will number 13 million; the wireless market will amount to 92 percent of the wired market; and online communications services will be worth 2.8 trillion won.

Taiwan: Information Technology

In 1995, Taiwan's ITRI ranked Taiwan among the world leaders in electronics products. It ranked fourth in information technologies, seventh in communications products, and fifth in consumer electronics products and in electronic components such as semiconductors, optoelectronics, displays, and IC packaging. As the fourth-largest producer of ICs, Taiwan had wafer fabrication factories producing $4 billion in semiconductors in 1995, was mass producing 16M DRAMs, and planned to have 20 8-inch wafer fabs operating by 2000. Although it plans to continue to be a world leader in electronics, Taiwan is beginning to move into other areas, including information technologies. Other critical products identified for support include medical diagnostic equipment, aircraft, robots, cogeneration equipment, and breathable fabric.

Of Taiwan's electronics output, information-related electronic components increased from a 38 percent to a 53.4 percent share between 1986 and 1995, and this share is expected to grow further. Although communication electronics has so far been a small proportion of the total electronics market, Taiwan is now targeting it as a future growth business. Between 1986 and 1995, consumer electronics fell from 30.9 percent to 7.3 percent of Taiwan's electronics output, after the government decided that electronic games and toys were intellectually unhealthy for its children. To sustain its economic development, Taiwan targeted 10 emerging industries in 1992: information, communications, consumer electronics, semiconductors, precision machinery and automation equipment, aerospace, advanced materials, speciality chemicals and pharmaceuticals, medical and health care, and pollution control and treatment industries. Of these, information, precision machinery, and speciality chemical industries are expected to become Taiwan's leading industries by 2002.

Malaysia: Multimedia and IT

Malaysia plans to invest more than $2 billion over the next decade to become the multimedia hub of Southeast Asia. In August 1995, Prime Minister Mahathir proposed the Multimedia Super Corridor (MSC) project to foster IT industries. MSC stretches south of the capital of Kuala Lumpur to where a new international airport and new federal capital are under construction-a 9-mile by 30-mile zone about the size of Singapore. This corridor will attract a workforce of 150,000. The Cyberjaya ("Cybercity") development company, Cyberview Sdn. Bhd., is a joint venture of five Malaysian parties and Japan's Nippon Telegraph and Telephone Corp. On May 17, 1997, phase one was initiated with a $1.6 billion investment in construction of the 6,900-acre Malaysian Multimedia University.

The electronic backbone of MSC will be a 2.5-10 gigabyte digital fiberoptic network that will link the corridor to Japan, Europe, and the United States. Multimedia experiments planned for Cyberjaya include the use of multipurpose integrated chip cards to serve as passports, identity cards, credit cards, and electronic money for such electronic administrative needs as the provision of driver's licenses. Some delays in the Cyberjaya project are expected as a result of Southeast Asia's current fiscal difficulties.

By creating an advanced information network, Malaysia's government hopes to lure leading R&D companies and software developers from abroad. More than 900 companies have applied to participate in the MSC program. Qualifying firms must be suppliers of multimedia and other information technology products or services and be willing to transfer technology to Malaysia. Nonmanual workers such as engineers should account for at least 15 percent of the workforce. Companies that joined the project by the end of 1997 will be exempted from corporate taxes for up to 10 years.

Forty-two foreign and local companies have met MSC qualifications to locate operations in Cyberjaya, including AT&T, Sun Microsystems, and NCR from the United States; Germany's Siemens; British Telecommunications; and Japan's NTT, Fujitsu, NEC,

Mitsubishi, Sumitomo, and Sharp corporations. NTT has already set up a subsidiary in Malaysia to benefit from the preferential treatment, including exemption from corporate tax and from mandatory rules on hiring local employees.

Singapore: Cluster Industries/Electronics

Singapore's 1991 Strategic Plan initially targeted 12 industries for development and support (aerospace has since been added):

— Commodity trading and shipping to strengthen Singapore's position as a leading international trading hub and regional headquarters for shipping and ship management activities.

— Precision engineering, electronics, and information technology to establish Singapore as the premier designer, marketer, and manufacturer of high-end precision components and systems, and high-value-added electronic products/components and as an R&D and product development center, and to support the export of software products and services.

— Petroleum and petrochemicals, construction, and heavy engineering to develop Singapore into a world-scale integrated petroleum and petrochemical hub, center for construction services for the Asia-Pacific region, and center for ship repair, oil rig construction, and manufacturing and servicing of oil and gas field equipment.

— Finance, insurance, and general supporting industries to establish Singapore as a major international financial center, regional insurance and reinsurance center, and a one-stop regional center for products and supporting services.

— Tourism to establish Singapore as a premier visitor destination with convention/exhibition and travel/tourism-related services. Singapore's Economic 2000 plan stresses working relationships among government, industry, and academia to support its strategy. Singapore's infrastructure goals include maintaining the employment and GDP contributions from manufacturing at 20 percent and 25 percent, respectively.

The key to this goal is its electronics industry cluster, including semiconductors, communications, display, and data storage businesses. Singapore's successful electronics development strategy produced revenues of over $45 billion in 1995. The electronics industry accounted for 51.4 percent of the manufacturing sector's output and employed 34.2 percent of the manufacturing workforce. In 1995, data storage devices were the electronic industry's most successful business, accounting for 23.3 percent of its total electronic industry output, followed by semiconductors with 21 percent. Final systems fabrication of computers and multimedia products accounted for 19.7 percent; consumer electronics, 12.4 percent; communications products, 6.3 percent; and office automation products, 5.8 percent. These successes pave the way for continued development in these areas.

Singapore is using a semiconductor strategy similar to Taiwan's, with balanced development of design, fabrication, assembly, and test processes. Singapore's semiconductor industry cluster includes 23 IC design companies, 5 wafer fabs, and 19 assemble and test companies. EDB plans for 20 wafer fabs to be operating by 2005 and intends to attract 2 or 3 more companies as joint venture partners. It has also targeted microprocessors and flat panel displays as key components. To support Singapore's continuing economic growth, the government is offering tax incentives for pioneering investments, incentives for skills training and R&D training, and special reduced taxation for specific industries and technologies.

Singapore also has introduced a value-added tax system to reduce overall taxation on individuals as well as on corporations. Singapore does not tax capital gains or Singaporeans living overseas. Singapore's 1991-1996 five-year plan budgeted over $3 billion to support new initiatives and projects. One EDB initiative seeks to upgrade Singapore from a manufacturing center to an innovation hub capable of creating new and better products and services for the region and the world.

A $500 million innovation scheme grants up to 70 percent of project costs to promote innovation within companies. A second initiative ensures that worker skills are available and land requirements are met and that first-rate infrastructures will be attractive to international investors.

China: A Determined Example of Asia's

National Planning for Economic Modernization Under its ninth five-year plan (FYP) for 1996-2000, China has established supporting technological modernization as a major goal. Scientific and technological objectives include the development of rural industries, improvement of traditional industries and basic infrastructures, strengthening of export competitiveness, development of advanced technologies, support for new industries, product development, and development of technical and support services.

The top three priorities are to encourage technology advancement in agricultural industries, develop a national information infrastructure, and improve factory automation processes. China's national expenditure on S&T investments amounted to $10.6 billion in 1995, a third of which came from the government. In its new national economic plan, China's goal is to increase the percentage of GDP invested in research and development from 0.5 percent to 1.5 percent by 2000. In today's China, spreading scientific knowledge is considered a "social systems engineering project" of profound and far-reaching significance.

Science, technology, and education are considered the primary forces that will make the country prosperous. Part of the State's role will be to strengthen the training of high-caliber industrial workers in scientific knowledge. S&T advances combined with improved worker quality are considered essential for social development via raising national competitiveness and improving citizens' living standards.

Technology Advancement Programs

Carefully husbanding its resources, China has borrowed program elements from around the globe to help it achieve its economic development goals. Seven national R&D programs have been established to more effectively transform research into industrial production through various stages of innovation and development. The

Ministry of Science and Technology coordinates implementation of these programs.

1. The Key Technologies Research and Development Program targets R&D in the areas of information technology, manufacturing automation, advanced materials, space technology, laser technology, energy technology, and biotechnology. Twenty-four key technologies and one hundred twenty-four specific technology items have been selected for development within national laboratories and engineering research centers, to be integrated with other ninth FYP projects to address identified problem areas in the national economy.
2. The National Basic Research Priorities Program promotes development of education, laboratories, and equipment to support math, physics, chemistry, mechanics, astronomy, geology, and biology. The program includes a component of international cooperation and technology exchange.
3. The 863 Program or Advanced Research Program was enacted in 1987 to benchmark world technology developments and identify and pursue indigenous innovation capabilities in the seven priority development areas mentioned in point 1 above, specifically to serve the country's economic development goals.
4. The Torch Program, initiated in 1988, provides incentives for renovating traditional industries, training scientists, commercializing key technologies developed in the 863 Program projects, and promoting international partnerships to commercialize Chinese research. A core concept in

this program is the establishment of high-technology industrial zones (HTDZs), so-called "Torch Zones."

5. The Spark Program was established in 1986 to facilitate rural industrialization, including raising the technical skills and management level of village and township enterprises, helping rural industries to develop by relying on advances in science and technology, and raising the educational level of workers. The Spark Program diffuses agricultural technologies to farmers through loans, information dissemination, and training programs.

6. The National Science and Technology Diffusion Program targets agriculture and related economic development. The Technology Diffusion Program was initiated in 1990 to ensure that advanced, appropriate, and mature S&T achievements are used throughout the nation's economy, especially in rural areas.

7. The Trial Production and Appraisal Program links science and technology with the economy through new product development and production. Trial production of new products and the appraisal of advanced technologies are typically located in HTDZs. New products are classified as state level or regional level. New products developed and produced nationwide for the first time are state-level products. New products developed and produced for the first time within a province, an autonomous region, or a municipality are regional-level products. The National Tax Bureau identifies a list of new state-level products whose taxes are reduced or remitted.

In October 1996, the "Law on Promoting the Transformation of Science and Technology

Achievements" was enacted to facilitate technology activities. The law creates a system for the government to manage domestic technology commercialization, protect foreign and domestic intellectual property rights, provide royalties to researchers for inventions, protect trade secrets, and support technology-based transactions.

Economic and Technology Development Zones

China's first HTDZ was developed in 1988, the year the Torch Program was instituted, to integrate research institutions with start-up incubator facilities and local and international firms that are committed to commercialising China's high-tech R&D achievements. There are now 53 Torch Zones. According to information from the Torch Program as of November 1997, some 13,000 tenant companies were located within the HTDZs, which had conducted over 10,000 Torch projects since 1991, about one-third funded by the central government, more than two-thirds funded by local governments. Revenue derived from the HTDZs from 1991 to 1997 was $10.7 billion (89 billion yuan), including $1.2 billion in exports.

In addition, China has a number of special economic zones and free trade zones spanning China's coastal cities and industrial centers that allow for duty-free imports of materials and components used to produce goods for export. China uses its various types of development zones to deliver state incentives for commercialization of high-technology projects, whether by domestic or foreign companies (although foreign ones must generally have domestic partners). The zones encourage research institutes, colleges, universities, and start-up firms, among others, to set up new high-tech enterprises and industries. Over 40 high-tech pioneering service centers have been established in the zones to generate new projects. As an example, Shanghai's Caohejing Hi-Tech Park specializes in microelectronics, bioengineering, new materials, automation meters, aviation, and space technology. It has more than 500 companies, of which 150 are funded by such major multinationals as AT&T, GE, 3M, ICI, Philips, Toshiba, and DuPont.

The government plans to encourage enterprises from the Shandong, Guangdong, and Jiangsu provinces to invest in new industrial zones to be built inland over the next five years. Township enterprises from coastal provinces have already invested about $3.6 billion in land. The plan is expected to create five million new jobs.

Developing State Enterprises into Global Players

Growing foreign competition is putting pressure on China's state-owned enterprises (SOEs), which employ between 20 and 40 million workers. In 1996, SOE sales grew only about 3 percent. World Bank statistics report that 50 percent of SOEs lost money in 1996 and that debt ratios have reached 80 percent to 90 percent of assets. Only 5 percent of China's SOEs had been made into stockholding corporations. The Chinese government wants SOEs to go public to raise capital for expansion, but the SOEs must be reformed before they are desirable investments for public investors. SOEs must improve management practices, acquire advanced technologies where appropriate, train employees in information technologies, and commercialize research. The government is attempting to reform the largest 1,000 SOEs, representing 2.8 percent of SOE employees, 63 percent of SOE assets, and 70 percent of SOE sales. Chinese officials estimate it will cost 500 billion yuan (about $60 billion) to reform the SOEs during the next five years. In 1996, 300 Chinese firms were targeted to go global, becoming joint-stock companies with improved technological capabilities.

Upgrading Infrastructures

Besides these various approaches to upgrading technology levels throughout its economy, China's leadership is also working hard to improve the country's infrastructure. Though it has some ambitious and far-reaching goals, even the basic improvements will be costly. The World Bank has estimated that China will need $500 billion for infrastructure developments between 1995 and 2000. The World Bank's 1997 loan figures showed that China was once again its top recipient of loans in fiscal year 1997, receiving $2.8 billion to carry out its development strategy targeting poverty reduction, environmental protection, and job-creating growth. Since China joined the World Bank in 1981, it has received a total of $28.12 billion in loans.

The Chinese government has identified 44 infrastructure and basic material industry projects. Loans for major infrastructure projects such as those involving electricity and transportation usually come from international sources. In the first half of 1996, China raised $8.8 billion in foreign loans. Between June and October, it raised nearly $5 billion more in foreign-currency loans and bond offerings. The China

International Trust and Investment Corporation, a quasi-government investment arm of the State Council, raised another $100 million in two syndicated loans and $360 million in yen-denominated bonds from Japan. The Ministry of Finance issued a global bond to raise $1 billion.

The Japan Export-Import Bank has approved billions in loans to China for infrastructure projects. Japan's Overseas Economic Cooperation Fund proposed its fourth three-year, yen-denominated loan package of $5.1 billion in 1996. The loans will finance projects implemented in the second and third years of China's ninth FYP. Japan's Export-Import Bank has provided a $1.925 billion economic development loan for construction of a thermoelectric power plant in Zhuhai. One $200 million fixed-rate bond issue by Morgan Stanley of the United States, for a highway in Guangdong Province, will be redeemed through toll payments. All of this is still a long way from the infrastructure outlays that the World China's "Golden" Projects for IT One of China's most far-reaching infrastructure development goals is building a state-of-the-art telecommunications and information system. The core of this program consists of three so-called "Golden" Projects established in the early 1990s for completion by 2003:

1. The Golden Bridge project is designed to modernize the information infrastructure by developing an economic information and data communications network spanning 500 cities and 12,000 large enterprises. The project will include satellite and optical fiber cable networks for these sectors: finance, customs, foreign trade, tourism, interorganizational

communications, transportation, state security, and S & T. The goal is to transmit data, documents, human voice, and pictures across the network.

2. The Golden Customs project will track quota permits, foreign currency transactions, and import and export statistics. It will link all foreign trade departments and support paperless trading.

3. The Golden Card project will replace cash transactions with an electronic service system for savings, withdrawals, and payment through credit and debit cards. By 1997, the China Electronic Information Industry Group had tested operations in 12 cities, had issued 30 million cards, and was testing advanced smart cards.

The development of China's information superhighway requires co-ordination among more than 20 government ministries and countless other organizations. The production and marketing information system is expected to link 360,000 state-owned enterprises and 8.6 million other firms with government offices via networks that will improve utilization of personnel, capital, and natural resources. In 1995, a smart card was developed that combined the functions of a credit card, automated teller machine bank card, and telephone credit card. It was issued jointly by Visa International, the People's Construction Bank of China, and the Nanjing Posts and Telecommunications Bureau. GPT Company of Britain won a contract in May 1996 to install 500 smart card telephones in Zhejiang Province, and has signed contracts for 2,000 more smart card pay phones each for the Beijing and Guangdong telephone authorities.

Authorities forecast that 200 million smart cards will be issued over the next seven years. Card production systems are already in place. Meinen, Zeigel & Company of Germany installed 15 manufacturing systems in China and Asia in 1995 with the capacity to produce 100 million cards annually. Gemphlus Card International of France is setting up plants in China, and France's Schlumberger Smart Systems is developing applications for China in cooperation with the China Hua Xu Golden Card Company, a subsidiary of the Ministry of the Electronics Industry (MEI).

IBM has established a joint venture with MEI's China Great Wall Computer Group and Kaifa Technology (Hong Kong), Ltd., to develop, assemble, and test smart cards in Shenzhen Science and Industry Park. Tandem Computer, Inc., of the United States was chosen in 1995 to provide hardware platforms for the Golden Card project. An optical memory smart card is to contain personal health care data by 2002. These Golden Projects are expected to overcome many compatibility problems as the information infrastructure is modernized.

Other Chinese ministries have begun additional Golden Projects. The Ministry of Health and Jitong Corporation are creating a network to connect large hospitals and research institutions, facilitating transmission of critical medical information and images. The Ministry of Construction will develop a network to track real estate transactions. The Ministry of Finance, the People's Bank of China, the State Tax Administration, and MEI will spend over $1.2 billion to computerize the tax collection system with the installation of 85,000 computers in 30,000 tax agencies across the nation. Companies participating in the project include AT&T, Compaq Computer Corp., Hewlett-Packard Co., Hitachi Ltd., IBM Corporation, Intel Corporation, MasterCard

International, Motorola Inc., Corporation, and Visa International.

Australia: Getting the Most from ICTs

A growth accounting framework to compare the contribution of ICTs to productivity accelerations in Australia and the USA. Using the USA as a benchmark, it attributes up to 0.3 of a percentage point of Australia's 1 percentage point acceleration in labour productivity growth to ICTs. ICTs have had no net effect on capital deepening, as increased use of ICTs has substituted for other forms of capital.

The contribution of ICTs is attributed to gains from business restructuring and innovations in product and process that they enable. The gains to date have been concentrated in distribution (especially wholesaling) and financial services. The evidence of spillovers and network economies is not (yet) strong or widespread.

The Australian experience suggests that the central tenets of policy reform - competition, openness and flexibility - have been important in driving the uptake of ICTs and assisting firms to use them in productivity-enhancing ways.

In the USA, ICT production gains have been on such a scale as to show up in increases in aggregate productivity growth. The productivity gains have also led to rapidly declining ICT prices, which has stimulated increased investment in them.

Australia's productivity growth also surged in the 1990s. However, Australia's takeoff predated that of the USA and the magnitude of Australia's acceleration has been greater than that of the USA suggesting that some different factors are at work in the two countries. Microeconomic policy reforms are widely considered to have played the major role in raising Australia's productivity performance. Some credit should be given to deft macroeconomic policy settings, especially in the face of the Asian financial crisis. Education levels in the workforce have also risen markedly over the past two decades and are likely to have played some role.

The tendency to link Australia's 1990s productivity surge primarily to policy reforms and not to an ICT boom has reinforced a view in some quarters that Australia has not accessed 'new economy' gains. Furthermore, the US evidence has been read to suggest that ICT production is needed to tap 'new economy' productivity gains. According to this view, the lack of a sizeable ICT production industry in Australia has been seen as a preventive barrier to ongoing higher productivity growth.

Some have advocated that governments encourage and develop Australia's ability to produce ICTs, in order to take Australia into the 'new economy' era (irrespective of the tech stock boom and bust). Australia has moved toward the international forefront in use of ICTs. 'Smart' ICT use can enable productivity gains through business restructuring and by providing a platform for further product and process innovations. As a user, Australia has benefited from the rapidly declining prices of ICTs and has generated productivity gains from the 'smart' use of ICTs.

Computers, telecommunication systems and the Internet have brought revolutionary changes to businesses, consumers, education, health, entertainment and many other aspects of life. A defining characteristic is that the costs of storing, accessing and exchanging information have been greatly reduced. In so doing, ICTs have reduced the costs of coordination, communications and information processing. But, increasingly, they have also facilitated changes in what businesses do and how they do it.

A particular analytical interest has centred on the links between ICTs and productivity growth. Many studies of these links have employed a growth accounting framework, based on national accounts approaches to productivity estimation. In these studies, ICTs cover equipment (hardware and software), but exclude the delivery of ICT-related services, such as telephony. The framework provides three avenues for ICTs to influence labour productivity:

- *Increases in capital deepening*: Labour productivity can rise as a result of higher capital use per unit of labour. Stronger investment in ICTs can raise capital deepening. However, many analysts have noted that this mechanism accords ICTs with no 'new' or special production qualities. As they have become cheaper, firms have substituted ICTs for labour and other forms of capital - as could happen for many other inputs.
- *Productivity gains in ICT production*: Producers' ability to manufacture much more powerful ICT equipment, with little increase in inputs, generates substantial MFP gains. If the gains are of sufficient magnitude and production is on sufficient scale, they can show up as contributions to aggregate MFP growth.
- *Productivity gains in ICT-using industries*: This is the most controversial source of ICT-related productivity

gains. It requires that use of ICTs generates MFP gains. The 'new economy' concept has always been vague; and whilst assessments have come to focus on ICT-productivity links, the debate on the nature and extent of those links continues.

On the one hand, 'new economy' enthusiasts believe there are MFP gains from such sources as increasing returns from ICT use and spillovers from network economies. On the other hand, sceptics have either denied or found little evidence to support the existence of MFP gains from use. Dale Jorgensen accepts that there is a new economy, but without MFP gains from use. He believes the new economy lies in the productivity gains in ICT production and associated ICT capital deepening as firms substitute cheaper ICTs for other inputs. There is, perhaps, some middle ground on the possibility of MFP gains.

For example, US Federal Reserve Board Chairman, Alan Greenspan, pointed to gains that he believes come from greater and cheaper access to information - greater certainty, through the availability of real-time information about customers' demands and the location of inventories and materials flowing through complex production systems, which leads to less wastage from extra production, inventories and staff; more efficient and compressed distribution processes; the development of financial instruments to manage risks; and lower search and transactions costs in business-to-business transactions.

The measurement of ICTs has important bearing on the source and extent of estimated productivity gains associated with ICTs. The measurement of the volume of ICTs produced affects estimates of output and productivity growth in ICT production. The measurement of the volume of ICT investment affects estimates of growth in capital inputs and therefore the productivity residual in ICT-using industries. In keeping with modern practice, the Australian Bureau of Statistics (ABS) uses hedonic (or constant-quality) price deflators to estimate real volumes of ICTs produced and purchased. Hedonic prices take into account changes in a number of characteristics of ICTs -processing speed, memory capacity and so on.

The quality-constant prices of ICT characteristics have declined markedly. This stems from the fact that, whilst there have been rapid technological advances (especially in the capacity of microprocessors), there has been relatively little movement in the nominal prices of equipment.

Hedonic prices have not been specifically generated for ICTs in Australia. The ABS uses the US price deflator for hardware, adjusted for exchange rate movements and a time lag, and an assumed 6 per cent a year reduction in prices of software.

Investment in ICTs became a sizeable proportion of total investment in Australia from the mid-1980s. Since then, the growth of investment has been very strong, especially in the 1990s, when investment in hardware grew by 35 per cent a year and software investment grew by 20 per cent a year in real terms. Australia became a high user by international standards in the 1990s. It ranked 3 in 1999 among OECD countries in terms of proportion of business investment devoted to ICTs. Australia imports most of its ICT equipment requirements. Australia ranks at the very low end of OECD countries in terms of size of its ICT equipment production industries.

The contributions of ICTs to Australia's productivity growth are now assessed and compared with the US experience. With some assumptions, the US case provides a benchmark that indicates the extent to which Australia's productivity gains can be associated with ICTs. There have been a number of US studies of ICT contributions to productivity growth.

A capital services measure of capital input is used and labour input is measured by hours worked. US studies also include a labour composition or 'quality' component, which captures changes in the hours worked by groups with different marginal products. A comparable component cannot be estimated for Australia. Since allowance for compositional effects (as in the USA) effectively 'factors out' this component from MFP growth, this component is added back in to US MFP growth estimates, to assist comparability with Australian estimates.

Australian data cover IT, without communications equipment, whereas US data cover ICTs. The US estimates used here cover the private business sector, whereas Australian estimates cover the market sector. The main difference between the two is that the ABS-defined market sector excludes Property & business services.

With similar uptake of ICTs in the two countries, the USA can then be used as a benchmark to assess the extent to which Australia's productivity gains can be associated with ICTs. Furthermore, it seems reasonable to assume, consistent with the US leadership in productivity and ICTs, that US estimates establish the upper limit on productivity accelerations that can be associated specifically with ICT production and use. First, however, there are some timing issues to sort out.

Most studies have used 1995 as the dividing year between periods of comparison of productivity growth and for assessing the ICT contributions to productivity acceleration -for example, accounting for productivity growth in the second half of the 1990s compared with the first half. The 1995 year corresponds to the takeoff point in advances in ICT technology, declines in ICT prices, growth in investment in ICTs and, as just seen, growth in ICT capital deepening. The 1995 year also corresponds to the takeoff in US labour productivity growth. But 1995 was a trough year in US labour productivity, at a point below trend. Estimates from 1995 to the end of the 1990s are from a trough to a peak and therefore overstate the underlying rate of labour productivity growth.

Issues with the boundary point and sensitivity can be set aside by analysing contributions to trend rates of productivity growth. The ABS method of estimating productivity growth over productivity cycles - from productivity peak to productivity peak - is one way of measuring underlying rates of growth.

Adopting this method puts the prime focus on accelerations in underlying rates of productivity growth, rather than on the ICT takeoff and its effects. The productivity-cycle method introduces a difference between countries in time periods compared, but it ensures that changes in underlying rates of productivity growth are compared.

There are several similarities in the US and Australian results:

— The estimated labour productivity acceleration is lower according to the productivity cycle method, compared with the pre- and post-1995 method.

— ICTs have made strong capital deepening contributions. The ICT capital deepening contribution has increased steadily from the 1960s in both countries.

— ICT capital deepening accounted for around a third of labour productivity growth in both countries in their respective 1990s cycles. ICT capital deepening made a contribution of a similar order of magnitude to the 1990s labour productivity accelerations in both countries.

— However, much or all of the increased use of ICTs in the 1990s has been offset by slower growth in the use of other forms of capital. There has been little or no increase in the overall rate of capital deepening in either country, especially in Australia. This contrasts with most other studies of the USA which have found that ICTs have contributed to a marked increase in the rate of substitution of capital for labour.

— MFP growth accounted for over half of labour productivity growth in the 1990s cycle in both countries. Faster MFP growth accounts for most of the 1990s labour productivity accelerations in both countries, and entirely so in Australia.

The main difference between the US and Australian results lies in the strength of the productivity accelerations. The acceleration in underlying labour productivity growth in Australia, at 1 percentage point, is twice that in the USA. With similar capital deepening contributions, the chief explanation for the difference lies in the much stronger MFP acceleration in Australia than in the USA.

It seems reasonable to assume, consistent with the US leadership in productivity and ICTs, that the US estimates establish the upper limit on productivity gains that can be associated specifically with ICT production and use. Assuming that no other factor has generated a productivity acceleration, the US estimates set the upper limit on ICT-related gains. Some of the 0.3 of a percentage point MFP acceleration must be attributed to production of ICTs.

The benchmark assessment does not in itself establish that ICTs have been at work in both countries. However, some supporting - though still circumstantial - evidence comes from an industry perspective, which shows an overlap in the USA and Australia in the industries that are both high ICT users and relatively strong productivity accelerators.

Whilst the evidence suggests that the aggregate MFP gains to date from ICT use are significant, albeit not spectacular, there is evidence of strong links in certain industries. . Several studies of the USA have found evidence of productivity acceleration in the 1990s in Wholesale trade, Retail trade, Finance, insurance & real estate (especially in financial intermediation) and Business services. These industries have also been characterised as intensive users of ICTs.

A similar set of industries emerged in the 1990s as major contributors to Australia's productivity surge. In the first cycle, the relatively strong productivity growth in the 'traditional' contributors to aggregate productivity growth -Agriculture, Mining, and Manufacturing - is evident. These traditional sectors were joined in the 1980s and early 1990s by two other strong performers - Communication services and Electricity, gas & water.

Whilst productivity growth remained relatively strong in all these industry sectors in the 1990s cycle (except for Manufacturing), they all experienced a deceleration compared with the previous cycle. On these estimates, none made a contribution to the productivity surge from 1993-94. A new set of service industries made the positive contribution. The stand-out performer was Wholesale trade. Other service industries - for example, Construction and Finance & insurance - also increased their rate of productivity growth.

Whilst there is increased scope for measurement error at the industry level - of both ICT use and productivity growth - it appears that there is no strong, positive relationship between ICT use and MFP across all industries. There is a strong positive relationship between increased ICT use and MFP acceleration in Finance & insurance and a weaker relationship in Wholesale trade.

The lack of systematic relationship undoubtedly reflects the fact that ICT use is not the only factor affecting industry MFP growth. It also signals that the productivity gains from ICT use appear - for the moment at least - concentrated in distribution and financial intermediation. The lack of a relationship across all industries also tends to support the view that the gains to date cannot be attributed to network economies, which could be expected to be more widespread.

The relationships between ICT use and productivity growth are complex. ICTs are often viewed as general-purpose technologies that require time to bring to their full potential and that provide a platform for other innovations in products and processes.

The Australian evidence supports the view that it is the changes in products and processes that generate the productivity gains. The Finance & insurance industry has been restructured to operate much more through ICTs (for example, ATMs, Internet and phone banking) than through traditional face-to-face contacts. Many new products (for example, financial derivatives) are now on offer.

An earlier study by Productivity Commission staff also found that ICTs played a part in the restructuring of wholesaling activities. Wholesalers were able to use bar-code and scanning technology and inventory management systems as part of the process of transforming wholesaling from a storage-based to a fast flow-through operation.

But, importantly, reforms were acting as the underlying drivers and facilitators of productivity gains and ICTs were just one component of change. It was not so much that wholesaling became much more ICT intensive or that new 'breakthrough' technologies became available. It was more that the competitive incentives to be productive became stronger and that new flexibilities became open to businesses to use ICTs as part of a more general process of restructuring and transformation.

For example, the motor vehicle industry was looking for efficiencies all along the 'value chain', including in distribution, to meet the increased competition from cheaper imports entering under lower trade barriers.

Another contributor in some areas was the reform of industrial relations processes that allowed greater labour flexibility through the introduction of split shifts and reduced the rigidity of job demarcations. At the general level, policy reforms have fostered productivity growth through three main avenues:

- sharpening incentives to be more productive, chiefly by strengthening competition;
- opening the economy to trade, investment and technologies developed overseas; and
- providing greater flexibility (for example, less regulatory restriction, more flexible labour markets) to adjust production processes and firm organisation to improve productivity.

These conditions have also provided the incentives for businesses to take up ICTs, as well as ready access to the latest ICTs developed overseas, and the flexibility to use ICTs to productive advantage.

A major implication of the evidence in this and other Productivity Commission papers is that, from a productivity and policy perspective, a prime focus on ICTs and the 'new economy' is somewhat misplaced. There are three potential pitfalls:

— too much attention on ICT production as a source of productivity growth;

— insufficient attention on the factors that drive ICT use;

— insufficient attention on other factors that are potentially the source of greater productivity gains.

On the first point, and in light of calls for policy action to foster the development of ICT production, the Australian (and the US) experience is now providing clearer evidence that there are also (MFP) productivity gains associated with ICT use. ICT production is not necessary to access productivity gains. The US estimates suggest that there have been roughly equal productivity gains at the aggregate level from ICT production and use in that country.

But the scope for productivity gains in production in the USA does not translate as readily to other countries as does the scope for productivity gains from use. The US production gains come from a very large scale of operations and a degree of technological leadership that cannot be readily established in other countries. Aside from some niche areas (particularly in software), ICT production requires not only large scale operation but also sales in highly competitive international markets. This makes it tough going for a relatively small economy like Australia's.

By being open to imports of ICTs, Australia has been able to gain quickly from advances in ICT manufacture and has been able to capture a sizeable terms of trade gain from the rapidly declining international prices in ICTs. Taking the benefits of productivity gains generated by foreign producers through lower prices is a real income gain to Australians. An international comparison by Bayoumi and Haacker found that Australia is among the world's main beneficiaries from ICTs, even though it is not a significant producer. Welfare gains from lower ICT prices, accumulated over 1985 to 2001, amounted to 5 per cent of GDP not far short of the highest beneficiary, the USA, at 5.6 per cent of GDP. Australia benefits as a high-using importer with rapidly declining prices. But the estimated welfare gains in some major producer countries.

Finland, Ireland, Japan, and Korea have been lower than in Australia. And some major producers (such as Malaysia, Thailand and the Philippines) have not experienced major welfare gains. The second point is that a direct focus on ICTs (and in particular on production) masks the importance of the preconditions required to drive the uptake and smart use of ICTs (where 'smart' implies business restructuring and complementary product and process innovations, based on ICT use).

Sharper competitive incentives to be productive help to explain why Australia has moved from being a technology laggard in previous decades to being at the forefront of new technology uptake in the 1990s. Taking full advantage of declining prices and advances in technologies and not restricting them through trade or other barriers is also conducive to ICT uptake. And the development of skills in the workforce can also be important in identifying and developing applications for ICTs. Strong competition also affects the distribution of productivity gains.

A competitive environment means that more of the gains are likely to be passed on in lower prices and thereby assist in dampening inflationary pressures. ICT-related or other productivity gains do not in themselves dampen inflation, as some new economy advocates claim. Healthy competition is a necessary precondition.

Flexibility is also important in enabling the productivity-enhancing reorganisation of firms (outsourcing, better management of supplier and customer linkages) and work arrangements (team work, multiskilling, performance-based remuneration, shift arrangements) and so on. The third and related point is that it is important not to lose sight of factors unrelated to ICTs that are the source of substantial productivity gains.

The Treasury stated that ICT prices have fallen in domestic currency terms by 9.5 per cent a year and raised the terms of trade by 0.3 per cent a year between 1985 and 2001. Since 1995, ICT prices have fallen by nearly 15 per cent a year and raised the terms of trade by 0.75 per cent a year.

Australia has enjoyed an MFP acceleration of around 1.1 percentage points associated primarily with non-ICT factors, but with some contribution from ICT use not production. To state the obvious, it would be not make sense to focus on chasing a gain of (at most) 0.3 of a percentage point associated with ICTs - especially by concentrating on encouraging ICT production - if that came at the cost of realising a 1.1 percentage point gain from catch-up and 'smart use' of ICTs.

But there is a big policy overlap between developing the conditions for catch-up productivity gains associated with restructuring and modernisation, on the one hand, and developing the conditions conducive to uptake and smart use of ICTs, on the other. Promoting effective competition, openness and flexibility is at the heart of both.

The Australian economy became more focused on productivity and more flexible at just the right time to take advantage of the advances in ICTs that came on stream in the second half of the 1990s. It was not so much that policymakers deliberately set out with an ICT strategy. Without many predicting or perhaps even realising it, Australia became 'ICT-ready' (and ready for any other technological development that could be usefully employed). Given a history of lagging in the uptake of technology and of relatively poor productivity performance, it is unlikely that Australia would have been as quick on the uptake of ICTs, or as able to use them in productivity-enhancing ways, had it not been for the sea-change that reforms brought.

Even though fostering the right business conditions should remain the policy priority, there are nevertheless ICT-specific policy issues to consider as well. These also cover the provision of ICT-related services and include:

— the optimal development of complementary innovations, based on ICTs;

— the optimal development of communications infrastructure;

— the implications of use of ICT networks for the strength of competition in markets;

— the development of appropriate ICT-related skills;

— adjustment issues concerning job flexibility for those with specific skills displaced by ICTs;

— appropriate protection of intellectual property rights in distribution via the Internet;

— access to networks, including the issue of the 'digital divide';

— regulation of network content; and

— security of tax bases through use of Internet and other networks.

In short, Australia has entered the 'new economy' era in the sense that some of its productivity gains are associated with ICTs. Australia's link with the 'new economy' has come, firstly, from high investment in ICTs. However, the substitution of ICT growth for growth in other forms of capital has meant that there has been no overall capital deepening effect on underlying, labour productivity growth. Secondly, there is evidence that there have also been MFP gains associated with ICT use.

The production of ICTs is not necessary to access MFP gains. And so Australia's lack of significant manufacture of ICT equipment has not been a barrier to entry into the 'new economy'. Australia experienced a strong productivity acceleration in the 1990s. Labour productivity accelerated by 1 percentage point and MFP by 1.1 percentage points. Most of the MFP gains (0.8 of a percentage point or more) are attributable to international catch up.

Microeconomic reforms have assisted this process by releasing the shackles on the economy that were holding back growth in productivity. A relatively modest part of the MFP gains (up to 0.3 of a percentage point) can be more specifically attributed to ICT use. These gains have been focused in the distribution and financial services sectors of the economy. There is not strong evidence of widespread productivity gains from use of networks, such as the Internet (at least as yet). Aside from the fact that production of ICTs is not necessary, government encouragement of local ICT production could be questioned on a number of grounds. Australia's cost structures, the competitiveness of the market and the need for large scale production and technological leadership would make it a tall task to establish significant and viable Australian production.

As an importer, Australia has also been benefiting from terms of trade gains from the declining prices of ICTs. Taking the benefits of productivity gains generated by foreigners through lower prices has been a source of real income gain to Australians. The welfare gains from ICTs have been greater to Australia than to most other countries, including many major ICT producing countries. This also raises the question of where the welfare gains would go if Australia were to foster local production.

If Australia became an exporter, at least some of the gains would go to foreigners. And it is by no means clear that Australian businesses would have the same access to the latest technological developments at the same declining price. This in turn could affect the rate of uptake of technologies and/or the rate of complementary investments in productivity-enhancing innovation. The Australian experience suggests that the policy priority should be to enhance competition, openness and flexibility in the business environment, rather than focus too strongly or directly on ICTs and the 'new economy'.

Policy reforms in Australia have provided competitive incentives for firms to take up ICTs, enabled ready access to the latest advances in ICTs and have ensured that firms have the flexibility to use ICTs in ways that help to transform their businesses and raise productivity. A focus on the right business conditions means that the 'smart' and productive use of ICTs and substantial gains unrelated to ICTs can then follow.

This approach focusing on the conditions in which business operates has taken Australia toward the international forefront of uptake and smart use of ICTs. It has generated large welfare gains by allowing maximum benefit from falling ICT prices and promoting associated productivity gains. There are always ways to improve further. But Australia has been on the right path to get the most welfare gains it can from ICTs.

Brazilian E-commerce Strategy

Brazil understood that develop local e-commerce ought

to be a strategy specifically designed for Brazilian environment. The most important fact was the launching of the Information Society Program as a framework for all activities regarding information technology in the country.

The Program assured both focus and economical feasibility for all actions the Country should perform to ensure our participation in the knowledge era. Thus, under this framework, many strategies related to market, production, human resources, e-government, Internet content, cultural and social aspects etc. were designed and implemented to reach the same goal – a more equal and dynamic social and economic development for Brazil.

Under the Information Society framework the actions taken to reach one target was mostly the same to reach the other, so development was amazingly quick in Brazil, surprising even those involved with the strategy.

Regarding e-commerce a strategy based on three main points was designed:

—Infrastructure

—Legal framework

—Implementation

At the very first moment became clear for Brazilians that two different lines of action regarding e-commerce implementation should be designed : one for B2B and another for B2C, although both depend on the same infrastructure and legal framework.

Infrastructure – certainly universalization of telecommunication was the most important way to provide a basic internet access for everyone in the

Country. The telecommunications privatization process, started in 95, established targets for the new owners that they have to accomplish, in the early years after the privatization.

It became a great success considering the growing rates in the period – end of 1994 to end of 2001 – from 13.25 million to 44.5 million) in fixed lines and from 755 thousands to 33.4 million wireless lines, with a total investment of US$ 10.9 billion.

Nevertheless, the most important decision taken by the Government and approved by the Congress was the FUST – a special fund to promote universalization of access not only for phone lines but also for Internet access. It was strategic because, due the huge social gap among classes in Brazil, certainly there would be non profit areas where the conventional attraction efforts for private investment will not work.

The fund itself is formed by a deposit from the incumbent operator companies, and will be rebated to them in a competition bid for the best projects to reach those non profit areas. The estimated annual investment is US$ 500.0 million.

Another important strategy was to ensure local capacity for developing software and manufacturing IT goods, focused on keeping our local trade balance under control.

For software solution development, Softex, a huge new design program, was settled around the Country to improve local human resources in software development, either considering the Portuguese language and local cultural peculiarities (specially regarding accounts and taxes) as well as to promote the start up of new software companies.

To face the huge investment necessary to reach the predefined goals in telecommunication privatization contracts, another important strategy was to attract foreign investments in manufacturing facilities as well as strengths the local manufacturing companies.

Certainly Internet facilities were another main issue. Brazil started with Internet, back to the end of the eighties, through the academic network program approach, Brazilian RNP, which was similar to USA and European programs in order to guarantee academic internet connection.

The Government used this knowledge to open competition, establish a well developed use of dot br, and have invested in constant renewal of IP network development. That led us to a very interesting position in the World Wide Web ranking especially considering our condition of developing country.

Nowadays Brazil is the 11 th in number of host, the 5 th in ccTLD registrar, as well as capable to run IPv6 in the academic network.

Legal framework - With infrastructure running and with adequate funding instruments, it was time to take care of the legal instruments that should be constructed – and how to deal with them – to improve our e-commerce and e-government. It was clear that overcoming the brick world concept regarding contracts, documents, financial transactions, credit bonds, signatures and certificates would be a must.

To help technically both the Government and the Congress, a special Internet Security Committee was settled, dedicated to establish a safety environment regarding contracts and signatures. This Committee produced a reference document -the "ICP Termo de Referencia" -with all technical and financial alternatives issues that have been used to support the formal Government proposal to the Congress.

With this step completed, during 2000 and 2001 the Government established the discussions and got approvals for the PKI,-the root structure, the certificate entity regarding government formal signatures and the alternatives for private relationship. The Government itself started using electronic signature at Jan, 1 st , 2001.

With the same approach the acceptability of electronic document and digital signature was submitted to Congress analysis and was approved. To guarantee a complete safety environment for government transactions, an agency – the AGP Brazil- was created, in order to accomplish a formal mission : "to establish and manage the policies and acts related to the permanent operation of PKI-Gov in Brazil".

Under this agency, the following activities took place:

— Establish formal criteria for Certifying Authorities [AC] and Registrar Authorities [AR]

— Establish the periodicity for AC and AR audit;

— Definition about charges and fines to be imposed for breaking rules

— Operational rules related to: ACs, ARs, digital signature, secure cryptography, certificate storage, certificate revoke, security copies and key recovering, key automatic update, key traceability, cross certification, validity for certificates, unretractability guarantee for electronic transactions and operations.

The concepts defined for electronic document followed the basic 1966 UNCITRAL model and was formalized by Federal measurement MP 2200-1 and MP 2002-2. A resume of the main rules can be described as:

"the cryptographic key pair shall always be generated by the owner, and his private key will be under his exclusive use, control and knowledge."

- all public and private electronic documents are legal;
- Document contents are presumed truthful, regarding the signature owner, if certified by ICP Brasil structure and will be valid as defined in art 131 Law 3.071 1/1/ 1916 of the Civil Code
- Document exchanged among private persons are free to use any certification if agreed among those persons"

Some other important decisions related to electronic transactions are in process and will define the best practices about the agency interaction with the market, advertising and public offers by electronic means and legal charges regarding systems invasion, electronic piracy, modification, destruction and unauthorized use of data.

New electronic procurement rules for government acquisition are also to be sent for Congress approval and will be a great incentive for the use of electronic auction, thus being one of the most important instruments to improve e-commerce among small and micro companies.

A new banking payment structure [SBP] regarding electronic money transference, currency use and related issues are already in use since June 7th, 2002 and was launched without any problem. This was not a surprise because Brazil was the first country to use banking automation back in the early 80`s. This was due to the high inflation rate at those days and the peculiar process Brazilians used to deal with the problem which demanded a unique solution that was not available around the world at that time.

The AC root structure is running and since January,2001 all documents transferred from or to the Brazilian President by the Ministers must be done by electronic means and with an electronic signature. After January, 2002 this procedure was extended for authorities in the next level of the Federal Government hierarchy regarding their transactions with their Ministers. The next levels will follow.

Nowadays is running a special effort regarding technology development for e-commerce which includes cryptography.

Implementation – With the first two legs of its strategy running, Brazil started the Implementation As stated before, two different lines of action regarding e-commerce implementation should be designed: one for B2B and another for B2C.

To deal with this scenario the Government established another committee the e-commerce committee. This is a private and public committee with a tripartite coordination with members chosen by the Government and by the representative associations of society.

The committee was launched in July, 2001 and is running under the following bylaws:

Six Sub-Committees

I - Payment means for e-commerce—Government Coordination

II – Logistics & National Integration—Government Coordination

III –Economic Aspects —Brazilian Industry Association Coordination

IV– Applications and Projects (social approach)—IP Association Coordination

V - Technology and Products for e-commerce —Software Association Coordination

VI –e-commerce for Small Business—National Commerce Association Coordination

With these responsibilities respectively :

- I -Payment means for e-commerce – Government Coordination Full acceptance of electronic offers inside and outside national border;
  - — On line currency and credit markets;
  - — Electronic stock and future/options market;
  - — Full offers of goods, information and services;
  - — Third part safety regarding electronic documents;
  - — Full legal guarantee
- II– Logistics and National Integration – Government Coordination
  - — Logistics,
  - — local and national transport network and services,

— distribustion, regional access, cost, investments, new rules and statistics related to e-commerce logistic and transport aspects;

— competition.

- III – Economic Aspects

— Brazilian Industry Association Coordination International aspects related to e-commerce;

— investments;

— financing and credit;

— costs, international legislation, statistics, international agreements intellectual property rights;

— arbitration (new law)

- IV – Applications & Projects (social approach) – IP Association Coordination

— e-procurement ;

— local IP access, training and local capacity for Internet use and trade – focus on shorten the social and economic gap using e-commerce for local development in the community commerce

- V - Technology and Products for e-commerce – Software Association Coordination

— New technologies development ;

— local software solutions;

— experimental joint development;

— R&D promotion;

— innovation promotion;

— venture capital promotion;

— focus on new products and new services

- VI – e-commerce for Small Business – National Csommerce Association Coordination

— e-procurement promotion for small business;

— low cost hardware ;

— training and promotion of local capacity (SEBRAE);

— joint work with V and IV sub committees for local solutions.

The committee is running and influencing many decisions related to Government and private entities, and like all other projects under the Information Society framework, is using all the facilities achieved around the Country to reach its goals.

B2B - It is important to understand that B2B in Brazil started shyly before the launching of e-procurement for the e-government program which increased the use of electronic auction and acquisition using previously existing electronic supplier database.

Initially the new activity was broadcasted among potential suppliers. Once e-procurement succeeded, it was a boom in the specialized media and even in the regular media, thus encouraging the use of e-commerce among more and more companies.

The 2002 forecast for annual average amount per customer is US$ 1,882. (IDC scenario) The investments in this area have been very important and some known brands are also operating in the country.

IT infrastructure, space and bandwidth supply Over 100,000 square meters and over US$ 600 billions investment The e-procurement is playing an important role in this matter, but it is still necessary facilitate the effective entrance of SME into this market to have a real increase of B2B e-commerce in Brazil.

A new program to be launched probably during July, 2002 shall be an important step ahead. It intends to establish a general website and e-procurement address for all municipalities in the Country at the same time, based on a local software platform.

After that, and with a simultaneous training program and the Fust fund to interconnect all municipalities, the opportunities for SME will be tremendously increased, forcing them to join to this new e-commerce technology.

B2C – B2C is a complete different world. First of all Brazilians, unlike Americans, due a cultural peculiarity are not used to buy by catalog, even by phone. Brazilians like to be among others, discuss their options and, depending on social class level, to be oriented by someone they trust, before their buying decision. Added to this peculiarity, the general low income and the yet not completed universiliation of telecom or internet access had contributed to reduce the growth rate of B2C.

However, comparing with other countries, Brazil is not following a peculiar path, since most countries, including USA, have been facing similar growing rates between B2B and B2C regardless their level of development.

The B2C in Brazil is responsible for a small amount of 15% on e-commerce income, but, considering the annual average income/customer, the numbers (IDC scenario) are not so bad:

— 2000 – US$ 619

— 2001 – US$ 725

— 2002 – US$ 873

Another important decision about to be taken by the Government is related to Digital TV standard definition.

In Brazil, due the "tight relationship" that Brazilian population has with the TV –92% of homes have TV (even in the poorest areas) – depending on the chosen standard, digital TV might be the most important instrument for B2C development. An old trust relationship among television media and people have been constructed during years, so the new digital facilities, if well defined, could be easily used as an alternative for e-commerce B2C, keeping the communication and orientation bond demanded by people and offered in Television approach.

In short, Brazilian e-commerce seems to be an important consequence of e-government growth. This statement can be explained first considering Brazilian people is already very familiar with banking automation and, because with the daily personal demanding of e-gov services, the population is learning quickly how to use IT facilities.

At the same time the e-government success is spreading a base of confidence in such technologies, encouraging small business' to invest in e-commerce facilities as well as to reduce the common personal fear simple people used to have against incomprehensive new technologies.

Brazilian e-government success is well known also outside the country due two unique successful programs

: our long time running Income Tax Internet, and the 2000 complete electronic major election – 108 million voting at same day in all 5,561 municipalities around the country, electing mayors and local chamber representatives, and getting the complete and non questionable results at the end of the very same day.

To better show the link between e-gov and e-commerce, programs like those implemented by the Brazilian Post Office are good examples: they are taking advantage and establishing new ways for improving e-commerce.

The basic one is the Open Door program which motto is "Everyone must have an e-address" even the homeless. An e-address. The idea is prepare the population to use internet, get electronic messages, government services and goods through the post office, as they are used to do in the traditional way. The Post Office is installing public internet kiosks with experimental local programs using local/regional students.

Chapter 2

E-Commerce and Economic Growth

The new economic paradigm, according to which new information and communication technologies (ICT) would deliver ever-higher rates of inflation-free growth, seemed to be among the first victims of the dotcom crash. But even after the crash, e-commerce has continued to grow.

While e-commerce clearly has a positive impact on the business sector, doubts have been raised about its impact on macroeconomic growth, and productivity growth in particular.

In previous technological revolutions, productivity gains have in the long run helped to improve living standards - one of the main goals of development. The US, which leads the world in IT and e-commerce, has had an impressive economic performance, particularly in terms of productivity growth, since 1995.

Much of the acceleration in productivity growth is structural and attributable to changes induced by ICT and the Internet, through improvements in all aspects of corporate organization, production, finance, marketing and logistics. According UNCTAD, ICT will continue to support rapid productivity growth, citing several reasons: the cost of computing power is expected to keep falling steeply for several years; most enterprises are still learning how to reorganize themselves in order to benefit fully from the Internet; and even if productivity growth does not maintain its recent phenomenal pace in the United States, the rest of the world has a lot of catching up to do in the application of ICT to business.

But there will be no productivity growth for many developing countries if they fail to catch up technologically with the industrialized world, as the Report shows. To assess the broader economic impact of e-commerce and the ramifications of developing countries' catching up or not, UNCTAD has conducted a quantitative analysis based on two scenarios: one in which developing countries fall behind technologically, and one in which they catch up with developed countries. The analysis is centred on cost savings and assumes that e-commerce can reduce costs of services, particularly in retail and wholesale trade, transport, and financial and business services.

Cost savings in services are simulated through a productivity growth scenario, which allows for the analysis of such macroeconomic variables as GDP, welfare, wages and terms of trade. The analysis is a unique application of a computable general equilibrium (CGE) model to e-commerce at the global level.

Under the first scenario developed countries would have welfare gains of $117 billion, while the developing world would lose welfare of $726 million. The Asian region, on the other hand, would gain $802 million, largely attributable to the transport services sector. Besides welfare and GDP losses, developing countries would also experience a reduction in wages and deteriorating.

The value of ICT for development lies not so much in the share of the global economy that this sector may come to represent, but in the changes that ICT will introduce in the functioning of enterprises across the economies that assimilate them. If developing countries were to catch up with developed countries in productivity, they would increase output, wages and welfare. A 1% productivity growth in the services sector in Asia, for example, would result in welfare gains of $12 billion, GDP growth of 0.4%, a wage increase of 0.4% and a 2- to-3% growth in services exports. By reducing costs, increasing efficiency, reducing time and distances, e-commerce could thus become an important tool for development.

If the Internet is only a 'space' - cyberspace - it is a space without borders in which private international law has no meaning, since the rules of private international law are made in order to deal with different legal systems and borders. Among the thorny issues raised by the advent of the Internet and e-commerce. Privacy and consumer protection are also problematic, given the lack of international agreements and of transborder or dispute settlement mechanisms designed specifically for electronic transactions.E-commerce currently operates in a tax- and duty-free environment, in an unclear legal and regulatory framework - a situation calling for urgent intergovernmental cooperation to clarify the situation. Income taxation largely depends on whether a business has permanent establishment (PE) in a country or not.

OECD countries have agreed that a website by itself cannot constitute PE, while a web server can, if it is owned by a business that carries on business through the server. However, "proposals by OECD countries have given scant consideration to developing countries' concerns in the field of e-commerce taxation", according to the Report, which also notes the "major differences" between EU and US approaches to international taxation rules on e-commerce.

As to consumption taxes, such as VAT or sales tax, there is a growing tendency to apply taxation in the place of consumption. This would actually work in favour of developing countries, as most of them rely heavily on such taxes for their government budgets and will be net importers of e-commerce in the medium term.

Although no customs duties are currently imposed on electronic transmissions, this is much discussed at the WTO, with a number of countries advocating a tariff-free environment for e-commerce and others expressing concern about possible revenue losses if products previously subject to customs duties are imported duty-free.

Potential fiscal losses on border tariffs and other duties imposed on digital imports could total $8 billion worldwide. While on average this is less than 1% of total government revenue, tariff losses would be much greater in developing countries.

B2B e-markets, e-finance flourishing

Business-to-business (B2B) e-markets, which have already outstripped business-to-consumer (B2C) e-commerce in volume, are expected to play an even more pivotal role in future, becoming the single largest component of B2B by 2004. Online B2B sales in the US are forecast to reach $3 trillion by 2004, of which an estimated $1.5 trillion will be via B2B e-markets.

The highest growth in B2B e-markets will likely be in such sectors as computing and electronics, utilities, motor vehicles, petrochemicals and paper, office products and food and agriculture. These markets will also undergo consolidation, the formation of strategic alliances and greater focus on the provision of differentiated and specialized products and services.

Online financial operations - which make it possible to handle huge financial operations and related payments traffic both nationally and cross-border at a fraction of the former costs and time - are also experiencing explosive growth, according to the Report. Current forecasts suggest double-digit growth rates for e-finance over the next few years.

The Internet banking segment is slated to expand 25% annually, as compared to 3% for the overall banking industry. In developed countries, half of all banking and 80% of all brokerage activities are expected to go online.

For emerging economies, the figures range from 30% for e-banking to 40% for e-brokerage. But financial service providers, especially from developing and transition economies, will have to address the high initial costs and technological complexity of establishing online payments before they can hope for "e-finance preparedness", warns the UNCTAD e-commerce report. The technology still cannot cope with the needs of high-value and micro-payments in B2B and B2C alike.

Online payments and e-financing technologies are at an early stage of standardization, with the industry still choosing between competing models and solutions. Promises of "Net-only" banking and payment solutions becoming a "killer application" are proving highly exaggerated, but banks and other traditional financial services providers are under pressure to adopt aggressive Internet strategies and rapidly increase their online services.

No economic sector has been subject to more far-fetched growth forecasts or sweeping statements about a bright future than e-commerce. Venture capitalists, financial analysts and the public in general have blindly used these inflated numbers to take decisions on investments in start-up companies and the stock market - often with disastrous results.

E-commerce data are largely provided by private sector companies, which regularly publish reports on the latest developments in e-commerce, including short- to medium-term growth estimates. Unfortunately, the numbers differ considerably, depending on which methodologies, definitions and indicators are used. Estimates of global B2B e-commerce last year, for example, range from $200 billion to $604 billion.

Ecommerce Strategies in Malaysia

Electronic commerce or e-commerce is recognised as an important agenda for Malaysia to start moving into the new Economy. Malaysia sees e-commerce as the new way to do business through the digital network. E-commerce will enable. Malaysian businesses to create new value, raise the level of productivity, increase competitiveness in export markets and facilitate new type of business process for reaching customers in the world.

In the 7th Malaysia Plan, ICT was recognized as a strategic tool to support the growth of the economy. The Plan targeted the development process of ICT and promoted extensive application to the public. In the 8th Malaysia Plan, e-commerce was specifically mentioned for the first time. Like any other technology, ICT can have positive or negative effects. ICT can aggravate the rich-poor gap but it also presents possible solutions to many problems. If properly harnessed, ICT can improve standard of living more quickly and more dramatically than any other time in history. It has therefore become compelling for a managed process in using ICT for positive development.

To better understand the fundamental technological changes and how it can improve the quality of life, the National IT Council (NITC) was established in 1994. The NITC acts as a think tank and an advisor to the government and is the key initiator of programmes and strategies aimed at creating an information rich society.

The work of the NITC is guided by the National IT Agenda (NITA), a strategic framework for IT programme development at the federal, state and local government levels involving the participation with the private, non-government and voluntary sectors.

The Government of Malaysia has already initiated efforts to lay the foundation for e-commerce in the country. The government in consultation with the private sector has initiated a legal and regulatory framework of cyber laws and intellectual property laws to create a predictable environment for the implementation of e-commerce. Six cyber laws have been enacted. They are the Digital Signature Act 1997, the Copyright (amendment) Act 1997, the Computer Crimes Act 1997, the

Telemedicine Act 1997, the Communications and Multimedia Act 1998 and the Communications and Multimedia Commission Act 1998. A bill on personal data protection is pending and efforts to harmonise existing laws and regulations with cyber laws are on going.

Malaysia has established a clear set of policy objectives that takes into account the ramifications of the convergence of telecommunications, computing and broadcasting. Reforms were undertaken by putting in place an enabling legislation, that is, the Communications and Multimedia Act 1998 and establishing a new independent regulatory agency for the convergent industry, which is the Malaysian Communications and Multimedia Commission.

The Communications and Multimedia Act 1998 provides the necessary policies to regulate, facilitate and nurture the development of the communications and multimedia industry, the growth of which is needed to support e-commerce.

The "Growth with Equity" development strategy has been successful in maintaining balanced development for over 30 years in the country. However, socio-economic inequities still exist and may be magnified if the development of ICT is not constructively managed. The government has set aside allocations to fund special programmes to address the digital divide such as community internet centres for rural folks and computing infrastructure to rural schools. In addition, the government has set up a Universal Service Fund to finance the cost of building basic infrastructure and internet access to rural and other underserved areas.

The adoption of ICT by the government in providing services to the public is a catalyst for greater use of ICT in the country. The public is encouraged to use ICT to access government information, transact services and make payments through various electronic delivery channels provided by the government. For the business community, an e-enabled government helps reduce their cost of doing business.

To accelerate uptake of e-commerce, the government is also making efforts to convince the non-ICT sectors, especially the small medium sized enterprises, which made up more than 84% of all enterprises to use more ICT products and services in their business. Besides increasing productivity and competitiveness in the non-ICT sectors, greater ICT use by non-ICT sectors will increase output in the ICT sector itself.

Malaysia participates at regional and international fora to discuss e-commerce and e-commerce related matters such as the WTO, APEC and ASEAN. Participation gives the country the opportunity to influence the development of international guidelines and new practices. The country also participates in cross border e-commerce projects such as the pilot projects for the exchange of customs EDI messages among customs authorities in Asia.

CHAPTER 3

Transformation in Information Society

The meaning of the 'Knowledge Society' is derived from geopolitical analyses, which often pick up the globalisation theme. The next meaning is rooted in deeper social and cultural analyses. These range from optimistic – and, perhaps, rather mechanistic – accounts of social change such as Manuel Castells' trilogy on the Network Societys; to much more sombre accounts, such as that offered by Ulrich Beck in his Risk Society, which emphasise the fragmentation of social meaning and atomisation of individual experience.

Closely allied are the gloomy scenarios offered by environmentalists – and even the violent protests against globalisation. Also linked, although indirectly, are notions of intellectual volatility, verging at times on the excesses of postmodernism – because grand narratives, over-arching conceptualisations, meta-theories have been made redundant by the 'acceleration' of knowledge and the ability to manipulate massive data-sets.

The university is implicated in all these different meanings of the Knowledge Society – for example, of the source of the basic science from which highly sophisticated information and communication technologies are derived; as a 'national' institution (because, despite their internationalist rhetoric, universities are creatures of the nation state) threatened by the decay of the welfare states that have nourished their development and challenged by market-led globalisation; as critical institutions from which alternative, even oppositional, ideologies emerge. So the university itself may have become a problematic and contested institution.

The idea of the Knowledge Society, accounts of changes in scientific production do not provide with the firm foundations on which we can build secure scenarios about the future development of higher education. Also, as with the Knowledge Society, the university is complexly embroiled – as the producer of (most) basic science; but also as an increasingly aggressive exploiter of intellectual property and as the mediator (or broker) of research results.

The new players in the Knowledge Society are not as easy to identify as is commonly supposed; and that the path the University should follow is far from clear.

There are three major rivals are identified by the ever-increasing number of 'observatories' that have been established:

i) *The first is the development of so-called 'borderless education' institutions.* Some of these are based on global consortia of traditional universities, or by mixed consortia of world-class universities (world-class – because the 'brand' is all important in this arena) and global corporations, either mass media or IT. Others, of course, are more directly rivals to the traditional universities – and may take the form of on-line 'universities' established by such corporations.

The fundamental analysis underlying all these efforts is that the problem is not the development of intellectual concepts and content – which can either be brought off-the-peg or provided by academic entrepreneurs / sub-contractors as part of a supply-chain – but the customisation, delivery and marketing of these intellectual 'products' – the potential of which is now massively enhanced by the power of information and communication technologies.

It is rooted in a one-dimensional technology-deterministic account of the Knowledge Society; it ignores the complexities of cultural transfer and of 'local' takes on 'global' knowledge (and consequently is restricted in its operation to a narrow range of disciplines – overwhelmingly business and management, IT and computer science and some fields of science and engineering); and it fails to understand the synergies and complementarities between traditional face-to-face and 'virtual' forms of learning

ii) *The second group of rival institutsions are private for-profit 'universities'*. The University of Phoenix is the inevitable totemic example, but there are several other examples. First, these institutions, because they are in the private sector, are – apparently – unencumbered by the burden of state, and public, regulation and, therefore, free to operate more entrepreneurially.

Secondly, private for-profit 'universities' like Phoenix, because they are not universities at all in a traditional sense, are also unencumbered by the burden of intellectual, professional and cultural norms which 'proper' universities, public or (not-for-profit) private, have to carry. This may be a genuine advantage – or, better, difference. Such institutions are free to unbundle activities such as research and teaching, course design and course delivery; nor do they need to worry about disciplines as communities of intellect, because they are able to concentrate simply on knowledge 'products.

But many of the constraints which apply to 'borderless education' enterprises also apply to private for-profit universities. In addition the analysis that animates their existence is again rooted in a one-dimensional account of the Knowledge Society, the geopolitical triumph of the market states;

iii) *The third 'threat' to the traditional university is seen as coming from the proliferation of 'corporate universities'.* Sometimes these take the form of re-badged company training departments, perhaps with some R and D elements thrown in. This kind of development has been encouraged, and legitimised, by the growth of a powerful 'human resources' discourse.

At other times the establishment of corporate universities reflect a more concerted approach to workforce development. A good example is the recent formation in Britain of the 'National Health Service University'. However, although both are important developments.

First, many 'corporate universities' are engaged in lower-level training and/or short-course based continuing professional development; they often contract with universities for the provision of more sophisticated courses.

Secondly, their activities are largely complementary to those of existing universities. For example, the NHS University in Britain is not going to set up in competition with University Medical Schools, or even Schools of Nursing.

These new functions – technology transfer and knowledge management – are familiar to all. The nature of teaching and learning, of academic courses, of research programmes has also been transformed. There are now open frontiers between the academy and society, the economy, culture. Work-based learning, the accreditation of prior experience and similar practices and phenomena are evidence of cross-frontiers flows. So, if we ask who are the new players, the answer is – in part – ourselves; we are the new players;

The second form taken by the hybridisation of higher education is an extension of the first. It is the emergence of new organisational forms within the University that parallel traditional patterns of academic organisation such as Faculties and Departments. Of course, that traditional taxonomy has complex origins – some parts are based on academic affinities and are 'policed' by (fairly) endogenous scientific communities; other parts reflect the division of professional labour in wider society (although this division of labour has not been imposed on the University from the outside; law schools and medical schools play a key role in not only the reproduction but also the definition of professions). It is difficult to claim that research institutes or graduate schools are novel forms (especially, of course, in North America). However, the balance is now changing.

More and more organisational units within universities are based on neither principle –academic affinities or the division of professional (or expert) labour. Instead they have more in common with project teams, think-tanks, task-forces – and, of course, market entities designed to exploit the intellectual property that is generated within the University. These old and new organisational forms coexist, sometimes as rivals but at other times as allies. Again, if we ask where are the new organisations in the Knowledge Society, the answer – in part – is in the University; we are creating many of these new organisations.

The second phenomenon is the potential for growing 'activist' knowledge organisations which are in opposition to both traditional universities and to the new 'market' universities. They are opposed to traditional universities because they associate them with social elitism (or the reproduction of social hierarchies according to the division of labour in a capitalist society) and with restrictive definitions of knowledge that again are elitist, frequently gendered still (despite the impact of feminism) and generally dismissive of alternative and popular knowledge traditions.

As a result these 'activist' knowledge organisations challenge notions of evidence, objectivity, balance, debate which have typically been regarded as fundamental to the University (even if these high ideals have not always been met). However, these organisations are equally opposed to the 'market' universities which we take to be the principal rivals of the public university. They reject many of the 'givens' which most have been bullied into accepting in this (apparent) twilight of social democracy and the welfare state – the materiality of motivation, the efficacy of incentives, the drive to efficiency, the calculus of cost and benefits (on which, of course, the case for developing 'market' universities is based). And, paradoxically, they reject these 'givens' taking full advantage of the technologies of mass communication which we take to be typical of the market economy.

These 'activist' knowledge organisations take many forms – from local community groups, now with access to global data-bases and communication networks, through fundamentalists of all kinds perhaps even to global terrorist networks (However much we recoil from the notion that they are knowledge organisations, they employ sophisticated technologies and develop their own ideologies).

These organisations also range from fundamentalists, which fundamentally reject the culture of liberality associated with elite universities and the parallel culture of rationality associated with university science and scholarship, to organisations such as Green Peace which believe with some justice that their rational use of scientific evidence is equal or superior to that of the World Bank or the IMF.

At their best these 'activist' knowledge organisations, in their enthusiasm for a more democratic distribution of knowledge resources and their opposition to the more baleful aspects of globalisation, may be assuming some of the ethical responsibilities which universities willingly accepted a generation ago but from which they have more recently distanced themselves.

In short, a naive and one-dimensional interpretation of the Knowledge Society – which, in fact, is a problematical category with multiple, and contested, interpretations. Furthermore these accounts attach too little weight to the fundamental – but, again, complex and ambiguous – changes that are taking place in knowledge production.

2002 E-Readiness Ranking

Today the e-rankings have become an established benchmark for countries seeking to harness the Internet 's potential to spur business efficiency, improve the provision of public services and encourage integration with the global economy. "E-readiness " is shorthand for the extent to which a country 's business environment is conducive to Internet-based opportunities.

It is a concept that spans a wide range of factors, from telephone penetration to online security to intellectual property protection. It is an idea that has outlasted the Internet "bubble " that sparked such exuberance -and delivered such disappointment -in the late 1990s. "Despite the dotcom bust, the Internet is still reshaping the way companies do business, and countries ' e-readiness will be a vital feature of the global competitive landscape," notes Daniel Franklin, Editorial Director of the Economist Intelligence Unit. Covering the world 's 60 largest markets, the rankings provide a useful guide for companies seeking to invest in technology-savvy countries, as well as governments looking to reap the benefits of the digital age.

Both the Economist Intelligence Unit and IBM have engaged in e-business research for many years, so collaborative work on the rankings was a natural fit.The rankings model is a joint undertaking. The Economist Intelligence Unit, however, has sole responsibility for scoring and ranking the 60 countries covered by the e-readiness rankings.

E-business is taking root just about everywhere -but some countries are pioneers, others laggards. In the latest edition of the Economist Intelligence Unit e-readiness rankings, which cover the world 's 60 largest markets, North America, northern Europe and Australia take the top ten spots. The new edition of the rankings -the third since their launch in 2000 -shows steady improvement and increasing convergence among the top-tier countries, where heavy investment in Internet technologies is bearing fruit.

Many less-developed countries lag behind, however, their e-readiness hindered by a range of factors, including poor infrastructure, inadequate protection for intellectual property, lack of finance and unfavourable business environments.

The new round of rankings affirms two conclusions suggested by previous editions. First, neither size nor location is destiny. Although the US comes first in the rankings, the rankings place a premium on agility rather than sheer economic might. Many nimble smaller economies in Scandinavia and Europe thus score highly, whereas less innovative giants like Japan rank relatively low.

And although geographic regions tend to fall into one category or another, there are always exceptions: standout countries such as Singapore or Chile, which outshine their neighbours in e-readiness. Second, government policy makes a difference.

Many less-developed countries, such as the Czech Republic and Mexico, are making good progress in e-business thanks in large part to proactive government policies. Indeed, for countries near the bottom of our rankings, improvement in the e-business environment owes much to public policy. Where governments have drawn up clear plans for IT investment and computer literacy, enhanced competition among infrastructure providers and enacted laws to deal with the grey areas created by the Internet, e-business fares better.

The white paper, published by the Economist Intelligence Unit in co-operation with IBM, presents the rankings of the world 's largest 60 economies (which account for 95% of global GDP), explains the methodology used and provides detailed findings for the top ten countries in each ranking category. The next edition of the Economist Intelligence Unit e-readiness rankings is scheduled to appear in January 2003.

The US leads the pack, as it did in the 2000 and 2001 Economist Intelligence Unit e-readiness rankings. However, due partially to changes in our methodology, and mostly to developments in countries ' infrastructure, regulatory environment and economy, there have been significant shifts further down in the rankings.

The Netherlands has moved into second place from tenth in 2001, for example, and northern Europe now claims most of the other top spots, thanks not only to sophisticated IT infrastructure and high mobile-phone penetration, but also to smart government policy and a good overall business environment. Asia, Latin America and Africa trail further behind, but a few standouts in each region have made significant gains.

North America and Western Europe dominate the top ten places in our rankings, with Australia the lonely outsider. These countries score highest both because consumers and businesses have embraced the Internet, and because their economic and political stability and openness to foreign investment make them good bets for all kinds of business, particularly e-business.

Singapore and Hong Kong lead the pack in Asia, taking 11th and 13th place, respectively, while Vietnam and Pakistan languish at the bottom of the heap, in 56th and 57th place. The same is true of Latin America, where advanced Chile ranks 28th, while Ecuador stumbles into 50th place. In the Middle East and Africa, Israel alone ranks among the top 30 countries.

The US may rule the roost, but many of the world 's largest economies, including Japan, Germany and France, are outpaced by smaller, more agile, competitors, such as the Netherlands, Switzerland and Sweden. What sets these countries apart is the broad accessibility and affordability of the Internet, thanks to state-of-the-art IT infrastructure and high per capita income.

The US tops the rankings because of the degree to which the Internet has become embedded in commercial culture. Nowhere is so much business conducted over the Internet so routinely. This explains why the US scored highest in the category for e-business supporting services (the consulting and IT services and back- office solutions used to facilitate online business) as well as in the social and cultural category (which considers, among other things, the degree of innovation and entrepreneurship in business).

Singapore and Hong Kong rank as the most competitive telecom markets in the world, and among the best equipped, yet don't figure among the top ten countries. While high-grade infrastructure is important, more important is how people use it. Infrastructure is still evolving.

Even top-ranked countries have not yet satisfied consumer demand for fast, cheap, secure and reliable Internet connectivity. High-speed broadband services are not universally available and Internet-ready mobile phones are still in their infancy -even in mobile- crazed Scandinavia. In emerging markets, meanwhile, monopolistic telecom providers still inhibit the competition that can speed innovation and drive down prices, and tight budgets thwart ambitious development plans.

Internet business thrives when governments are committed to a clear, consistent strategy to develop IT infrastructure. Adequate funding is crucial, but so too is firm political leadership that builds public support.

Successful e-business depends on a strong legal framework that protects private property and encourages entrepreneurship. Increasingly, it also requires Internet-specific legislation. In the crucial category of legal and policy environment, Australia comes first, followed by Sweden, Switzerland, Finland and the UK. Other countries - even those without a strong e-business culture, such as Mexico and Chile -are enacting smart Internet legislation, recognising that good laws promote industry growth.

Methodology With every year the model for the Economist Intelligence Unit 's e-readiness rankings has grown in sophistication. This year, working in association with IBM 's Institute for Business Value, the Economist Intelligence Unit adjusted the rankings framework to shift away from the dotcom era 's emphasis on websites and e-commerce to the new imperatives of corporate efficiency, security and global connectivity.

Some countries demonstrate strength in all categories, while others stand out in a few categories but lag behind in others. What follows is a category-by-category assessment of country performance, along with an explanation of the Economist Intelligence Unit 's e-readiness criteria. Pointers are given, as well, to indicate how countries could do more to seize the advantages that the Internet offers.

Connectivity measures the access that individuals and businesses have to basic fixed and mobile telephony services, personal computers and the Internet. The affordability, quality and reliability of service -all functions of the level of competition in the telecom market -also figure as determinants, as does the security of content delivered and transactions conducted via the Internet.

For e-business to take root, countries at a minimum need to ensure secure access to the Internet. Where phone lines are inadequate, computer ownership extremely low and Internet connections prohibitively expensive, e-business has failed to take off. But even in wealthy countries where the infrastructure is reliable and secure, there is tremendous room for improvement. High-speed broadband services are not universally available, and Internet-ready mobile phones are still in their infancy -even in mobile-crazed Scandinavia. No country entirely meets consumer demand for fast, cheap, secure and reliable Internet connectivity.

Deregulation promotes Internet access. Singapore and Hong Kong have the most deregulated telecom markets in the world, followed by northern European countries and the US. At the other end of the spectrum are countries where the state maintains a stranglehold on telecom providers. Turkey 's government, for example, is dragging its feet on selling Turk Telekom, which controls not only the country 's fixed lines but also mobile telephony and Internet service provision. Such fixed-line monopolies hinder e-business in much of the developing world, as they are most often the largest Internet service providers as well.

The two faces of mobile usage. Three out of four Swedes carry a mobile phone. The reasons are clear: the country is tech savvy and gadget loving, and its liberalised telecom market offers lots of choice at low prices. All this bodes well for e-business.

Mobile phone penetration in the Czech Republic is not far behind, at 68%. Yet here the reason for mobile usage is altogether different: the incumbent fixed-line monopoly provides poor service at high prices. In the Czech Republic, as in many developing countries, mobile-phone penetration is high simply because the fixed-line alternative is so unattractive. Mobile usage on its own is not a good indicator of a country 's e-business environment. Uniform standards are important in encouraging mobile usage -and here the US falls far short of Scandinavia.

In evaluating the general business climate, the Economist Intelligence Unit screens 70 indicators covering criteria such as the strength of the economy, political stability, the regulatory environment, taxation, competition policy, the labour market, the quality of infrastructure, and openness to trade and investment. The resulting business environment rankings measure the expected attractiveness of the general business environment over the next five years. Calculated regularly as part of the Economist Intelligence Unit

Country Forecasts, these rankings have long offered investors an invaluable comparative index for 60 major economies.

Good for business, good for e-business. Not long ago, the Internet was seen as the engine of a new world of business that would leave "old economy " companies in the dust. The consensus now is that the Internet makes sense only when applied within the framework of traditional business rules. That said, it is clear that all types of companies and every industry can apply e-business solutions to improve efficiency and streamline operations.

Today, business is e-business, and vice versa. For this reason, countries that score highly in the Economist Intelligence Unit 's business environment rankings -those with stable governments, strong economies, developed legal and regulatory systems, and flexible labour markets -are generally also the best places to do e-business. Countries where competition is restricted and legislation is cumbersome are less e-ready.

The Netherlands scores highly in all the categories that the Economist Intelligence Unit considers crucial for doing business. It has a stable political framework. Its economy is characterised by low inflation, steady growth and openness to foreign trade. Competition policy is well developed. Taxes are low by European standards and financing is readily available. Infrastructure, especially telecom infrastructure, is excellent.

The Netherlands is well ahead of its neighbours in labour market deregulation. Thus the Netherlands takes first place in the business environment rankings. Not surprisingly, it is also near the top in the e-readiness rankings. The Netherlands has perhaps the strongest B2B infrastructure in Europe, and Dutch multinationals are using cutting-edge technology to improve everyday business practices. ING Bank, for example, equips its insurance salesforce with wireless Internet access.

Shell, a Dutch oil giant, has developed innovative ways of combining real-world and web-based training. Compare the Netherlands with one of Western Europe 's e-business slowpokes, Italy. Italy places 22nd in both the business environment and e-readiness rankings. It suffers from political instability, huge public debt and an over-regulated labour market. In this environment, e-business takes longer to develop. Only 6% of Italians shop online, and B2B e-commerce accounts for less than 1% of total commerce.

Many of the countries that score highly in the e-readiness rankings also allocate a large portion of public spending to information technology, or enact incentives that encourage private-sector infrastructure investment.

Relatively small economies, such as Austria and the Netherlands, must dedicate a larger share of total spending to IT infrastructure than massive economies, such as the US and Germany, in order to maintain similar levels of infrastructure; their ability to commit these funds indicates a strong commitment to e-business. Even countries further down on the list -including Korea, Portugal and Brazil -are also devoting tremendous resources to IT development, signalling their determination to become e-business leaders.

Logistics and delivery systems play a role. E-business relies on more than phone lines and PCs. It requires electronic payment systems and populations that habitually use credit cards. It also mandates efficient and secure postal, courier and other logistics systems involved in the delivery of goods purchased online or shipped as part of just-in-time manufacturing systems. Those ranking highly in this category have efficient, expansive, reliable and cost-effective delivery systems. Innovative start-ups need financing.

To move business online, companies need the help of other companies, from website designers, to payment facilitators, to hosting providers. These small, innovative firms depend on start-up capital. In Western Europe, North America and Australia, financing is readily available from a variety of sources and on generally good terms. In many emerging markets, however, banks function poorly, stock markets are embryonic and venture capital is practically unknown. Lack of financing is hampering e-business development throughout much of the world.

E-business development depends both on a country 's overall legal framework and specific laws governing Internet use. Governments that support the creation of an Internet-conducive legal environment -both through policy and enforcement -get high scores. Those more concerned with censoring content and controlling the web score lower. There 's a role for government. It 's easy for governments to declare ambitious Internet-development plans, but such declarations need to be followed by deeds. Even where funds are in short supply, action can be taken to ensure that the legal system supports e-business.

Developing a consistent and predictable legal and regulatory framework to address emerging e-business legal concerns is a good start. This can include ensuring a level playing field in the telecommunications industry, where old monopolists often retain effective control of the market, or passing legislation that extends to the Internet proper measures to protect intellectual property rights, or directing law-enforcement agencies to protect online security.

Putting public services online can help demonstrate the benefits of e-business while saving taxpayers time and money. The UK and Singapore are standouts in shifting paperwork-intensive processes to more streamlined web-based procedures. A good place for governments to start is to simplify the registration of a new business so that it can be accomplished in a single step via the Internet. This frees local entrepreneurs from red tape and makes the country a more attractive investment destination for foreign capital.

Literacy and basic education are preconditions to being able to navigate the web. In addition, the rankings consider a population 's "e-literacy "-its experience using the Internet and its receptivity to it -and the technical skills of the workforce. And because Internet business involves risk-taking, the rankings assess the national proclivity to business innovation and entrepreneurship.

Basic education is not enough. Internet users must have some degree of education. However, basic literacy is not enough. In poor countries where literacy rates are relatively high, such as China, Sri Lanka and Kazakhstan, e-business is often hampered by a shortage of both technically skilled workers and an "e-literate " population that has had exposure to the Internet.

In countries where both literacy and e-literacy rates are high, e-business is thriving. Scandinavians, and northern Europeans in general, are highly educated, tech savvy and multilingual. These factors bring the region nearly even with the US in our rankings. Many countries could do better. France, for example, receives high scores for education and literacy yet earns only an 8.25 in this category. There are several explanations. The French tend to start using the Internet at an older age than the typical American or Scandinavian, and many French cling to Minitel, the country 's long-established proprietary service. Less than one-third of the population speaks English, the lingual franca of international e-business.

No business or industry can function efficiently without intermediaries and ancillary services to support it. For e-business, these include consulting and IT services, and back-office solutions. The rankings also take into account whether there are consistent, industry-wide technology standards for platforms and programming languages.

Israel, a major exporter of software and high-tech products, is one of the few non-Western countries at the forefront of e-services development. The country is tech savvy, with an exceptionally high share of scientists, and entrepreneurial. Moreover, Israel boasts one of the most vibrant venture-capital sectors outside Silicon Valley. The result has been an ever-growing number of e-consultants, e-marketers and technical-support providers to underpin Israel 's high-tech sector.

Governments help set tech standards. An absence of global technology standards is emerging as an inhibitor of e-business growth and efficiency. Although the legend of the Internet is one of self-government, international mediation will be increasingly necessary to reap the benefits of global connectivity.

The US General Accounting Office recently joined the debate over the future of XML, the most widely used mark-up language. The GAO 's brief was to establish whether XML should be used to standardise government data and promote interoperability. But the agency expressed doubts not only about XML, but also about a plethora of competing standards. The report appears to have shaken up the notoriously slow-moving standard-setting bodies, which have promised to address the shortcomings.

In short, the Economist Intelligence Unit 's e-readiness rankings lend themselves naturally to an action plan for governments seeking to capture the benefits of the Internet and the changes it has wrought. Connectivity is a necessary first step.

Although it is consumers who ultimately drive adoption of the Internet, governments can help ensure that the proper infrastructure is in place, and that its reliability and security are protected. Protecting competition in the communications industry helps speed e-business.

E-business cannot thrive where other forms of business fail. So governments aiming to promote Internet usage need to adopt policies that facilitate growth, promote investment and reduce red tape. Measures that encourage entrepreneurship, including the availability of financing for innovative firms, are helpful.

Creating a conducive legal and regulatory environment is crucial as well. This means not only ensuring that traditional legal safeguards, such as protection of intellectual property rights, are extended into the digital world, but also training and funding the police and judicial personnel needed to enforce them. Adopting a coherent and far- reaching government "e-strategy "- particularly one oriented to universal Internet access -provides a vision of the digital future that can inspire both business and civic enthusiasm.

Making public services available online, in a citizen-friendly format, helps sustain that enthusiasm and gives governments an opportunity to lead by example -as well as to save time and money. Adding computer literacy to the basic education curriculum, and technological specialisation to the range of training options, promotes needed skills. Supporting countrywide industry standards helps promote data sharing without stifling competition, as does joining the international dialogue on global standards.

Yet, as the Economist Intelligence Unit e-readiness rankings suggest, savvy policy and creativity can often trump sheer size and power. Wealth is an obvious advantage, but lack of funds is no excuse for ignoring the potential of the Internet.

Estonian Transition in to Information Society

Societal inclination towards a fast acquisition of modern technologies, willingness to experiment with new solutions and internationally successful promotional campaigns have introduced Estonia on the international arena as a rapidly evolving information society. For example, the issue of technological developments and their impact on society has been analysed by different international analytical reports and Estonia has been ranked highly:

— McConnell International (2001), for example, indicates that in the fields of e-leadership, human capital and overall e-business climate the majority of conditions in Estonia are suitable to the conduct of e-business and e-government.

— The latest (2001) Human Development Report issued by the United Nations Development Programme (UNDP) also ranks countries next to human development index (where Estonia holds 44 th position and belongs to the group of high human development countries) also according to the technology achievement index.

Although Estonia was not ranked by the UNDP, according to the provided formula Estonia would be on the 30 th position belonging to the group of potential leaders. Indeed, the broad picture seems to confirm this concept, as figures and early growth rates are in some cases remarkable (particularly in the category of consumer goods and exports), and several initiatives that have been undertaken by either government or corporate agents are remarkable, inspiring other countries to imitate Estonian practices.

The early launch of the Estonian information society developments is frequently used as best practice for other countries. Without hesitation, the rapid development of the telecommunications market is a clear success story:

— A reasonable state policy has generated rapid catching-up both in the fields of fixed lines and mobile communications;

— Estonia has been one of the first countries amongst the CEE countries to open the telecommunications market for liberalisation, giving a good basis for further development;

— Public initiatives in the fields of eLearning (e.g. Estonian Tiger Leap) and eGovernment are also good examples that other (especially Central and Eastern European) countries attempt to imitate. Like other transition economies, Estonia is experiencing very rapid developments in the technical sphere with a number of problems arising at the same time on the social scale, such as the digital divide. Recent developments in the Estonian telecommunication market are characterised by the fast development of both telecommunications market and Estonian information society as a whole:

— Rapid increase in the number of telephone lines;

— Accessibility to modern telecommunication services (GSM, ISDN, DSL) and reduction of the prices;

— Total liberalisation of the telecommunications market (expiration of the exclusive rights granted to Estonian Telephone Company) since January 1, 2001;

— Promotion of technological development by the State through legislation (Cable Distribution Act, Telecommunications Act, Digital Signature Act). In general, the proximity of advanced Scandinavian technology forerunners is a significant driver. The rapid uptake of novel technologies, enhanced wireless communication infrastructure, a high number of conventional telephone lines and Internet hosts has created a moderately favourable platform for building up appropriate forms of applications.

As a well functioning telecommunications sector is considered important for enhancing the competitiveness of an economy and the quality of life, Estonia has paid much attention to the information society developments and directing these after regaining its independence.

Main issue in the beginning of 1990s was insufficient technological infrastructure and in order to support its development a Concession Agreement was signed. This helped to attract significant investments into extension and digitisation of the public telephone network.

During the 1990s the state has adopted also several important legislative acts and established the necessary state structures and has in this way organised the telecommunications The most influential enterprise in the Estonian telecommunications market AS Eesti Telekom was restructured already in 1991-93; in 1997 the state enterprise Eesti Telekom was re-established as AS Eesti Telekom and the decision was adopted to organise an initial public offering (IPO) to sell up to 49% of the shares.

The IPO took place at the beginning of 1999, and institutional and private investors purchased 49% of the shares owned previously by the Republic of Estonia. At the moment AS Eesti Telekom has 100% ownerships in AS Eesti Telefon (Estonian Telephone Company) and in AS Eesti Mobiiltelefon (Estonian Mobile Telephone Company).

Since the beginning of 2001 the number of telecommunications companies increased remarkably and currently the most important companies in the market are AS Eesti Telefon, Levicom BroadBand OÜ (TELE2) and Uninet AS. Estonian mobile telephone communications market has been liberalised from the very beginning and currently there are three operators on the market.

As for year 2000 there are 522 000 conventional main lines in Estonia and 557 000 mobile communication subscribers with the market turnover for carrier services being 259 million Euros. Since its early days telecom sector has shown a constant growth, though conditions for further expansion are somewhat more restrictive nowadays.

On the one hand, the market is reaching saturation point, though it might be just a temporary situation in light of the launch of the next generation mobile services; on the other hand intensive competition in the sector pushes down the prices. The predicted growth rate of the total telecom market was about 10% for 2001.

Access to the Internet is mainly realised through the use of dial-up services in Estonia, although DSL services are available in major cities. There are 8 major Internet Service Providers (ISP) in Estonia. Technology uptake and applications When looking at the ICT manufacturing in Estonia, it follows, that foreign orders are very important for the Estonian ICT sector - 73% of the subcontracting activity originates from abroad.

Typically, subcontracting involves assembly of various communication equipment and software outsourcing. As a result, subcontracting revenues constituted 60–100% of the Estonian turnover of telecommunications equipment production, industrial automation, consumer electronics and components, and about 15% of the computers and office machinery sub-sector in 2000. Due to high foreign demand, the export of the Estonian ICT industry has increased rapidly.

On the downside, most of the rise can be assigned to a single company's activity – Elcoteq Ltd provides 83% of the total Estonian ICT exports and 96% of telecommunications equipment exports as the statistics for the year 2000 indicates. Of domestic industries, manufacturing, the telecommunications sector, banking, wholesale and retail trade, and governmental structures are the important drivers of the emerging Estonian ICT cluster, as they demand most of the production generated by the ICT sector.

On the services side, the most popular application areas of Internet are banking services, but public administration's efforts in IT sphere have also generated new web-based services in public domain. As 41% of Estonians aged 15 to 74 are identified as Internet users, there seems to be challenge for both public and private sector organisations in introducing innovations in services fields, namely through the use of ICT.

The most popular electronic service in Estonia is Internet banking. Hansapank has indicated 365,000 Internet banking clients and Ühispank 150,000. To some extent the clientele basis is overlapping, but is still reasonable to believe that total number of Internet banking users exceeds 250,000, covering more than 18% of total Estonian population.

Factors that have put Estonia to the position of the leader concerning Internet banking among former Eastern block Countries and outdoes a lot of Western European countries, are simple-to-use software, free of charge transactions during the services' introducing time to the market and the impact of Nordic countries' IT culture on Estonia.

Other popular services offered via digital channels are digital taxation board portal and insurance payment systems. Digital taxation board is represented both in the system of Hansapanks Internet banking interface Hanza.net, Ühisbank's U-net as well as separately, via Tax Board's own portal. In the former case personal identification of Hansapank's and Ühispank's clients is used for electronic tax-related transactions, in the latter case special security codes are issued to clients upon request.

The number of income tax declarations submitted through Internet banking portals exceeded 36,000 for the declaration period of year 2000. There are other interesting services provided by the private sector, e.g. Mobile parking is another recent innovative initiative launched by the Estonian Mobile Telephone (EMT) and parking surveillance authorities.

In order to use the system, after parking a vehicle a SMS has to be sent to the parking centre, and finished upon further notification, also via SMS. The parking fee is subsequently added to telephone bill or deducted automatically from client's mobile bank-account.

LocateGSM is a service offered in cooperation with EMT and GIS developer Regio Ltd. This is a web-based mobile positioning system (MPS) enabling to display the location of EMT mobile subscriber on a map. This way the system is offering good bases for further development of different location-based services.

In addition there are also other remarkable initiatives carried out in the public sector. These are mainly dealing with the modernisation of the communication within the government, or provision of services to companies and individuals on digital bases (e.g. e-Citizen project under planning, electronic ID card initiative).

In 2000 the first phase of the project of "Information Systems for Government Sessions" was developed and implemented, forming thus a solid basis for Government's work digitalisation, as well as making available Government protocols and information concerned to general public.

The project aims at engaging citizens more actively into policy decision processes, as well as motivating public debates concerning nationwide and important initiatives. The citizen portal encourages submitting ideas, visions, directions etc. as well as comment on bills released by ministries already during the process of bill drafting. Steps towards modernising the governmental information exchange system were taken starting year 2000, at the initiative of the pilot project X-road (cross-road).

The objectives of X-road pilot project are to interconnect state databases, to enable requesting information to authorised user via Internet from any of the databases after authorised accession. This project is especially important as elements of the state information system were founded technologically independently, but also at different points in time, thus calling for operative modernisation and co-operation.

Parallel to X-road project incentives on bringing several main registries (Business Registry, Real Estate Registry etc) on full-electronic Internet basis are being implemented. The access is guaranteed to all users, and the information obtained has full legal power.

For projects like these governmental structures are important users of telecommunications equipment and services, office machinery, computers and software, whereas the government's affection for novel technological solutions has had a positive effect on a number of public sector initiatives.

Despite of the rapid spread of Internet connections, relatively high level of users and extensive investments into Internet stores, the turnover of electronic commerce is insignificant. According to Global eCommerce Survey e-commerce penetration is 6% in Estonia. For the USA the relevant figure is 33% and for Finland 17%. Factors impeding the development of e-commerce are sustainability of buying habits, limited product range in Internet stores, inconveniences in paying for goods and deliveries and security risks when using bankcards.

Forming a new electronic commerce culture is a world-wide problem and in this light Estonian developments are comparable to the most successful European countries. One of the strongest Estonian advantages in these developments is the widespread Internet banking (favours the rise of positive attitude towards e-commerce); the most important discouraging factors are the smallness of the potential market and conventional shopping habits.

Consequently, bringing more services onto digital basis is substantially dependent on the potential demand for these services. Presently the demand is derived mainly by the clients of Internet banking, who have their personal banking accounts for conducting electronic-transactions via Internet based web portal.

Evidently, the fast development of the Estonian banking sector and the high-tech solutions elaborated by the banks' own product development departments have reinforced the need for quality software, and trustworthy and secure products, thus having also positive effects on generating innovative solutions.

Also, collaborative actions undertaken by the banks and telecommunications operators have established strong links between these two sectors, paving the way for future m-commerce related activities. However, in this context the relations with content providers are insufficient, meaning that these relations have to develop towards a more active involvement of external content service providers in order for a large-scale functioning m-business or m-leisure to appear.

CHAPTER 4

Information Development in India

For most developing countries, the internet has been of relatively little significance for the large majority of businesses, except possibly for some larger countries. The reasons are not hard to find. For most countries, the primitive state of communications infrastructure is a difficult barrier to internet development. In most, business operations involve mostly small firms, often the last to benefit from improved means of communications even in richer countries. And, not least, poor countries generally lack the pool of technically trained people necessary to fuel change.

With the possible exception of China, India has been affected more by changes in IT than any other developing country, yet the country remains very poor by any standard. The country's businesses have until early in the 1990s been heavily influenced in their growth by the government's licensing regime, several companies having become very large firms operating nationally mainly through their ability to garner licenses.

The structure of many of these firms, therefore, has been dictated not by market demands, but rather by the availability of government licenses. In addition, many companies have benefited from the government's past policy of protection from international competition, a program that together with licensing has yielded gross inefficiencies and bloated enterprises. All of this is changing. The licensing regime is largely gone, and protection is beginning to be pared away. Foreign direct investment, while still not exactly encouraged in some sectors, is far more welcome than it was. The results have been dramatic. Large conglomerates have had to give attention to their competitive viability in a much tougher economic environment. Reorganization and restructuring to achieve more competitive focus is becoming the rule.

In IT more specifically, India has in some ways become a world leader, yet the degree of penetration of such new phenomena as the internet is still quite modest. Even so, at least the larger manufacturing companies and, perhaps more importantly, financial institutions have begun to use new technologies to improve efficiency and better serve customers. There seems little question that the gradual opening of the Indian market has been forcing businesses to pay more attention to competitiveness.

In some ways India is not representative of the larger developing world. Although illiteracy is still widespread, India has a long history of support for technical education and, as a consequence, has produced large numbers of technically qualified personnel. The country is, in fact, a not inconsequential exporter of engineers and scientists; Silicon Valley alone boasts around 150 Indian millionaires, for example, and American immigration rules allowing thousands of visas for technical people have benefited disproportionately Indians. At home, the large group of technically-qualified persons in India, to some degree utilizing their Indian-American contacts, has formed the backbone of a rapid growth in IT investment in India, a growth that is continuing today.

India possesses a substantial middle class, variously estimated at between 150 and 200 million people, depending on criteria. This group is concentrated in perhaps 150 towns and cities scattered around this very large country, and it forms the major source of customers for a variety of businesses, either directly or indirectly. In an increasingly competitive environment, this group appears to have provided strong economic incentives for businesses to find ways to improve efficiency.

IT provides an important vehicle to accomplish this goal and IT providers are being pushed incessantly to improve access and broaden services. Finally, the IT industry has expanded relatively free of the kind of government regulation that has affected other industries. As a result, the industry has been the source of considerable entrepreneurialism and has fostered development of the growing venture capital industry described above.

Moreover, as in the United States, the IT industry itself has been the source of productivity gains for the economy as a whole as manufacturers emulate production techniques in the West and output increases rapidly. The importance of the IT sector in India also is a feature not replicated in most other developing countries.

Because the internet provides the greatest possibility for overall economic gain among IT sectors, we begin with a description of the internet and how it is currently being utilized. Not surprisingly, India has lagged far behind many other Asian countries in the adoption of the internet. In a population of one billion people, there are fewer than two million internet subscribers, a figure that contrasts with India's closest comparator in size, China, which has more than three times as many telephone lines and four times as many internet users.

In fact, by the year 2000 India had only around 26 million fixed-line telephone connections and fewer than five million personal computers in place. Clearly, if the internet is to become a major vehicle in transforming the Indian economy, there is little question that rapid further development of India's communications and data transmission network is essential. Just as obviously, there is still a long way to go in this development.

Of major importance is the state of economic development in the country; India on average is still a very poor country, with a monthly per capita GNP of only 180 US dollars on a purchasing power parity basis. Despite the existence of a sizable "middle class," most people in India worry about obtaining the essentials of life, not in gaining access to telephones, much less internet service. Even so, given the availability of an adequate telecommunications network, India's internet audience could increase substantially.

But, that network, too, historically has been a major constraint. As noted, there exist relatively few telephone connections, and it is well known that the value of the internet increases geometrically with added connections. More importantly, however, the reliability of the system nationally has certainly not been adequate to support internet use, even if more connections were to become available.

The country has lacked a high-speed data communications backbone to speed transmission and interconnectivity. In some ways, these constraints are a "chicken and egg" proposition: without a better national telecommunications network, there is little incentive to connect; without more connections, the incentive to build a more adequate high-speed network diminishes. Breaking this deadlock promises to be an important determinant to internet growth and, more broadly, to the attractiveness of the country as a destination for high-technology foreign investment.

Another constraint to Indian internet development has been the structure of telephone tariff schedules. As in many other countries, tariffs have been based on time charges which can make internet usage a very expensive proposition. These tariffs have been changing and are now based on larger units of time. But, even now, the cost of internet service from the telephone monopoly is not cheap. Five hundred hours annually of dial- up service can cost $200 for a slow-speed connection, a figure that compares with a U.S. standard of perhaps $180 for unlimited time. Beyond the 500 hour yearly base, time is billed at about 35 cents an hour, also not an insignificant charge for users.

Internet expansion suffers from the generally poor condition of other parts of India's infrastructure. Internet use for commercial purposes is based importantly on increasing the speed of transactions, eliminating steps in the distribution chain and delivering products faster and more reliably. It is the last step of this process that is at risk in an India-like environment, because the physical infrastructure to deliver products from supplier to customer speedily is largely absent.

Even if high-speed telecommunications were in place, which as yet it is not, much of the transactional advantages of the internet in commercial practice would be lost owing to poor roads and inefficient rail facilities. To be sure, internet use provides opportunities for both consumers and businesses to compare easily large numbers of products and prices. But, without the ability to deliver products expeditiously, this advantage can be largely negated.

Widespread internet use within India is not necessarily a barrier to increasing and potentially benefiting from use of the internet by Indian companies. For example, with the much improved access to international gateways now becoming available businesses can easily expand their potential customer base globally through the internet, even if their local clientele is not yet connected.

In fact, buyers and, particularly, industrial purchasers in many industrial countries today are routinely posting detailed product and component specifications on specialized websites open to all with access to the internet. The purpose of such sites is to widen the net of possible suppliers, thus reducing costs. For Indian companies, therefore, opportunities to expand business relationships with foreign firms could be enormously enhanced through the internet, even though internet use in India remained relatively constrained.

Company utilization of the internet in India thus far is limited, but corporate interest in future use is intense. Firms are establishing special groups internally to investigate how the internet might be used both for internal control and for developing more efficient means for dealing with customers and suppliers. Generally, little will actually be done until the current efforts to upgrade India's telecommunications infrastructure are further advanced.

One exception, a company that has gone further than most, is Reliance Industries, a firm mostly engaged in chemical production and distribution, and a company actively involved in building a fiberoptic network linking Indian major cities. This company, in addition, expects that the internet will become a primary mechanism to improve operations, and it already has in place an internet-ready communications and control system. But, much of the system today uses leased telephone lines, not yet the internet.

For example, of the company's 20,000-odd customers around India, 3-4 thousand are major buyers, accounting for perhaps 75 percent or more of total sales. These major customers for chemicals are now linked electronically to an internet-based market exchange introduced by Reliance, one of several now existing in the country. In addition, through leased- line facilities, customers can process orders, and Reliance can deliver dispatching details, better manage inventory, carry out invoicing, and provide technical service, all done electronically. This customer network will be transferred to the internet at the earliest possible moment, since the internet should provide substantially lower operational costs.

To provide some measure of the benefits already apparent from this system, Reliance has been able to reduce receivables from 310 days to 90 days, only one area of savings. Cost improvements come primarily from a general tightening and acceleration of processing within the company and between the firm and its customers. Savings do not occur as a result of reducing manpower.

In addition, the speed of order delivery has been improved greatly and inventories reduced in a system that is now integrated into the firm's overall management control function that links not only important customers but also over 50 of the company's own operations. These results for Reliance are similar in nature to cost reductions experienced by companies in industrial parts of the world, even though thus far the internet has not been much utilized.

One might anticipate even greater savings in India, as compared with more industrialized countries, since operational efficiency prior to the introduction of electronic controls is likely to have been far lower than comparable figures for companies in the developed world.

Although the introduction of Reliance- like systems lags in India among larger manufacturers, there are other areas of the economy where considerable progress has been made, despite the as yet primitive nature of the country's telecommunications network.

A few Indian private banks and financial institutions represent a sector that has become a leader in using electronics to offer new customer services. Though still early in the process, banks see the internet as a vehicle not only to improve current services but, in addition, to bring into the banks new types of businesses. For example, some banks look forward to the time when client companies will choose to delegate most "back office" functions directly to their banks. Moreover, banks are attempting to link with Indian commercial web-sites to offer clearing services to clients of these sites.

One interesting example of bank activity is HDFC Bank, started as an off-shoot of India's Housing

Development Finance Corporation six years ago. The bank now has 125 branches and is adding new ones rapidly, including 60 last year.

Branches have been connected to the home office from the outset through a private data network operated for the bank by Wipro Infotech Software and Services Company, a large Indian software developer. HDFC Bank targets high-worth individuals and larger corporate clients but is also developing a sizable retail banking business. Telephone transactions of the type familiar in more developed countries (automatic payments, transfers, deposits, account balances, etc.) were introduced two years ago, but these functions are now also available through the internet.

Although precise cost estimates for serving customers via the internet are not available, banks have studied savings that are possible through telephone transactions, as compared with other means. For example, if a teller-based transaction costs, say, 150 rupees, the same transaction done via an automatic teller machine runs only about 15 rupees and via electronic connection 10 rupees, less than 7 percent of the teller cost. One other interviewed bank offering similar electronic services confirms these cost figures.

Internet-based services are a more recent introduction, but already demands for the services are expanding quickly. Today, HDFC Bank claims over 100,000 retail internet customers, almost half of whom utilize the service more than once monthly. Another aggressive bank, ICICI Bank, also is active both in telephone and internet service for its customers. Its internet customer base grew from 6,000 to 250,000 in a single year. As more customers are added in these banks, unit costs of transactions promise to fall rapidly, because the expense of adding more server capacity is minimal. In other words, the marginal cost of serving an internet customer is still falling.

In another aspect of its business, HDFC Bank is working closely with the Bombay Stock Exchange, which itself is in the process of automating transactions. Before automation was introduced, weekly reporting to the exchange was accomplished by brokers submitting floppy disks two days before each week's end.

Today, through clearing accounts maintained at HDFC Bank and elsewhere, clearing is instantaneous, and 400 brokers maintain accounts at the bank for this purpose. While such developments in the financial sector are encouraging, they should be kept in perspective. Private banks in India account for barely one- fifth of total deposits.

Although this proportion has been increasing, the vast preponderance of Indian banking is still done in state-owned facilities, which, thus far, have shown only modest interest in increasing efficiency. There has been talk of increasing the proportion of private ownership in state banks in order to increase productivity, but resistance to such moves by still powerful unions and others has stalled much action. Website Development Despite the lack yet of extensive broadband facilities in India, growth in the number of new websites has been explosive.

There are today hundreds of Indian commercial websites. Although financial figures are unavailable, it is likely that most of these sites are not yet profitable and are based on the joint expectation of much improved internet infrastructure and perceived first mover advantages. As in the United States, some of these sites will succeed, but most in all likelihood will never reach financial viability for a variety of reasons. Some will fail because they were formed too early to take advantage of newer infrastructure advancements to reach potential users. Advancements, in general, are not yet in place. Some will fail owing to their inability to change long-established commercial customs of their hoped- for clients quickly enough. And, still others will fall by the wayside because their creative motivations were not matched by realistic means to gain revenues from their clients, another cause familiar from the American experience.

Still, as in more developed parts of the world, enough of the new websites could survive to at least begin to change how business is being conducted in India. In the process, these websites may be a harbinger of widespread efficiency gains in an economy plagued by slow transactions, sluggish order processing and unnecessarily high inventory levels. A brief review of some of these websites follows.

Business-to-consumer websites (B2C) Although there has been extensive development of websites intended to attract household consumers, their future viability can be seriously questioned. Part of the reason lies in the extremely limited penetration of personal computers among Indian households.

Although the numbers are rising rapidly, there are fewer than 4 million personal computers in all of India and, of these, perhaps only 20 percent are used by households, including those used for home offices. Telephone access, the only means, has been expensive and unreliable, and methods of product delivery to customers are as yet underdeveloped. Even though a substantial middle class may exist among India's impoverished millions, a group who might eventually be attracted to electronic transactions, these handicaps present a formidable barrier to rapid development of B2C growth.

All of these problems, of course, are in the process of easing, but the transition will require substantial time. Meanwhile, B2C websites hope to make sufficient inroads among urban dwellers to at least survive until better times are possible. It will decidedly be an uphill fight. Some observers note that while the population of personal computers is relatively small and the technological means to connect them is still rather primitive, there are 37 million cable television subscribers.

As the fiberoptic network now being laid out is completed, it is thought, these subscribers might furnish the foundation for successful B2C expansion. But, even if cable viewers could be connected to the fiber-optic grid, the paucity of personal computers would still provide a difficult environment for B2C transactions to expand.

One can conclude, therefore, that extensive development of B2C websites probably is premature at this stage of India's development. This conclusion is supported by results from a recent study by the Gartner Group, as reported in India News. Of the few internet subscribers in India, only 2.2 percent had engaged in B2C commerce or paid for services online. Only 3.6 percent had ever placed orders over the net, usually for such services as movie booking or for products like books, audio cassettes and CDs, and software. Customers were largely well-to-do families Business-to-business websites

(B2B) Use of the internet between businesses, on the other hand, offers greater promise, and a profusion of Indian websites is one result.

As in the case of B2C sites, many of the B2B sites are likely to end up as casualties for many of the same reasons. But already there are indications that acceptance of the internet as a way of revising business practices to gain efficiencies is quite widespread. Many businesses are fully aware of the trade-related commitments the Indian government has made as a condition of joining the World Trade Organization and of the falling trade protection that will be one consequence.

The internet is seen by many of these firms as one possible vehicle among many others for gaining increased competitiveness. Even so, present use of the internet, either for direct inter-company communications or through business websites, is still early in its development.

A few examples of websites now in existence provide background. Typical of cross-sector sites, ones involving a number of quite different sectors, is Indiamarkets. com, started by IMO Communications. Development of Indiamarkets began in March, 1999, with venture funding from the Warburg Pincus Fund among other sources.

As the company's own literature puts it, Indiamarkets is "India's first comprehensive business-to-business infomediary, an aggregation of vertical supplier communities representing over a hundred diverse product categories. The site, launched only in January, 2000, offers a gateway to promote business between potential trading partners and provides transaction-enabling content that facilitates judicious business decisions." To accomplish its objectives, the site offers a variety of on- line services: sector-specific news, reviews of state policies affecting the sector, a buyer posting facility, a supplier posting allowing one to compare offerings from across India, and an auction facility to sell machinery or excess inventories.

By late 2000, the site claimed to have 30,000 subscribers, $600 million in inventory up for sale, over 2,000 "hits" and 150 transactions arranged daily. IMO also is opening 70 business centers around the country to provide services to businesses without access to computer networking. Indiamarkets.com faces a number of problems common to such sites.

Of primary importance are the site's planned sources of revenue, mainly to come from a combination of advertising on the site, an "enhanced" listing for companies who pay an annual fee and, most importantly, planned fees for transactions completed using the website. Transactions fees had not been put in place by October, 2000, but arrangements had been made with Citibank for a payment gateway on the site for easy clearing. This will be facilitated by credit checks through Dun and Bradstreet.

Whether or not users of the site will be willing to pay fees remains to be seen. However, IMO studies show that, aside from user savings from lower prices, transactions costs are reduced by 6 to 7 percent through use of the site, a not insignificant figure. Such sites also are likely to lower prices by bringing added competition to markets from better and more complete information.

The website, of course, also will be subject to its own competitive environment, as more B2B sites offering services to the same clients open up. Thus, while the availability of various savings might make customers more receptive to fees, the size of those fees could be constrained by competitive considerations. Much depends on the degree to which the more generalized website, exemplified by Indiamarkets.com, succeeds in competition with sites that are more focused on particular sectors.

One such portal is Kagaz.com, constructed by Ecomedia Infosystems to service only the pulp and paper industry. Kagaz.com is a subscriber site, with a subscriber base now numbering about 10,000 (half of whom are foreigners), each of whom pays a small monthly fee for access. The site offers news, data, and bulletin board-type notices on paper availability.

India has relatively few paper manufacturers, but there are about 80,000 paper traders who act as middlemen between manufacturers and converters, cutters and printers. Traders exist because of their local knowledge of customers, taxes and regulations.

The ultimate objective of sites like Kagaz.com, of which there are now an abundance in India, is to offer a full e-commerce portal where transactions can be facilitated for a fee. For example, when new deals are arranged between sellers and buyers, Kagaz guarantees the deal and accepts payment, which is released when delivery has occurred. The problems faced by Kagaz.com are typical of many other such sites.

The very low overall penetration of personal computers and internet connections in India is matched by the spotty existence of PCs among potential customers of the site. Most traders, for example, have no access presently to a PC. Yet, these traders ultimately are the foundation of the site's hoped-for business, because they, not manufacturers, are the ones who maintain inventories in the system and understand intimately their customers needs and peculiarities. The intention for now is to work through these traders, not to work around them. Therefore, one major marketing task of Kagaz.com and like sites obviously will be to broaden the base of internet-connected and conversant traders and dealers.

Such a task will not be a simple one, even if the expansion of high-speed data links across India in the next two years proceeds as anticipated. The trader community is likely to be tradition-bound, accustomed to carrying out business successfully in time-honored fashion.

Breaking old habits doubtlessly will prove much more difficult than has been the case in more industrialized societies, where PC use was common long before the advent of internet possibilities. Even so, if portals can demonstrate significant cost savings through internet use, a substantial marketing effort, competition should force change over time.

Business-to-government websites (B2G) The Indian government and some state governments have made a commitment to increased transparency and simplified procedures through their adoption of internet-based access to government functions.

Today, for example, governments account for over 28 percent of IT spending in India. In much of this effort, regional units have been in the forefront, computerizing operations to streamline services and, hopefully, reduce bureaucracy. Among the functions being made available through the internet are government procurement bidding and various application procedures, both familiar from more economically advanced countries. Whether or not such efforts do, in fact, reduce bureaucracy and lower government costs remains to be seen.

With burgeoning fiscal deficits at both national and regional levels, saving are obviously needed badly. In India, however, government service has often been seen as a sinecure, where employment is a continuing obligation. Transferring internal operations and some public functions to electronic forms may not have much in the way of employment effects, at least not in the short run.

Still, to the extent that the internet makes dealings with government at all levels easier and more transparent for non-governmental entities, and particularly for businesses, gains in efficiency could be substantial as internet use expands throughout the country. Moreover, to the extent that increased transparency and efficiency are accompanied by lower government employment and fewer opportunities for corruption, one might also anticipate that such advances will be fiercely opposed.

One rapidly expanding business for Indian companies is the provision of back-office services to international clients. The basic business has a long history globally; Ireland, the Caribbean and the Philippines, for example, have provided such services to companies in the United States for many years.

The typical task involves the transcription of raw data into electronic databases, where paper records are shipped in by air, local residents transform the data into electronic form, which is then transferred back to the developed country company via the internet. The business today involves a wide number of industries including, to name just a few, airlines, banks, insurance companies and medical establishments.

Currently, India employs between 50,000 and 100,000 people in what are termed "internet-enabled services," producing $500 million in export earnings. Growth has been so rapid that some observers anticipate employment of well over one million within ten years generating income of $10 billion.

Although such expectations may be overly optimistic, India does have some competitive advantages: like the Philippines, India has an abundance of English-speaking people, many with university educations, who are willing to work for a fraction of the cost similar workers earn in the client's home country.

Internet-enabled services have changed in recent years to involve other areas. For example, the transcribing of voice dictation by medical practitioners and others in the United States has become a big business.

A more sophisticated trend recently has been the transfer to India of some research and development operations, made possible by the instantaneous transfer of data and information through the internet. All of these services also rely not only on English language capability but also the availability of a reservoir of well-educated, yet under-employed, people. For example, typical employees in the Indian industry include graduates of university programs in science, liberal arts and even such professions as medicine or law.

Because the internet is only now just beginning to make its impacts felt across India, any discussion of development impacts is, at best, premature. Unlike in software development,now well established as an internationally competitive industry, use of the internet either by individuals or most businesses is still at a primitive stage. This picture almost certainly will change rapidly, however, as high-speed data networks are completed linking at least the larger cities. How rapidly, of course, will depend on the speed of finishing not only the underlying network but also "last mile" connections to individual homes and businesses. For larger businesses, this process is likely to proceed quickly, as the gains are clearest there. For others, one can anticipate that existing cable networks will provide the most likely vehicle, but the process will take longer.

The extent of gains from wider internet penetration is, at this stage, a matter of conjecture. Even in the United States, estimates of productivity gains as a consequence of information technology generally and the internet more specifically vary widely.

The range of opinion runs from Nobelist Robert Solow's well-known remark 13 years ago, "We see the computer age everywhere except in the productivity statistics," to much more optimistic statements from a variety of other economists more recently. Clearly, productivity has jumped in the United States in the past five years from some set of causes, but the sources continue to be elusive. It suffices here to note that the U.S.

Congressional Budget Office and the Office of Management and Budget both project productivity gains in the next ten years to be about 0.5 percentage point higher than the average for the years 1973 to 1995. 6 In the developing world, estimates are even more perilous, but it does seem clear that one cannot simply extrapolate the industrial country experience to developing countries. Some observers believe that efficiency gains are likely to be smaller in poorer countries. They point out that developing countries depend more on production in small and medium-sized enterprises, and these are less likely to experience substantial gains from internet use, at least not in uses internal to the organization, as compared with larger organizations.

Moreover, poorer countries typically rely more on commodity production and exports, which, in comparison with the manufactured goods produced and marketed by industrial countries, are less likely to find material productivity improvements from use of the internet.

Finally, the point has been made that introducing technologies from industrialized countries, possibly including the internet, can result in smaller productivity gains in developing regions, as compared with gains in the technology- innovating area. These technologies tend to be biased toward skill- intensiveness, which produce fewer gains in productivity when transferred to a developing country.

These observations are, of course, entirely speculative at this stage, since the internet is in its infancy in most poor regions. But, there seems little doubt that gains from the internet could be substantial and, despite more skeptical conclusions, could affect developing economies in even more profound ways than is the case for industrialized regions.

The case of intracorporate use of the internet is illustrative. In industrial countries, use of the internet for coordination between geographically widespread units represents only an incremental change from the way in which business had been done. For larger companies, management control typically had been exercised through dedicated networks long before the internet came into existence. Companies like Texas Instruments have operated sophisticated global networks linking their subsidiaries for decades. For such firms to move from these networks to the internet was really only a small, if less costly, step. In fact, many of these firms thus far have continued to use older networks in preference to the internet.

For a developing country like India, on the other hand, even dedicated networks are a relatively new phenomenon and are far less pervasive than in more industrialized parts of the world. Delivery of reliable telephony, the backbone of any dedicated system, has occurred only recently.

As a consequence, use of the telephone system as a vehicle for internal management controls has not been widespread, as the earlier Reliance Industries example illustrates. Assuming the internet, utilizing still- to-be-provided broadband facilities operated privately, becomes widely available in coming years, reliable opportunities for better management controls should become more popular.

Even smaller companies may be well placed to take advantage of it. The result might well be a much more productive industrial system made possible through better managerial controls. Again, however, at this stage much is conjectural.

The gains from improving transaction capabilities between firms should be even more striking in a developing country environment, particularly in a large country like India. Part of these gains will come through the B2B portals noted above and are similar to gains found already in industrial countries. Part will be the result of company-specific uses of the internet to increase awareness of procurement needs among a larger audience of potential suppliers. Again, tightening relationships between buyers and suppliers has been under way for many years in developed countries, starting with Japan and later being transferred to firms in other industrialized countries.

It antedates internet development in these parts of the world. In India, on the other hand, the distribution system at all levels remains antiquated and inefficient. The gains to be made from tightening this system, even apart from fixing the abundant remaining problems in physical distribution, are likely to be substantial.

In addition, although services in India are far less important as a proportion of GDP compared, say, with the United States, the internet still promises to yield efficiencies in the service sector. The examples of banks given above provide concrete evidence.

Clearly, financial clearings, among other financial services, can be enormously accelerated through the introduction of electronic banking, with commensurate savings in working capital requirements throughout the economy. To be sure, the larger benefits are not likely to be in consumer banking for some time to come, since internet penetration is so limited, even among the well-off, and overall income levels so low.

For businesses, on the other hand, the much greater ease of accomplishing financial transactions through the internet promises important gains. Similar benefits could be available in other services, including insurance processing, government licensing and permits, health care and transportation, among others.

Adding more competition to existing markets promises to be another development contribution, especially in the Indian context. Aside from a few large firms, markets in India tend to be regional and even local, isolated from one another by poor communications and inadequate roads.

The internet can at least partially alleviate these problems, in the process widening sources of information and, in all likelihood, lowering prices. The active interest in several B2B portals, as evidenced by the number of "hits" and associates transactions, provides some evidence that these benefits already are being found.

To be sure, much remains to be achieved in physical infrastructure improvement to assure that gains are truly widespread, but even in the short-run the evidence seems to be that through better information markets are broadened and prices reduced.

Finally, India's efforts vastly to improve connectivity internationally by allowing private parties to offer their own gateway facilities can be seen as belated recognition that the future of global commerce will more and more be intimately dependent on high-speed access to the internet.

The need for improved international connectivity goes well beyond the requirements of internet-enabled services, although for India these are likely to be rapidly expanding areas of business.

The wider reality is that if Indian manufacturing companies are to become more internationally competitive, as they hope to be, ready access to wideband internet services will be of paramount importance. Buyers in the industrialized countries that

Indian companies hope to service expect to be in instantaneous and continuous contact with suppliers through the internet, and firms that have inadequate electronic connections already find their possibilities compromised.

The Indian government has recognized this requirement and is moving quickly to improve both international gateways and the country's fiberoptic infrastructure, both largely through incentives directed to private sector providers.

As in most countries, computers and IT have been around for a long time in India. But, considered as an industry gaining global recognition and as having an internationally competitive future, IT's much-publicized growth in India has been a much more recent phenomenon.

Software exports, the earliest harbinger of a more widespread IT expansion, began only in 1985, when Texas Instruments established its subsidiary in Bangalore. This move was followed not only by other foreign software companies setting up operations in that city and elsewhere but also by a number of domestically-established software companies.

In more recent years, as the internet has expanded globally, these earlier investments have been followed by an explosion of start- up internet companies and by early efforts of a few well-established manufacturing companies at using the internet and other forms of communication to improve efficiency in their operations.

IT manufacturing also has occurred in India for many years and has included investment by multinational companies, as IBM's early involvement in

India suggests. Today, many foreign producers of computers and peripherals (HP, IBM, Compaq, Canon, etc.) have manufacturing operations in the country, often in joint ventures with Indian companies.

There are in addition a number of wholly Indian companies, exemplified by HCL, a company that formerly had a joint venture with HP but has now taken over the enterprise. A variety of other manufacturers exist, including producers of peripherals, electronic supplies and fiberoptic equipment, among others, including Modi Xerox, Tata Liebert and Wipro as examples.

Manufacturing growth in computers and peripherals has been less than spectacular in India. This is a reflection partly of the thus far limited growth in the domestic end user market and partly of the inability of the volume-limited manufacturers to be competitive. In addition, in recent years unit sales of equipment have grown faster than the dollar figures would indicate, as unit prices have fallen in response to more competitive moves by both domestic manufacturers and multinationals.

Historically, IT manufacturing has been a protected industry in India but, as in other technically-based industries, this policy has been changing. By and large, manufacturing in India has not been internationally competitive. As one consequence, India has been unsuccessful in following the lead of other Asian nations in developing robust export markets for IT equipment or components.

However, as a signatory to the IT Agreement of the World Trade Organization, the government has committed to a zero duty regime by 2003. This, together with a simplification of procedures for transacting business in the sector, could have positive competitive outcomes for the Indian industry, but it remains to be seen who will be the major beneficiaries: local businesses, foreign investors, or some combination of the two.

One possible vehicle for bringing IT manufacturing to the fore, through direct foreign investment as in Singapore or Taiwan (China), has not been successful for a variety of reasons. Foreign investors might have taken the lead in introducing leading edge technologies and manufacturing methods. But, when such investors did attempt to break into the Indian market, their hopes often were dashed.

Disagreements over intellectual property protection was one cause of difficulty, as IBM's early departure illustrates. This development, a result of India's sensitivity to foreign influence, alone discouraged other investors for many years afterwards.

More recently, attempts at joint ventures between Indian firms and outside technology investors, such as that between HP and HCL, often have failed, owing in part to inconsistent objectives among the participants. Foreign investors were interested mostly in producing for local markets, whereas Indian companies wanted eventually to develop export markets as well.

Unlike software development, which can begin small and technically simple, efficient hardware output in IT depends on a minimal scale of operation and continuous access to technological innovations largely derived in industrialized countries. Protection doubtlessly was conceived as a way eventually to develop adequate scale but, as in most other cases, has resulted only in inefficient producers without easy access to technology.

Moreover, manufacturing is more susceptible to India's familiar inadequacies in high-ways and port facilities which, particularly if exports are a goal, can add materially to delivery costs for goods shipped by methods other than air transportation. The reality in any case is that IT hardware production is as yet an insignificant industry in India. This situation, of course, could change rapidly if the internet and associated computer technology use expands as some anticipate will occur in India.

After all, the same technological talent that produced international competitiveness in some software areas, could be brought to bear on hardware design and production. But, success in hardware will come with considerably more difficulty than in software, where government influence has been minimal and where production has relied almost entirely on highly skilled engineers and technicians working in relatively small groups.

Software Development For now, India's major comparative advantages in the IT sector is software development. Software had its modest beginnings, at least as an internationally competitive sector, with the Texas Instruments investment in Bangalore noted earlier (See also the accompanying box). Today, the business is both large and expanding rapidly, directed almost entirely to overseas clients, and involves both domestic and foreign firms.

Most companies, multinationals and domestic firms alike, today use dedicated satellite links in their contacts with either their home offices or customers. Eventually, however, the speed and cheapness of internet connections may substitute for dedicated means, as international internet connections become better established and security issues are overcome.

Texas Instruments (TI), the first of several multinationals to establish operations in India, began as a wholly-owned operation intended to enable the company to continue software development 24 hours a day and to do so with decreased costs. At the time, engineering salaries in India were only 10 percent of those prevailing in the United States, which translated into software development costs of fifty percent less than in the US.

Today, owing to its early positive experiences, TI assigns not only much more sophisticated applications of software but also has expanded to include the design of integrated circuits. Although still dedicated entirely to TI's internal needs, the much-expanded facility in Bangalore now employs 350 people in a world-class computing and communications environment equal to any in the company's global operations.

Infosys Technologies, Limited, began in 1981 as essentially a two-man applications software shop for large companies. By 1985, sales had already reached $18.1 million. In the 1990s the company added satellite transmission capabilities to ensure reliable and fast connections with clients in the industrialized world. Rapid growth has continued, with fiscal year 2000 sales at $203.4 million, over 90 percent North America and Europe.

Today the company employs around 5,000 software professionals in seventeen development centers located throughout the world, up from just 585 professionals in 1985. In fosys is not the largest of India's dedicated software firms, as both Tata Consultancy and Wipro have greater sales, but in terms of its growth rate, employment expansion and customer base, it is a prototypical Indian applied software company.

The sector's growth has exceeded 50 percent annually in the period shown. Today, software shipments count for over 10 percent of India's total exports and two-thirds of sales for the entire IT sector, including equipment, training and maintenance.

The software market in the United States and Europe is simply orders of magnitude larger than in India. Moreover, potential customers in developed countries have dealt with software consultants for a long time. They tend to have a clear picture of software development costs and are, commensurately, receptive to the cost-saving opportunities Indian companies potentially make available. Professionals in India earn perhaps $12,000 annually, high by Indian standards but one-quarter or less of western salaries for like work. And, according to sources in the United States, the quality level of major Indian software producers can exceed typical standards in the U.S. for the types of programming undertaken.

Fast growth has been paralleled by a rapid expansion in the need for technically trained personnel in the sector. Professional employment for software production, according NASSCOM, reached 280,000 in 1999, up from only 6,800 when Texas Instruments formed its subsidiary. Companies have projected a need for another 140,000 professionals in the next year, far more than the 85,000 becoming available from various Indian educational institutions under the most optimistic projections. McKinsey consultants, who have done a major industry study for NASSCOM, estimate that India could absorb 2 million software engineers in various capacities by 2008. Clearly, the rapid expansion of both private and public institutions for technical education now going on in India is badly needed.

Development Contributions of Software Operations

Taken in a narrow context, the software sector cannot be said to have had a major development impact on a country as large and as poor as India. Direct employment in the industry is minuscule in relation to the country's population and is concentrated in only a few metropolitan centers. Most of the sector's output is directed abroad, applications software presumably intended to improve operational efficiencies in US and European, not Indian, companies.

Few ordinary Indians can be said to have been affected one way or another by the software sector's astronomical growth and increasing international prominence. And yet, a case can be made for taking a somewhat broader view of the sector in terms of its potential effects on the larger economy. Some of these impacts are apparent already; others may take somewhat longer to come to fruition.

Aside from India's very large informal sector, software development is probably the only sector to have grown up largely free of inhibiting governmental regulation or interference. In fact, central and state governments have provided such incentives as tax exemptions, investment concessions and setting aside areas for technology parks, among other steps, to encourage the sector's growth.

Nurtured by these incentives, the sector has provided the primary example in India of the growth potentialities that can occur by allowing relatively unfettered entrepreneurialism to flourish. One consequence has been a commensurate growth in venture capital availability, as investors see the chance of multiplying their investments by a hopefully propitious selection of opportunities. The example set by the software sector has not been lost in government circles, where a similar growth pattern in a number of other high technology areas is a fervent hope, if not quite yet an expectation.

Plans that are afoot include the creation through private companies of a fiberoptic "backbone" linking the nation's cities and towns, a rapid expansion in the availability of fast internet connections, the building of a system of "info-kiosks" to bring internet availability even to rural areas, and an overall improvement in telephone service nationwide.

The hope is for India to become an international leader not only in software development, by now an accomplished fact, but to leapfrog many other developing countries by establishing a world-class telecommunications infrastructure and associated technology capabilities.

Matching these plans to reality, however, will require enormous efforts, including close coordination among and between central and state government units, and very large amounts of private investment capital. To attract the capital, private investors will need to be assured that they can move ahead without inordinate interference from various governmental units. It is not entirely clear, even in high technology sectors, that this freedom will be forthcoming, despite a new telecommunications policy. This is particularly true in areas where, in the past, government has maintained a monopoly, as in local telephone provision. Still, the point to be made here is that the success of the software sector has provided a useful role model for developing further high technology sectors and the message has not been lost even among the entrenched bureaucracies in the various capitals. Long distance voice and data communications, for example, have been opened up to private competitors, following the earlier lead of wireless communications.

The software sector also has been a source of additional export earnings for India, and one not dependent on the country's grossly inadequate rail, road and port network. Software now contributes ten percent of total export earnings, and it is a percentage that is growing rapidly as the industry expands at rates exceeding 50 or 60 percent annually, far higher than other, more traditional export industries.

Yet, although export growth by India's companies has been rapid, the Indian share of software production in global markets is still minuscule. In the year 2000, for example, Indian exports of software to developed country markets represented less than 2 percent of total production in those countries. Clearly, there remains ample opportunity for rapid growth to continue for some time to come.

Although direct employment in the software sector is both small in relative terms and specialized, there are a number of indirect employment effects that can be mentioned. Most obvious are the opportunities in other areas that have opened up as the sector has expanded, including jobs in construction, infrastructure improvements and suppliers. No estimates of such "trickle down" effects exist, but the impacts cannot be trivial if one judges by the large construction projects supporting the sector's expansion that can be seen around such cities as Bangalore, Mumbai, Hyderabad or New Delhi.

The fact that India is demonstrably competitive internationally in the production of sophisticated software brings other advantages to the country. Indian technological sophistication, though still narrowly defined, has begun to alter international perceptions of the country. Instead of viewing India as a country burdened by decades of heavy-handed government regulation of the economy, foreigners now view the country somewhat more favourably, though not yet as a country where future growth will approximate that of China and several of the Southeast Asian countries.

Whether or not much enhanced foreign direct investment and technological transfer will follow such changes in perception is, of course, decidedly problematical in today's political and economic environment in India. A weak set of national and state governments is plagued by high fiscal deficits and seems unwilling or politically unable to rein in the subsidies that are largely the cause. This weakness, together with a long-standing suspicion that foreign investment represents a continuation of imperialism under a different guise, continues to make life difficult for those investors who have shown recent interest in establishing a greater Indian presence.

Even domestic investors have had difficulty with the crowding out effects of Indian deficits. Add to all of these concerns the paucity of Indian public investment to improve physical infrastructure or general educational standards, and it should come as no surprise that investors still see India as one of the world's more difficult economic environments. The positive example of software obviously has much to overcome. Even so, the software sector's success has at least given greater voice to demands for educational improvements to support not only this sector but also other related sectors.

The immediate impact has been in the expansion of technical colleges and universities as well as more attention to lower- level training institutes. While not helping directly with the more basic problems of illiteracy and inadequate primary and secondary education, such moves certainly do support not only software producers but also other technology- based sectors that have been receiving attention as sources of more general economic growth in India.

Internet use has been relatively slow to evolve in India. This slowness has been characteristic not only of personal use of the internet but includes business use as well. Although there are abundant internet sites devoted to business-to-business (B2B) and business-to-consumer (B2C) transactions (reviewed earlier), few are yet successful in a financial sense.

Moreover, employing the internet for internal corporate transactions is still in its infancy in India, mostly because the underlying communications facilities are as yet not fast enough or sufficiently reliable for most corporate uses. It is fair to say that most data links used within large companies in India are not internet-based, but rather are dedicated leased telephone facilities.

Awareness of internet potentialities as a valuable tool for future business communications is now widespread. In fact, planning for internet use by corporations is advancing rapidly. On a more general scale, the internet is being seen as a necessary vehicle for improving the country's global prospects and, therefore, essential for contributing to further economic development, a view involving not only business interests but, as importantly, government ministries. As a consequence, several initiatives have been advanced to accelerate India's development of required infrastructure to support wider internet use, particularly by business interests. Several of these initiatives are reviewed briefly below.

Fiberoptic backbone: As noted, one of the major impediments to more advanced uses of the internet, particularly for business use, is the primitive nature of the country's communications system. While telephone quality has been much improved, India has lacked the necessary infrastructure for high-speed data transmission. It has been clear for some time that if such a system is to be built, it will not be done by governmental interests, national or local. In the face of large fiscal deficits in both national and state budgets, public investment has remained low. Nor has there been any expectation that the national telephone monopoly would find the enormous amount of funds to support the creation of country-wide, high-speed data networks.

To break this obvious logjam, permission has been given for private companies to lay optical fiber cable along road and highway rights-of-way at no charge and to allow private right-of-way arrangements with such other entities as power distributors and Indian railways. Moreover, permission has been granted to private parties to enter the long-distance telephone business. One result of such changes has been a number of privately funded efforts to build an interconnected system of fiberoptic cables to link at least the major cities in the country in relatively short order. Problems still remain on so-called "last mile" connections, but the apparent hope is that, for larger businesses, these problems will not be insurmountable and, for residences and small-businesses, ways can be found to link through existing cable television lines or through information kiosks. One example of a company that has entered the fiberoptic cable business is Reliance Industries, a company cited earlier regarding its present and future use of the internet. This firm is committed to developing a national fiberoptic network linking 115 cities which, together, represent about 50 percent of India's GDP. This $3-4 billion set of projects in a short time will permit Reliance to offer long-distance and local telephone service, internet service and high-speed data transmission. Eventually, the company expects to enter the already competitive business of selling back-office services. Reliance is only one of several private companies in India determined to profit from the provision of internet infrastructure.

Wireless services: By 2005, it is estimated that 1.2 billion people worldwide will be able to access the internet using mobile communications. And, for many, mobile connections may well be cheaper and more convenient than fixed lines. For relative latecomers to the cellular telephone explosion, like India, who can initiate digital systems from the start, wireless services may be one method for avoiding some of the disadvantages stemming from inadequate and often expensive dependence on landlines.

Wireless services in India, which have been digital from the beginning, are furnished largely by several large, private providers. The state-owned operator, MSNL, is only now beginning its own services Although growth in the market for mobile communications has been disappointing, mostly owing to high costs of both equipment and service, this picture is changing. Costs have been coming down, and the response thus far has been encouraging for providers. Today, there are perhaps 2-3 million subscribers in India, a very low number compared even with other developing countries. Growth, however, has approximated 85 percent over the past year, a figure that obviously is based on the low user base noted above. To provide a comparison, China has 54 million subscribers.. Whether or not mobile communication becomes at all important as a vehicle to access the internet remains to be seen in India. Thus far at least, mobile internet service is yet to be offered.

Fixed telephone service: In a recent enumeration of internet readiness, the Economist Intelligence Unit ranked India fiftieth of the sixty countries ranked. A major reason for the low rating was India's connectivity ranking, a measure taking into account not only the state of the existing telephone network but also other factors affecting access, such as dial- up costs and literacy rates. In this ranking, India was rated 3 on a scale of 10 in connectivity, along with such other countries as Egypt, China and Pakistan, among others. There are about 2.0 main telephone lines in India per 1,000 inhabitants, a strikingly low number but one that has increased by 60 percent in the past four years. One corollary of low telephone density is that service has not yet reached thousands of villages. And, while major cities are largely serviced, the quality of many lines is poor, largely owing to low quality last-mile connections. While telephone access and quality of service have both been improving rapidly, the system is still often subject to dropped connections, obviously a bane for reliable internet services.

Provision of telephone communications in India has until quite recently been a province exclusively of government as was the provision of internet services. Although local land- line service remains in the public domain, both long distance and internet services have been opened up to other providers. One consequence has been an explosion of internet service providers (ISPs); in 1999 alone new ISPs established over fifty sites. Interestingly, the potential presence of this new competition apparently motivated Videsh Sanchar Nigam, Limited (VSNL) dramatically to expand its own presence by adding thirty cities to its ISP network and to lower fees. One can anticipate a similar reaction as private long-distance providers gear up to enter aggressively into that market.

As to local services, the market is still reserved to the Department of Telecommunications, except in Mumbai and New Delhi, where Mahangar Telephone Nigam, Limited (MTNL), is sole provider. MTNL also is a public sector company under the Ministry of Communications. Both the DOT and MTNL have been under great pressure from within the government to expand telephone access, and the result has been a quite rapid expansion of services. Still, insofar as the internet is concerned, competition for the public companies to increase the quality of services and lower prices is likely to come not from within but rather from cable television providers linking with some of the private companies laying down fiberoptic cable across the country. Here a number of constraints unfortunately apply.

International Linkages: Until recently, all telecommunications gateways in India were the province only of the government through VSNL. Needless to say, with internet and other users seeking high-speed connections, the demand for international band width already far exceeds the supply. And, demands are increasing rapidly, even with only limited use of the internet thus far. Most Indian websites, particularly those being designed to service non-resident Indians, have attempted to evade this bottleneck by establishing their sites in the United States. But, in the longer run, if the internet is to become the vital communications means hoped for, the gateway constraint must be breeched. Recent changes in Indian telecommunications policy have opened up international gateways anywhere in the country to private internet service providers (ISPs).

These new carriers hope to team with foreign providers of undersea cable to rapidly expand international services. Although limited only to internet providers, not voice traffic, and burdened by somewhat excessive security requirements, the new licensing provisions promise to reduce the supply-demand gap in the near future.

There is, of course, much more to business success than access to the internet. Firms exist in an environment that is either supportive of their competitive efforts, not supportive, or something in between. Even with a completed high-speed fiberoptic network connecting most cities and with much- improved international gateways, both expected within the next two years, India's economic environment could, at best, be ranked as "something in between." For purposes here, it is unnecessary to run through the litany of well-known difficulties businesses face (continued government interference at both national and state levels, remaining protection, even in the IT sector, inadequate public investment owing to high fiscal deficits, the associated 'crowding out' effects in capital markets, government subsidies, sectors reserved to very small firms, labor laws, etc.).

The fact is that today few firms in India outside the software, textile and chemical industries are truly competitive internationally, especially among locally controlled companies. Even within the IT sector, domestic manufacturers of personal computers, peripherals and other equipment are concerned that opening markets in response to India's joining the WTO could be devastating if and when lessened levels of effective protection are introduced. Adjusting to increased international competition, in other words, could present difficult problems for many Indian companies.

Two negative factors affecting the growth and success of the internet in affecting productivity improvement seem particularly important. The first has been mentioned earlier, poor physical infrastructure for moving products within the country and, for export and imports, through ports.

The inability to ship goods easily and cheaply is a major constraint in building a true national marketplace in India and a constraint that will not easily be overcome. Some efforts have been made to improve ports through private sector initiatives, but much remains to be done both here and, particularly, in highway construction. Given low public investment and the apparent discomfort in relying on private methods of financing infrastructure projects, this constraint is likely to persist for some time to come.

The other factor that ultimately promises to compromise success, certainly as compared with several other Asian nations, is educational achievement. Fewer than 60 percent of Indian children complete the fifth grade, and 45 percent are illiterate. These percentages compare poorly with such competitive countries as Thailand, Indonesia or, especially, the Philippines.

Although lack of literacy has not thus far been a major problem for those parts of the IT sector that have been successful, particularly the software industry, the much wider impacts from the internet that are anticipated across the economy will depend increasingly on availability of trained or trainable workers. In some ways, India appears bifurcated between an educated middle-class, from which the technical schools draw, and the vast majority of the population with little, if any, formal education.

Appendix

Strengths and weaknesses of Asia's developing economics

Some of Asia's strategies to rapidly modernize and industrialize its economics, with some of their successes and difficulties. Despite the variations in the development schemes of the individual nations, there are several common themes. In general, industrial development in Asia seems to have been most rapid and most successful when conceived as a long-term effort that requires active governmental involvement to define goals and optimize limited resources, attract industry, encourage continuous technological progress through its various stages, and develop global competitiveness. Despite the stunning economic and technological gains achieved in the past quarter-century by the Asian countries described above, the recent downturn in 1997-

98 exposed serious weaknesses in infrastructures and financial systems, as well as overcapacity in industries such as electronics and petrochemicals. Table 1 lists some of the general obstacles to continued development. Table 11 summarizes specific strengths and weaknesses of the NIEs as they relate to continued growth potential.

Table 1. Asia's Obstacles to Continuing Growth

Overcapacity	:	The region is overbuilding in such manufacturing areas as autos, semiconductors, consumer electronics, and chemical processing.
Weak Capital Markets	:	Capital is channelled too often to state-owned companies or private conglomerates. Small businesses are starved for funds.
Rising Costs	:	Tight labour markets are pushing up wages, while rising affluence is increasing demand for goods and housing.
Poor Infrastructure	:	Asia needs better highways, pollution control, port facilities, and power plants.
Widespread Corruption	:	It hampers small businesses and scares off some foreign investors.
Inadequate Training	:	Some countries have poor elementary schools, while others cannot teach workers to act innovatively.

Mature and Newly Industrializing Asian Economies

A number of uncertainties face the countries of Asia as their economies mature. Japan, the dominant player in Asia and the most advanced, is struggling to solve problems in its real estate markets, financial institutions, and social security and health care systems for its aging population. Japan's ongoing economic woes despite its hard-won business and technical strengths caution Western and Asian observers to seek a balanced view of Asian economic growth policies.

The major strengths and weaknesses of Asia's NIEs can be summarized as follows.

Korea

Korea's chaebols are the strongest global players among Asia's NIEs. They have benefited from 25 years of government support and protected markets and are now recognized as major global players. Samsung leads in computer memory products and will expand its semiconductor capabilities. Other chaebols also are performing well in international markets, despite the country's fiscal woes. Korean industry is becoming increasingly autonomous as it moves abroad. Nurturing the growth of smaller companies has had some limited success. An outstanding educational infrastructure and hard-working citizens figure prominently among Korea's competitive advantages.

On the other hand, Korea faced declining exports and increased labour problems during the downturn. At the same time, it is paying the political price for its heavily regulated, highly politicized, and, by Western standards, corrupt banking system. Korea's currency and financial crisis resulted in loans worth $55 billion, including $21 billion from the International Monetary Fund (IMF), $10 billion from Japan, and $5 billion from the United States. Many financial companies closed operations. In addition, both security and economic threats from North Korea figure into the equation.

Korea's chaebols need to restructure and become more focused to meet the growing strength of global competition. Korea's 12th-ranked chaebol, the Halla group, filed for bankruptcy on December 6, 1997, with $5.3 billion in debt, 20 times the group's equity. Hyundai had guaranteed as much as $1 billion of Halla's debts. Daewoo faces financial problems in 1999. By law, the 30 largest chaebols are now required to lower their debt-payment guarantees to 100 percent of their equity.

Taiwan

Taiwan has successfully established a global position in electronics products and key components and has a significant number of firms capable of taking their operations into the global market. Taiwanese firms' original development strategy has made them leaders in new product introductions. The country's key component and product strategy ensures that adequate resources will be available for continued development of technological and product capabilities. Taiwan's economic successes are tempered somewhat by its ambivalent political status vis à vis mainland China, both in terms of its relations with other countries (few countries want to alienate China) and in terms of the political and economic aspirations of its people. Solution of this political problem does not appear to be imminent; meanwhile, however, Taiwan continues to engineer its rapid economic growth, based in no small measure on tapping business opportunities in China. In the long term, China hopes for Taiwan to provide a key technology base for its continued development.

Singapore

Singapore appears to have developed the most comprehensive approach to attracting MNCs and keeping them involved in its economy. The government provides incentives to establish management and operational headquarters in Singapore, actively aids companies in moving factory and marketing operations across the region, and provides incentives for firms to conduct their research activities in Singapore. Singapore is making major investments to establish the most advanced telecommunications system in Asia, while continuing to promote technology-based, value-added manufacturing. Singapore aspires to become the primary financial center for the Asia-Pacific region. Its goal is to become the "intelligent island" in the age of information technology. Some say its "economic miracle" has come from a totally managed society that critics argue is overregulated.

Malaysia

Malaysia achieved very high growth rates until the financial crisis that resulted from heavy foreign investment in high-tech manufacturing. Malaysia's vision still is to be totally developed by 2020. It plans to build the most advanced information technology infrastructure in the world. In spite of its recovering growth rate, the earlier rapid development has caused structural economic issues such as a huge current account deficit.

Malaysia is aggressively pushing to build an independent technological lead in multimedia. This follows a similar approach taken earlier in the automobile industry. By making a strong financial commitment, providing 10-year tax holidays to technological leaders, and developing next-generation infrastructure and products, Malaysia will continue to be an aggressive player in Southeast Asia.

China and Hong Kong

China's strong commitment to upgrading its technology base and infrastructure encourages foreign firms to locate operations close to its 1.2 billion-consumer market. In China today, fewer than 5 percent of the people own a dishwasher, clothes washer, vacuum cleaner, micro-wave oven, or car. There is one telephone for every 25 people, one fax for every 200 people, and one PC for every 400 people. High-tech industrial parks, such as the China-Singapore Suzhou Industrial Park near Shanghai, and special economic zones, such as Shenzhen, are central to China's strategy.

Hong Kong provides direct access to China. China fever abated somewhat in 1997, 1998, and 1999. For example, the total value of new pledged foreign investment contracts dropped 20 to 30 percent in 1996 and 1997. Few people can predict the long-term impact of Hong Kong's return to China. There are many questions about Hong Kong's ability to continue to provide world-class service under Chinese rule. It has become increasingly expensive to operate in Hong Kong, and the education base there has its own shortcomings. However, Hong Kong is expected to aid China's ability to upgrade its business skills and provide a key channel for raising capital.

Contrasts Between the Asian NIEs

There are sharp contrasts among the United States, Japan, and some of Asia's newly developed economies. Singapore stands out as the country with the highest percentage of population in the workforce. While Japan has the second highest percentage of workers, its aging population is likely to cause a decline in workforce percentage. In education, Korea has the highest percentage of university graduates in the work force, but still struggles to improve the indigenous innovative capability required to develop advanced technologies. This difficulty has a negative impact on GDP growth.

The countries in Asia are rivals in pursuit of Western business, which has resulted in overcapacity of operating facilities. This situation has provided an opportunity for Western firms to exploit low-cost sources of supplies in Asia, especially in electronics components. Continued development by the United States of close relations with Asian countries provides continuing economic opportunities. As Henry Kissinger has noted, "We are, or could be, closer to each of the contenders in Asia than they are to one another."

Less Developed Asian Economics

Less developed Asian countries such as the Philippines, Thailand, and Indonesia have benefited from the successes and rising wages of their more developed neighbours. They, too, are taking on the challenges of managing rapid industrialization. Those countries that are able to overcome political problems and build effective development strategies will also participate in Asia's future economic expansion. Growth in regional and global demand require continued expansion of Asia's industrial base. Rising wages and full employment in the NIEs provide continued opportunities for the LDCs of Asia. For example:

— The Philippines has benefited from the regional expansion of firms from more developed countries. However, political unrest and official corruption continue to be problems. Corrective actions seem limited as long as the powerful landed gentry resist moves toward economic reform and discourage foreign investment. While the closing of the Subic Bay and Clark military bases chilled relations with the United States for a time, the infrastructure that remained has served the Philippines well in attracting industry and jump-starting its economic growth. However, the thriving industrial complexes now located at the bases are in serious need of expanded infrastructure.

— Thailand had its financial crisis because of a banking system burdened by a host of bad loans. Pressures on its currency affected the fiscal stability of such neighbouring countries as Malaysia, the Philippines, and Indonesia. At the present, rising wages are making manufacturing in Thailand less competitive, and it is struggling in its effort to move up the ladder to higher-value products. It is further being constrained by an educational system in need of serious improvement.

— Indonesia still is in a state of political as well as economic crisis, although signs offer hope. As the people's economic and political aspirations continue to rise, Indonesia's leaders are addressing the difficult structural changes demanded by the IMF in return for a $43 billion rescue package to stabilize Indonesia's currency. The country also seriously needs an improved communication system because of its geographical structure. Its 13,500 islands stretch 3,200 miles east to west and 1,100 miles north to south.

— *Vietnam*: The addition of Vietnam to the Association of Southeast Asian Nations (ASEAN) appears to have been the most successful of the ASEAN expansion efforts to date. Vietnam is at the center of the most dynamic economic region in Asia. It is fast developing a market economy driven primarily by foreign investments exploiting its low wage rates. Vietnam is a country still debilitated by the ravages of war, with an almost nonexistent communications and transportation infrastructure. Its GDP per capita is about one-quarter that of Indonesia or the Philippines. The situation should, however, quickly improve because of major investments from Hong Kong, Taiwan, and Australia.

— *Cambodia, Laos, and Myanmar:* Although ASEAN has been a stabilizing and supportive force for areawide economic development, it has yet to have much impact on the least developed countries of the region. The concern for human rights in both Cambodia and Myanmar is politically distracting. At this time, prospects for development in these countries are limited. Myanmar may have some advantage because of its location and the completion of the China highway that will link South China to Thailand through the northeast corner of Myanmar. Indonesia and Thailand are expected to see shrinking economies in 1998 because of serious financial problems and the collapse of regional markets. However, 1999 forecasts put most Asian economies back on the road toward rapid growth. Even if the forecasts are too optimistic in the short term, many observers already see signs of recovery and restructuring in most countries that bode well for Asia's long-term economic recovery.

Table 2. Real GDP Growth in Asia (percent)

	1997 actual	*1998 actual*	*1999 forecast*	*2000 forecast*
China	8.8	7.8	6.6	7.0
Hong Kong	5.3	–5.1	–1.3	3.1
Taiwan	6.8	4.9	3.9	4.8
Indonesia	4.6	–13.7	–4.0	2.5
Malaysia	7.7	–6.8	0.9	2.0
Philippines	5.2	–0.5	2.0	3.0
Singapore	8.0	1.5	0.5	4.2
Thailand	–0.4	–8.0	1.0	3.0
Japan	1.4	–2.8	–1.4	0.3
Republic of Korea	5.5	–5.5	2.0	4.6
India	5.5	5.6	5.2	5.1
Australia	3.6	5.1	3.1	3.2
New Zealand	2.1	–0.3	2.7	3.3

Asian Model for Development

The Asian experience shows that there is no perfect set of actions that guarantees economic development without risks and setbacks. Governments must be flexible in dealing with the ever-changing competitive terrain by adjusting development strategies as conditions change and the relative strengths of competing countries grow. The lessons that can be learned from the Asian experience are worth noting. These lessons revolve around the strategies and trends in low-cost labour, infrastructure investment, worker skills, support for technology, and the business climate. They also reflect the growing impact of globalization and regional cooperation.

Competitive Strategies and Trends

Low-cost labour

The search for low-cost labour continues to be the primary driver of economic development across Asia and other developing areas of the world. It dictates constant changes and updates in strategies to attract and retain investment and increase standards of living. As development occurs and labour costs increase, there is a corresponding growth in the purchasing power of consumers for products and services that in turn creates a significant market opportunity. The growth in the purchasing power of Asia's population of 3 billion, especially its growing middle class, during the early and mid-1990s created a significant market opportunity. Domestic and foreign corporations invested in Asia in hopes of capturing an early market position.

Asian countries with rising labour costs turned to technology-led economic growth strategies as a way to continue to increase their standards of living as some types of investment inevitably began to move to lower-cost producers. Singapore has developed its own strategy to build and manage "world-class" industrial parks in Vietnam, China, Indonesia, and India to benefit from the move by helping firms expand low-cost operations across Asia. The impact of the economic slowdown on this scenario is mixed. Labour costs in some Asian countries have fallen, increasing their attraction for some types of investment. On the other hand, the purchasing power of much of Asia's middle class is stagnant or in some cases declining, negatively affecting market opportunity.

Infrastructure investment

Demand for all forms of infrastructure investments drives corporate and country strategies and is an important part of the Asian development model. Basic industrial infrastructure is a competitive advantage in attracting business to a country. Before the economic slowdown, infrastructure investment began to allow Asian economic growth to expand from a limited number of urban areas to broader geographical areas.

As Andrew Tranzer noted in 1996, "East Asia is now capturing over 60 percent of the world's private capital flows to developing countries, an inflow worth $100 billion in fresh capital every year-not to mention managerial and technical expertise (East Asia central banks collectively hold more than $600 billion of foreign reserves)." Despite the setbacks of 1997-98, Asian countries still are investing in building the infrastructures needed by tomorrow's information societies. It is expected that the Asia-Pacific region (excluding Japan) will spend a trillion dollars on infrastructure in the next 10 years. Singapore's IT 2000 strategy calls for the creation of a national information network with all homes, schools, businesses and government agencies interconnected in an electronic grid. China plans to spend more than $40 billion installing the equivalent of a Bell Canada-size network each year until 2000. China's government also has established its "Golden" projects to boost its communications systems, record-keeping, commercial transactions, and so on into the information age. And the Philippines is taking advantage of military bases vacated by the United States.

Where extending advanced infrastructures across an entire economy is too costly and complex to accomplish in the short term, science and technology "parks" have allowed countries to rapidly build state-of-the-art mini-economies within a geographically restricted area. Reduced tax rates, advanced infrastructure, and policies such as one-stop regulatory permitting give Asia's high-tech industrial parks an advantage in attracting or keeping global competitors.

Worker Skills

Ability to compete globally is not a function of national size, as Malaysia, Korea, Singapore, Taiwan, and Hong Kong demonstrate. There are many reasons for the success of their companies, but it is becoming increasingly obvious as their labour costs have risen that their primary competitive advantage is their growing knowledge base and number of skilled workers.

Today every country can easily tap into global technology, acquire advanced manufacturing practices, adopt the best financial techniques, acquire investment money from international venture capitalists, and employ knowledgeable workers from around the world. In today's globally competitive environment, the best jobs go where the most qualified workers are available. Conversely, advanced education in science and technology results in the highest-paying jobs and the most benefit to the economy. Countries with inadequately trained workers tend to find themselves locked into low-paying, low-value-added assembly-type jobs and industries. Lester Thurow expressed it well when he said, "The skills of the workforce are going to be the key competitive weapon in the 21st century" in Head to Head: The Coming Economic Battle Among Japan, Europe, and America.

Support for Technology

Asia's success in applying advanced technology resulted in part from substantial investment and commitment to specific emerging industries and critical supporting technologies. In the early stages of development, Korean government-funded research institutes provided an important mechanism in building the research strength of its chaebols. ITRI in Taiwan has been responsible for supporting the electronics industry and entering the semiconductor industry. In Singapore, government research institutes target industries and subsidize R&D for foreign firms willing to conduct local research and build a local technology base. In addition, Singapore's EDB directly subsidizes high-tech development programs. Malaysia's "multimedia corridor" called "Cyberjaya" provides various types of support for companies locating in it, including a new multimedia university.

Development of multitechnology/multimedia products often also requires strategic alliances for more rapid and efficient development, since internal development may be too slow in getting to market in a timely fashion. Taiwan's entry into the semiconductor business has included every major player in the world. Asian NIEs have effectively targeted growth industries and related technologies for development. Many of the targeted areas are in electronics, multimedia, and information fields. Taiwan is only one example of the practice of targeting. Its Critical Components strategy targeted 48 critical components and 24 critical products to provide global leadership in 10 emerging industries. The Taiwanese government has provided R&D, prototyping, and ramp-up incentives and support to semiconductor and LCD technologies.

As a result of this kind of targeting, Taiwan, as well as the other NIEs addressed in this study, is achieving first-rate competitiveness in global electronics, multimedia, telecommunications, and information markets, successfully challenging traditional leaders. Hong Kong's Vtech has over 50 percent of the world's electronic learning aids market. Taiwan's Acer ranks among the top 10 PC companies in the world, competing directly with U.S. and Japanese leaders. In key computer components, Singapore's Aztech Technology controls nearly 90 percent of the world's sound card market. Korea's Samsung is the world leader in DRAM technology.

Business Climate

The growing ease of doing business in Asia has facilitated economic growth. Singapore's "one-stop shopping" strategy has been very attractive to MNCs. Hong Kong's high-quality services and management infrastructures provide a critical bridge for companies seeking to do business in China's industrial parks and special economic zones. Similar strategies are being used across Asia to allow efficient local administration of industrial development policies. Offering attractive investment incentives is an important component of Asian industrial development strategies. Investment incentives offered by Asian NIEs include tax holidays, exemptions, and reductions; another factor that draws investors is improved access to new markets. In terms of sheer size of investments, China, despite large declines in the past three years, has been the Asian country most successful recently at attracting foreign investment, about a third of all manufacturing-related investments in developing nations.

Environment

Sustained and sustainable economic growth is also linked to the ability to integrate environmental and productivity decisions. A clean environment, particularly as it affects production of high-technology products, is increasingly a competitive issue in Asia. In Beijing, NEC had to isolate and air condition its entire factory to keep pollution from affecting the quality of its IC production.

Globalization and Cooperation

The Asian experience suggests that to improve competitiveness, local high-technology companies can and must rapidly begin to expand operations beyond the national economy, since economies of size and scale demand their involvement in as many markets as possible. Localization of business activities must then focus on marketing and distribution. The Korean experience also indicates that as companies go global, they must intensify efforts to develop next-generation technologies. Research centers must be established not only at home but also in major technical centers abroad, as Japan and Korea have done in the United States and elsewhere.

Regional cooperation is an increasingly important element in competitive Asian development practices. With eight cooperative growth triangles, superior technologies and development practices are moving rapidly throughout the Asian region. For example, the Southern China Growth Triangle unites Taiwanese technology and management skills with Hong Kong's distribution and service skills and Southern China's low-cost production expertise.

Singapore and Malaysia provide capital and leadership in the development of the Southeast Asian region through ASEAN. ASEAN is now sponsoring the Association of Indian Ocean Rim Countries and the South Asia Association for Regional Cooperation, which involves India, Bangladesh, Nepal, Sri Lanka, and Pakistan.

Project-based cooperation also exists. For example, in February 1997, a submarine optical fiber network was completed that links nine Asian nations (Japan, Korea, Taiwan, Hong Kong, the Philippines, Thailand, Malaysia, Singapore, and Indonesia)-a length of over 12,000 kilometers. The $650 million project, built by a consortium of companies from the United States, Japan,

France, and Great Britain, began in 1994 as part of an effort to build an Asia-Pacific Information Infrastructure. Another area in which cooperation is evident is the financial support extended by the healthier Asian economies to those experiencing fiscal difficulties at this time.

Obstacles to Continued Growth

Despite aggressive strategies to upgrade technologies and attain global competitiveness, Asian countries face various obstacles to sustaining their economic growth:

— Overcapacity and strong price competition have resulted from heavy investment in a small range of industries including automobiles, semiconductors, consumer electronics, and chemical processing. In addition, the Asian economic slowdown has cut recent forecasts of automobile sales in 2000 by nearly half for Thailand, Indonesia, Malaysia and the Philippines.

— Many local firms are ill prepared as they restructure to meet World Trade Organization membership requirements for local market access by global competitors. The IMF also is committed to opening the Asian financial system to global competition, with Japanese deregulation that began in 1998.

— The scarcity of local capital makes it difficult for developing nations to build infrastructures or properly capitalize their own local firms. Short-term foreign loans placed countries like Thailand in serious financial jeopardy, since signs of economic slowdown cause foreign capital to exit rapidly and generate pressures for currency devaluation. Small entrepreneurial firms cannot grow without access to such funds.

— There is a shortage of talent needed for advanced stages of development. Weak school systems and a lack of creative thinking are exposed as labour costs rise and higher-level skills are needed. Simple lack of experience operating in an international milieu increases risks.

— As some of the experiences of Japan and Korea have demonstrated, heavy regulation and administrative guidance directed at protecting local markets can prove to be dysfunctional to industry restructuring in the face of increased global competition and rapid technological and market change. Protective government regulations are difficult to dismantle, but if not dismantled can ultimately impede growth by slowing market responsiveness. As product life cycles fall from years to months, bureaucratic interventions or management delays can rapidly cause local firms to lose competitive advantage.

— Many Asian business relationships and activities (1) are illegal under the 1977 U.S. Foreign Corrupt Practices Act, (2) inhibit competition, restructuring, and rationalization of growing Asian economies, or (3) impede working relationships with potentially helpful multinational corporations and organizations such as the IMF. While seeking to stabilize the Asian economies, the IMF has a longer-term objective to reduce the incidence of political corruption. On December 17, 1997, 34 OECD nations signed an antibribery treaty that will make payments to government officials a criminal act following the U.S. Foreign Corrupt Practices Act. Such pressures to change traditional or accepted business practices can greatly stress rapidly developing economies. Despite these obstacles, overall, Asian countries are rapidly adopting proven strategies for economic development. As more and more nations commit to developing high-tech industries, national and corporate competition is increasing in both emerging and established industries. The focus in India, China, and the Philippines on software, challenging U.S. domination of this industry, is an example of the constantly changing competitive landscape.

While the aftermath of the financial and monetary crisis is expected to continue to slow Asia's growth rate in the next two to three years, economic expansion is not expected to stop; in fact, most Asian countries are counting on technology development to help them grow out of their present difficulties.

Considerations for U.S. Policymakers

The recent stability in the U.S. economy has generated steady growth and provides full employment. The breadth and depth of the U.S. technology base continues to be second to none. Long-term competitiveness, however, relies on education, infrastructure, innovation, and initiatives that encourage both domestic operations and global leadership. As the U.S. market diminishes in relative global importance, it must sustain its innovative and technical capabilities in order to support continued economic stability and growth. Asian (and other) nations are challenging U.S. leadership in emerging high-technology industries: as Japan has successfully targeted steel, automobiles, and semiconductors, Taiwan has successfully targeted computer-related technologies, and Malaysia is targeting multimedia technologies. Such challenges cannot be overlooked. As nations compete for leadership in advanced technologies, the United States must ensure that its "crown jewels" are not lost to foreign competition. Therefore, it is essential for the United States as well as less developed countries aspiring to higher standards of living to be mindful of the lessons of the Asian model of development. Asian global strategies are addressing five fields that all countries should consider crucial to success in high-technology industries:

1. Educating and effectively utilizing knowledge workers, creating new knowledge, and protecting related intellectual property.

2. Increasing their access to global markets to ensure competitive economies of scale and recognition of evolving product and market standards.

3. Developing advanced infrastructures to attract and support global technology leaders and to facilitate development of local firms that can compete in the global marketplace.

4. Attracting and investing the capital needed to build essential infrastructures and to develop technologies and capacity for emerging growth industries.

5. Using legislative and fiscal incentives to induce high-technology companies to locate and participate in local R&D and value-added operations.

There also are market opportunities to consider. Since many countries lack the technology base needed to enter emerging businesses by themselves, strategic alliances offer U.S. firms opportunities to participate in the establishment of future industries in many locales.

Careful management of international market alliances will be imperative to future U.S. economic success, as will open markets, rapid responses to market and technological change, and continued cost competitiveness. Like Japan, the Asian newly industrializing economies' growing technological base offers a source of a new and unique R&D. While the United States finds itself in a comfortable economic position today, it can expect growth in global competition supported by aggressive industrial development strategies from newly industrializing countries in Asia and elsewhere. The new competitive paradigm will demand continued infrastructure and technology development, global market access, and creative new responses to both competitive and cooperative challenges from the Asian countries of the Pacific Rim.

CHAPTER 5

Policy Issues and Legal Framework of E-Business

On 28 May, the European Commission adopted the eEurope 2005 Action Plan. At the Seville Council (21 June 2002) the Council endorsed the objectives of the Commission's Action Plan for eEurope 2005 as "an important contribution to the EU's efforts towards a competitive, knowledge-based economy, calling upon all institutions to ensure that it will be fully implemented by the end of 2005 and invites the Commission to present in good time for the spring European Council in 2004 a midterm review to evaluate progress and, if necessary, make proposals to adapt the Action Plan".

The eEurope 2005 action plan states that by 2005 Europe should have modern online public services, e-government services, e-learning services, e-health services, a dynamic e-business environment and, as an enabler for these, widespread availability of broadband access at competitive prices and a secure information infrastructure.

To achieve these objectives, the 2005 Action Plan comprises four separate but interlinked sets of action:

1) *A dynamic e-business environment:*

- The Commission in cooperation with Member States will review and adapt legislation at EU and national level, starting in 2003 with an e-business Summit By the end of 2003:
- The private sector is called upon to develop interoperable solutions for transactions, security, signatures, procurement and payments;
- The Commission will examine the possibilities of setting up a European on-line dispute resolution system and further work with stakeholders on creating consumer confidence;
- The Commission will examine how European companies could be provided with additional functionality relating to the .eu domain name (e.g. trusted cyber identity, trust marks and an authentication scheme).

(2) *On-line public services*

- Member States are to ensure that by 2005 all public services (administrations, schools, universities, museums and libraries etc.) have broadband Internet access;
- By end 2003, the Commission will issue an interoperability framework based on open standards to support the delivery of e-government services to citizens and enterprises.

(3) *A secure information structure*

- A 'Cyber security task force', constituted by Member states and the private sector, should be operational by mid 2003. This task force will work as a centre of competence on security issues and develop a concept for a European computer attack alert system and facilitate transborder co-operation in the field of information and network security;

- Development of a 'culture of security' though good practices and standards by end 2005;
- The Commission and Member states will examine the possibilities to establish a secure communications environment for the exchange of government information by end 2003.

(4) Broadband

- Analysis and support for development of broadband deployment and Ipv6;
- The Commission will ensure spectrum availability and efficient spectrum use for by wireless broadband services ad cooperate with Member States with the regard to the introduction of such services.

The Copenhagen Summit in December 2002 should adopt the eEurope Benchmarking Report. The vast majority of the actions in the eEurope 2002 Action Plan should be realised by the end of 2005.

On July 12, 2000 the European Commission adopted a proposal for a Directive on 'processing of personal data and protection of privacy in the electronic communication sector'.

The proposal is part of a package of proposals for initiatives which will form the future regulatory framework for electronic communications networks and services. It aims to adapt and update the existing Data Protection Telecommunications Directive to take account of technological developments.

Unlike the Telecommunications Directive the scope of the future Directive would not be restricted to telephony and data networks, but will also cover satellite, terrestrial and cable TV broadcasting networks, irrespective of the type of information concerned.

The key provisions of the proposal relate to the following:

- Location Data
- Processing of traffic data
- Security and confidentiality
- Ex-directory default
- Unsolicited commercial communications and spamming
- Privacy-compliant software and hardware

The vote in European Parliament (plenary) took place on May 30, 2002. There will be no conciliation procedure. Formal approval by the Council is likely to take place within six weeks. The main controversially discussed issues can be summarised as follows:

- *Unsolicited Commercial Communications:* Parliament accepted the Council's common position, thus approving an opt-in system for e-mail, faxes and automated calling systems, which means that users should give prior permission for receiving unsolicited electronic communications for marketing purposes.
- *Directories*: Consent of the subscriber to be listed in a public directory would be needed under the new proposal replacing the existing opt-out regulation. The Common Position follows the Commission's proposal. Parliament accepted the Council's common

position, saying that users should give prior permission. The EP has maintained the possibility for Member States to allow reverse search functions.

- *Cookies*: Use of cookies would only be allowed provided the user is given, in advance, clear and comprehensive information and is offered the right to refuse the processing. Parliament accepted the Council's common position that users should have the right to refuse them, specifying that users should be provided with clear and comprehensive information on their purposes.

- *Data retention*: In line with the EP's amendment, electronic communications service providers would be allowed to process traffic data in order to market any electronic communications service (also other then their own) or to provide value-added services, provided that the subscriber or the user (depending on the data to be processed, the type of service etc.) has given his consent. Under the common Position Member States may provide for retention of data for a limited time to safeguard national security, to solve criminal cases etc. On the contentious issue of data retention, it was agreed by Parliament that Member States may only lift the protection of data privacy in order to conduct criminal investigations or safeguard national or public security, when this is a necessary, appropriate and proportionate measure within a democratic society. In a recital, Parliament added that lawful interceptions of electronic communications should be subject to adequate safeguards in accordance with the European Convention on Human Rights and Fundamental Freedoms and with the rulings of the European Court of Human Rights.

- *Security*: Electronic communications service providers would be required to inform their subscribers of any security risk where they do not intend to take a measure to remedy it. This does not discharge them from remedying any new and unforeseen security risks. The European Parliament asked for a review of the Directive within three years of its application.

Distance Marketing

In October 1998 the Commission proposed a directive on the distance marketing of consumer financial services, modifying Directive 90/619/EEC, 97/7/EC and 98/27/EC. Aim of the proposal is to come to a harmonised framework for distance contracts on financial services in order to avoid the adoption by Member States of different consumer protection regulations for this new form of trade and guarantee the functioning of the Internal Market.

The aim of the proposal is to ensure a high level of protection for consumers of retail financial services (e.g. insurance, banking and investment services) marketed by telephone, by electronic means such as the Internet or by mail. This is to encourage consumer confidence in such services and provide financial service suppliers with a clearly defined legal framework valid for distance selling throughout the Single Market without hindrance.

The proposal should facilitate the development of innovative forms of trade in financial services within the EU and make it easier for consumers to buy financial services in other Member States.

The scope of the proposal covers the provisions of financial services at a distance. The key provisions related to the following:

- Prior information
- Right of reflection
- Right of withdrawal
- Settlement of disputes.

On May 14, 2002 the European Parliament approved in the second reading the Council's Common Position without any major amendments. The Council met to a high degree Parliament's demands from the first reading.

The European Parliament adopted only two amendments to the Council's common position, one of which states that the performance of the contract may only begin after the consumer has given his approval. The agreed solution is essentially based on the principle of maximum harmonisation, providing only a small scope for Member States to be able to introduce or maintain national rules.

The end result is that the text allows for:

- A high level of harmonisation of information requirements related to Article 3 of the Directive.
- The abandonment of the principle of minimum harmonisation, as initially called for by many Member States during the Luxembourg Council in April 1999.
- Far reaching harmonisation of the right of withdrawal payment of the service, unsolicited services, unsolicited communication, redress etc.

- Providing for the possibility of amending or further harmonising the provisions of the Directive in light of experience gained.
- Clarifying the relation of this Directive to the e-commerce Directive. Other changes included a clarification the text and layout of the Directive.

On 25 March 2002, the EU Telecommunications Council adopted the .eu regulation. Now the European Commission has to set up the infrastructure needed for the domain. A call for private, non-profit organisations to run the .eu registry can be expected soon. The .eu Top Level Domain will provide Europe's companies the possibility of identifying themselves as European or pan-European companies on the Internet.

The creation of .eu will also open up for the possibility of registering more names on the Internet and will thus boost internet use and e-commerce in Europe in line with the objectives of the eEurope Action Plan, endorsed by the European Council in Lisbon on 23 and 24 March 2000. The .eu regulation creates the legal framework for a Registry which will be the body that will run the domain in practice.

The Commission is in regular contact with the Internet Corporation for Assigned Names and Numbers (ICANN) so that the creation of the ".eu" code on the Internet can become a reality once the registry is in place. ICANN will be responsible for the organisation and management of Internet naming and addressing systems, known as Internet Governance.

Cross-border alternative dispute resolution

On request of the Council, the Commission is currently

working on the development of practical, efficient and inexpensive procedures for out-of-court settlement of consumer disputes should be promoted to strengthen consumers' confidence in e-commerce.

EEJ-NET

The European Commission officially launched a European Extra-Judicial Network for settling consumer disputes out-of-court (EEJ-NET). The European Network will cover any consumer dispute over goods or services. It is expected to reduce costs, formalities, time and obstacles in cross-border disputes, thereby boosting consumer confidence in electronic commerce. Rather than to harmonise and create general standards for out-of-court dispute resolution schemes the main provision of the EEJ-NET is to use the existing national out-of-court dispute resolution schemes and link them to national bodies to provide a EU-wide complaints network. The system is basically built on mutual recognition between the national redress bodies and exchange of information.

FIN-NET

On February 1, 2001 the Commission announced the launch of an out-of-court complaints network for financial services. The network will bring a number of national existing out-of-court dispute resolutions systems on the basis of a voluntary MoU.

Commission Recommendation on the resolution of consumer disputes On April 4, 2001 the European Commission adopted a non binding Recommendation on the resolution of consumer disputes. It applies to bodies which attempt to resolve disputes by bringing consumers and suppliers together to convince them to find a solution by common consent.

European Commission Green Paper of April 19, 2002 on alternative dispute resolution in civil and commercial matters. The Green paper is part of the Commission's policy of facilitating access to justice within the creation of an European area of freedom, security and justice. The paper covers ADR methods in civil and commercial matters, including employment and consumer law.

DG INFSO will be proposing a Communication on the promotion of Online Dispute Resolution (ODR) which is expected in July 2002. DG INFSO is particularly concerned with the promotion of Online Dispute Resolution in the context of eEurope and the desire to provide effective alternatives to the court system for settling disputes that arise across jurisdictional borders. These cross-border disputes will be more prevalent in the Information Society and in particular through electronic commerce.

The Communication will focus on the importance of developing awareness and trust in ODR services and will emphasise the need for a balance between flexibility and respect for basic quality criteria.

Taxation (VAT)

At the ECOFIN Council on May 7, 2002 Ministers adopted the long debated directive and regulation to modify the rules for applying value added tax (VAT) to certain electronically supplied services, including subscription-based and pay-per-view radio and TV broadcasting.

Aim of the new rule is to subject non-EU suppliers to the same VAT rules as EU suppliers, in accordance with the principles on the taxation of e-commerce agreed at the 1998 OECD Ottawa Ministerial Conference. The new rules thus modernise the existing VAT rules to provide a clear regulatory environment for all suppliers. They also contain a number of simplification measures aimed at easing the compliance burden for business. Member States have to implement the new measures by 1 July 2003.

The new VAT rules will apply to 'all electronically supplied services' such as software and computer services generally, plus information and cultural, artistic, sporting, scientific, educational, entertainment or similar services as well as to broadcasting services.

According to the new rules:

- EU suppliers do not have to charge VAT when supplying electronic services or broadcasting services to non EU-customers;
- Non EU suppliers will have to charge VAT on services electronically supplied to EU customers at the VAT rate of the Member State where their customer usually resides. They can register in the Member State of their choice (so called Member State of identification) and pay all VAT due on a quarterly base. The State concerned will then reallocate the VAT revenues to the Member States where the consumer is located.

In 2006 the Commission will either have to adopt measures on mechanism for charging, declaring, collecting and allocating VAT revenues on electronically supplied services which will ensure taxation at the place of consumption for all transactions, or it will have to extend the period of time during which the recently agreed rules will apply.

The Commission proposal for a Council Framework Decision of 27 April 2002 on "Attacks against information systems" is meant to provide basic framework for police and judicial co-operation on attacks against information systems linked to terrorism. It addresses the three most common threats: unauthorised access, disruptive attacks and malicious software. Other security threats, like accidental and environmental threats, misrepresentation and illegal interception are however not addressed in this Framework Decision.

The proposal seeks to approximate criminal law across the EU so that Europe's law enforcement and judicial authorities can take action against this new form of crime to protect users. It also aims to encourage and promote the security of information infrastructures, while trying to find the right balance between the need to curb cybercrime on the one hand, and protecting civil liberties and other societal interests on the other (privacy protection, users rights, development of new technologies).

The main provisions include:

- *Interference with information systems*: the offence of interference with information systems is divided into two aspects: attacks aimed at the serious hindering or interruption of the functioning of an information system (such as "denial of service attacks" where there is a deliberate attempt to overwhelm an information system or viruses directed at blocking an information system), and attacks aimed at the deletion or alteration of computer data.

- *Penalties*: Member States are required to take the necessary measures to ensure effective, proportionate and dissuasive penalties. Some offences might justify a maximum term of imprisonment of more than four years, such as offences that are committed in a group; cause substantial economic loss, physical harm to a natural person or substantial damage to critical infrastructure.
- *Jurisdiction*: the proposal intends to ensure that each Member State has jurisdiction for cases where a person physically present in the EU attacks an information system in a third country; or a person physically present in a third country attacks an information system in the EU.
- *Operational points of contact for high tech crime*: it provides for a legal obligation on Member States to establish 24 hour / 7 days week operational points of contact to facilitate the exchange of information on attacks against information systems. What is illegal "off-line" should also be illegal "on-line". The current proposal thus follows in its approach the latest Commission proposals for framework Decisions on the approximation of criminal law related to child pornography and racism and xenophobia.

The proposed Framework Decision on Cybercrime is the result of an extensive public consultation within the EU Forum on Cybercrime, involving all major players. It also takes into account other international activities such as the work of the G8 and the Council of Europe's Convention on Cybercrime which aims to harmonise national legislation on cybercriminal activities, promote international police co-operation and share electronic evidence across borders.

The Green Paper of October 2, 2001 on Consumer Protection puts forward a number of options for future action to increase consumer protection and hence increase consumer confidence in the internal market. It covers B2C transactions.

Digital Rights Management

Digital technologies have transformed the copyright environment and have given rise to a potentially huge market for content. The advent of broadband networks and their capacity to transmit large volumes of multimedia content at high speeds emphasises the importance of ensuring that digital content is available under the appropriate conditions, which meet the interests of both rightholders and users.

The Copyright Directive supports the use of DRMS by protecting technical measures, and by requiring Member States to take into account the application and non-application of technological measures when providing for fair compensation in the context of the private use exception for which fair compensation is required. The Directive also calls for voluntary measures by industry to protect copyrighted material while ensuring interoperability and compatibility of different systems in the protection of copyrighted material.

Against this background, the European Commission is open to playing a facilitating role aimed at encouraging the different stakeholders to tackle outstanding DRM issues together and find common ground.

The promotion of open, flexible and interoperable Digital Rights Management Systems (DRMS) was the subject of a workshop organised by the European Commission in Brussels on 28 February 2002.

Representatives of the content, information technology, and consumer electronics industries, as well as several user and consumer associations, participated and set out their views on how to make DRMS acceptable to all market players and how to bring about co-operation between them.

Software patents

The proposal for a Directive to lay down rules relating to the patentability computer-implemented inventions would harmonise the way in which national patent laws deal with inventions using software. Such inventions can already be patented by applying to either the European Patent Office (EPO) or the national patent offices of the Member States, but the detailed conditions for patentability may vary.

Under current EU law, computer software can only be protected by copyright but the legal protection of computer-implemented inventions is unclear (some Member States allow protection by patent and others do not). The proposed Directive is expected to clarify the legal protection of this kind of inventions.

The main provisions of the proposal relate to the following:

- To benefit from patent protection, inventions would have to be new, involve an 'inventive step' and be capable of industrial application. It implies that a computer-implemented invention which makes a "technical contribution" to the state of the art, which would not be obvious to a person of normal skill in the field concerned, is more than just a computer program "as such" and can therefore be patented.

- The mere computer implementation of a technique or business model already known would not be patentable.
- Patents would not be granted to computer programs on their own, i.e. an isolation from a machine on which they may be run. This marks a different approach to the direction taken until now by the EPO and some case law in Member States. The proposal therefore reflects concerns that if 'isolated' computer programs could be patented, this would blur the distinction between the scope of copyright and patent protection, and that if enforced, patents including such claims could be used to prevent "reverse engineering" and other activities considered legitimate in respect of computer programs already protected under copyright law.
- A patent would normally be granted to specific innovative components of a software and not to the entire software itself.

This is an important distinction with copyright law. While copyright protects the entire code of an operating system, game or piece of business software against unauthorised copying, distribution and use, a patent would cover only the specifically-patented components.

The proposal would require the Commission to monitor the impact of computer-implemented inventions and to report to the Parliament and the Council on the operation of the Directive within three years of its implementation by Member States. This provides an important safeguard which would allow any necessary adjustments to be made.

The Directive would have no direct legal effect on the European Patent Office. However, once the Directive was implemented, the Commission would consider taking action to resolve any inconsistencies in the context of the European Patent Convention. This has already been done on a previous occasion, with no particular difficulty. In any case, European Patents, once granted, become subject to national laws, so any patents granted after the Directive took effect and which were inconsistent with its provisions would need to be amended to bring them into conformity.

Public sector information

Increased access to, and exploitation of, information by the public sector is an essential basis for many digital information products and could become an important 'raw material' for new services and in particular for the wireless Internet.

A European approach to the conditions under which public sector information can be accessed is necessary because of the current national fragmented rules and practices. In October 2001 the Commission issued its Communication "eEurope 2002: Creating a EU Framework for the Exploitation of Public Sector Information" aimed at improving access to, and re-use of, public sector information.

The Communication focuses on economic and internal market aspects of public sector information and proposes a set of actions to overcome the market barriers that exist at European level caused by differences in national regulations and practices. Improved use of public sector information will held the European information industries to create added-value information products.

On 5 June 2002 the Commission issued a first provisional version of a proposal for a directive on improving access to, and re-use of, public sector information. This proposal aims at establishing a minimum set of rules governing the commercial and non commercial exploitation by any EU citizen or legal person.

Key provisions of the proposal are the following:

- Public sector bodies and bodies governed by public law would have to make available their documents in any pre-existing format or language, through electronic means where this is possible and appropriate. This does however not imply an obligation to create or adapt documents.
- The directive shall apply to all documents that are generally accessible. Excluded shall be documents that do not fall in the scope of the public tasks of the public sector bodies concerned, documents containing personal data and documents held by public service broadcasters, educational and research establishments and cultural establishments.
- Any applicable conditions for the commercial re-use or exploitation shall be nondiscriminatory.

Legal Framework for E-commerce and Internet

Much of the experience in creating such an enabling legal and regulatory framework on a national level is found in and derives from the industrialized, developed countries, the issues explored here raise particular challenges for policy makers in the developing world. Much of the international experience described points to certain advantages in harmonizing legislation, or at least moving towards an environment of interoperability. Yet there is also strong demonstration that in certain areas, particular national requirements must also be taken into account.

The variety of issues and requirements for the elaboration of the legal and regulatory infrastructure for e-commerce and the Internet highlight the necessity of a comprehensive approach to legal reform issues.

As de Tocqueville observed, law matters. Law gives effect to policy. As such, laws affecting e-commerce are in important and integral part of the enabling environment for e-commerce. And, the policies undertaken and the manner in which they are reflected in law will affect how e-commerce develops, how it is used, etc.

But laws alone are not enough. There are other attributes that make the legal and consequent institutional structures work in their respective environments. Among these are a history of market development (culminating in mature markets), and known outlets and predictable results for resolving disputes including respected, independent, credible judiciary and other mechanisms for resolving disputes that have the confidence of the general public. It cannot be said with certainty that all of the other, exogenous factors that support the legal, regulatory and institutional precedents in developed countries (mature markets, credible outlets for resolving disputes, etc.) exist to the same extent in all developing countries – and care should therefore be taken that while creating the essential legal infrastructure, other aspects of the market reform enabling environment not be ignored. The process of legal reform that is an integral part of developing an enabling environment for e-commerce.

The report by UNDP regarding ICTs and development, e-commerce is and should be viewed as a tool of development, not a reward. Efficient provision of ICT infrastructure and services will enhance production, which will contribute to growth and even help in alleviating poverty – a primary goal of the World Bank.

In this sense, the Internet, and e-commerce, are transformational. No longer are "old economy" concepts of capital formation and capital flows necessarily applicable. Now, productive assets do not need to be equated with natural resources, nor does value-added processing necessarily need to take place after export. But, for the equation to work, ICT infrastructure and services need to be provided on an efficient basis (which depends in part on removing barriers to entry), reducing users' costs.

Finally, in the context of the reform agenda, it is instructive to take account of the types of e-commerce activity likely to be undertaken. The following table 1describes the types of e-commerce activity that should be incorporated into an e-commerce legal and regulatory enabling environment.

Consideration should be given to the types of e-commerce that are to be encouraged. Additionally, as will be argued later, it is important that the legal framework not be designed for just one type of activity. Rather, a commercially neutral approach should be taken.

Difficult policy decisions need to be made and communicated to constituents. If the precepts of the ICT reform process are accepted (that efficient provision of ICT infrastructure and services aids in production and growth), this will undoubtedly lead to a the identification of a number issues that will need to be addressed in the reform process. Regardless of whether it is e-commerce, there are common elements of the reform process.

Table 1
Types of E-commerce and Related Internet Activities

	Government("G")	Business ("B")	Consumer ("C")
Government	G2G – coordination	G2B – infor mation	G2C– information
Business	B2G – government procurement	B2B-e-commerce between business	B2C – e-commerce in consumer markets
Consumer	C2G – e.g., tax compliance	C2B – price & other comparisons	C2C – auction market

In the fist stage of reform, a change to the status quo is introduced through new policies. How to give effect to these policies results in reform issues that need to be dealt with. How these issues are dealt with is the strategy of introducing the reforms.

Finally to give effect to reforms, they need to be implemented. Because law is the embodiment of policy, the process of legal reform needs to start right at the beginning, during the shaping of the new policies. And while clearly some of the reform issues that will arise at the beginning of stage two, those engaging in law reform need to take part in developing the strategies and in their implementation being in part, the passage of new laws.

The importance to successful reform, especially legal reform, of broad public consultation, stakeholder "buy-in" and "local ownership" can not be overemphasized. To have a law, or series of laws, on the books, that stakeholders (government, regulators, owner/operators and users) do not understand or agree with will impair the success of the reform program.

In addition to the elements of the process of reform is the sequencing of reform. There are many variations on reform sequencing, taking into account urgency, parallel processes, local circumstances and the like.

Practical considerations may dictate modifications. Whatever the circumstances, however, where there is a legal element to the reform process, it is logical that in order to effect the shift from the market supported by the "old" legal framework to the market supported by the new legal framework, certain things have to happen. First, the policies giving rise to change need to be elaborated. These will, in turn, give rise to new legislation that reflect, embody and give effect to those policies.

To the extent that the laws provide for or anticipate regulation, a regulatory framework can be elaborated to implement the law. Finally, it is assumed that new entry will come into the market based on the certainty provided by the legal and regulatory framework.

The basic theme in legal reform is to create an enabling environment of predictability and certainty through good governance and respect for the Rule of Law that encourages use and confidence in the e-commerce market place. A non exhaustive list of underlying principles behind legal reform in the area of e-commerce follows:

— Preference for market-based approaches (regulate only what is necessary and when it is necessary; incentives should derive from the market)

— Make use and entry easy (infrastructure and services liberalization play a key role)

— Promote Certainty/Confidence (transparency)

— Enhance transactional enforceability

— Harmonize/Standardize (reference to international best practice, model laws, etc., interoperability of laws (not necessarily carbon copying) will facilitate use and growth of commerce beyond national borders)

— Neutrality as to commerce (the legal regime established should apply equally to and facilitate B2B, G2G, G2C, etc., this also allows "future-proofing" of legislation to facilitate the introduction of new forms of commerce that can be conducted electronically)

— Neutrality as to technology (the legal regime should also be "future-proofed" in terms of the introduction of new technologies deployed to conduct e-commerce – laws drafted today, based on today's technology may prove inadequate for new technological innovations)

— Protect Intellectual Property

— Protect Consumer Rights

A number of legal issues typically arise in developing a legal framework to enable e-commerce. First, there is both a national and an international dimension to the reform agenda. At the international level, a number of international, regional, and even private organizations affecting the content of national law.

Attention should also be paid to mandatory requirements (conventions, treaties, directives) that emanate form these bodies, as opposed to syntheses of good practice (e.g., model laws). These international elements point to the important considerations of harmonization, standardization and interoperability in facilitating entry into the global marketplace.

Clearly the UNCITRAL model laws and the EU directives (described below and in more detail by others) are in part aimed at accomplishing this. As successful reforms in e-commerce are out of necessity comprehensive, cutting across traditional technology and commercial boundaries, the role of regulators and regulation will need to be critically examined.

To name but a few areas where this will be important are regulation of communications services and infrastructure (telecommunications), public key infrastructure, domain name registration, and general principles of competition – and where appropriate the exercise of regulatory forbearance where market forces are operating.

A specific issue common to any e-commerce framework is how personal data privacy is protected. There are varying approaches, for example the "opt-in" vs. the "opt-out" approach. Experience has demonstrated a divergence of treatment regarding privacy, for example between the EU approach and the approach in the United States. It is therefore evident that different policy approaches lead to different legal approaches.

However, this particular issue also demonstrates problems of "interoperability" (the basic incompatibility between opt-in and opt-out systems) resulting from different legal approaches. Other issues include, protection of intellectual property rights, alternative dispute resolution, liability for content, taxation, jurisdiction and distribution of goods are all other important issue that will need to be addressed in framing a legal enabling environment.

Because of the borderless nature of e-commerce and trade facilitated through e-commerce, the value of minimum or common international standards has long been recognized as contributing to the interoperability of national legal regimes in developing truly global commerce.

Model laws, conventions and regional laws from a variety of sources contribute to the emerging body of international best practice that developing countries can look to for examples in framing their e-commerce legislative environments. Too often, however, there is a tendency to adopt international precedent (whether model law, directive or other precedent law) wholesale, without adapting it to local dynamics.

Certainly there is value in learning from the experience of others, but as argued above, the reform process should be a critical, thoughtful, deliberative and iterative process, balancing bespoke needs with underlying principles such as harmonization and interoperability. The result of adopting model laws verbatim, without a holistic approach, can be as ineffective to the growth of e-commerce as a framework that does not take account at all of the international dimension.

In addition, there is a large body of intellectual work regarding e-commerce and development, including legal issues of e-commerce development. They are too numerous to mention here, although the annual E-Commerce Reports of UNCTAD stand out as being well written and presented, comprehensive in scope, sufficiently detailed and addressing cutting edge issues.

The WTO played a major role in opening markets for telecommunications services. The role that liberalized provision of services plays in increasing access, lowering prices and facilitating new entry is well recognized.

Now the WTO and its members are debating new challenges brought by the online world. Whereas the various GATT agreements covered trade in goods, and the GATS covers trade in services, how should downloadable software be treated, for example? It is also an area which developing countries have an opportunity to make their voice heard in the debate.

UNCITRAL is probably best known in the e-commerce area for the two model laws it has promulgated: (1) UNCITRAL Model Law on Electronic Commerce with Guide to Enactment 1996 , with additional article 5 bis as adopted in 1998; and (2) UNCITRAL Model Law on Electronic Signatures with Guide to Enactment 2001.

The E-Commerce model law covers, inter alia, legal recognition of data messages and digital signatures, and certain elements of encryption. The Electronic Signature Model law covers, inter alia, PKI certification and certain elements of data privacy protection.

The Guide to enactment of the Electronic Signatures Model Law is particularly instructive about the issues surrounding PKI certification, for example. It should be emphasized that these are "model" laws, and while a synthetic project taking account of many legal systems and a broad range of experience, they can, bearing in mind minimum requirements of interoperability, be tailored to meet specific local needs ITU.

At the ITU's recent World Telecommunication Development Conference in Istanbul, ITU-D (Bureau of Telecommunication Development) was mandated, inter alia, with examining how to promote a favourable legal environment for e-services and applications in cooperation with other international organizations and financial institutions.

Hague Conference on Private International Law. A new draft Convention on Jurisdiction and Foreign Judgments in Civil and Commercial Matters is under consideration by the Hague Conference on International Law which, if promulgated in its current form, could have far reaching effects in the on-line world.

Provisions of the draft Convention could, in effect, lead to the intellectual property rights protection of one country being applied in another country where the rights protected might be different.

ICANN, though not an "international" organization like UNCITRAL, nonetheless plays an undeniably central role in global e-commerce through its domain name processes, especially in domain name registration and regulation of ".com", ".edu", ".org", etc. It's affiliated organization, IANA, is responsible for top-level county domain names ("ccTLD").

The following issues to be dealt with on a national level that are of particular importance to developing countries. These are not exhaustive, but representative. The four issues are

(i) convergence implications and competition law,

(ii) fundamental features of regulatory reform,

(iii) the role of intellectual property rights in development and

(iv) the use of alternate dispute resolution mechanisms.

Other legal issues of significance in the e-commerce enabling environment at the national level, but not discussed here in any length, include recognition of electronic contracts and issues of contract formation (e.g., recognition of "click through" and "browse through" concepts); recognition of digital signatures; protection of personal privacy; consumer protection; taxation; customs, import and distribution; limits on foreign direct investment; and content liability.

The list of laws that would need to be considered in building the national legal enabling infrastructure for e-commerce will naturally be dictated by local requirements and circumstances. It should be borne in mind that there may already be laws affecting commerce in the "off-line" world (contract formation, consumer protection, tax and dispute resolution, for example).

However, there are certain issues that are peculiar to the "on-line" environment, such as "click through" contract formation, P/PKI certification, digital signature recognition and domain name registration.

Convergence/Competition. It is now axiomatic that there is a phenomenon known as convergence among technologies and services brought about by digitalization. Where sector-specific, or technology-specific regulation may have been appropriate before, the converged nature of technology and services implies a greater reliance on competition policy, law and regulation to guard against abuses of dominance or other anticompetitive behaviour in the market place. It is important to note, however, that the object of competition law is not to protect certain actors but to ensure a competitive market by enhancing efficiency to stimulate development.

For example, a yet-to-be-privatized state-owned telecommunications service provider (or a private monopoly, for that matter) may through its dominant position exert control over the provision of leased line access to ISPs. If this results in discriminatory treatment among ISPs, or, the price of leased line access is not cost-based, or is otherwise slowing market entry of ISPs, the issue could be viewed as a matter of telecommunications regulation or as a competition law issue (abuse of dominance or anticompetitive behaviour).

Accordingly, to ensure fairness, resort could be made to the competition law of general application. If there is not a competition law of general application, consideration should be given to putting on in place. Comprehensive Regulatory Reform. The areas of regulation that touch upon e-commerce are many. These include, to name a few,

— regulation of the telecommunications infrastructure and services over which e-commerce is conducted; domain name registration; public/private key infrastructure certification regulation; data privacy protection regulation;

— competition regulation

— banking and financial sector regulation (including credit, payments systems, exchange controls, anti-money laundering; and

— import restrictions and intellectual property rights.

In designing regulatory functions and institutions, international best practice demonstrates that certainty and confidence in the regulator is enhanced through transparency and where there is functional, financial, legal and institutional separation of the policy setting, regulatory and ownership functions. This is to ensure against political and industry capture.

Intellectual Property Rights

From a developmental standpoint, it is recognized on the one hand that where intellectual property rights, such as copyright, are not protected by national law, holders of copyrighted software (or hardware with imbedded software) will be reluctant to export to that jurisdiction. Accordingly, developing countries wishing to expand economic growth through e-commerce, but where the protection of intellectual property rights is unclear, will face challenges of encouraging vendors to invest in those countries.

On the other hand, it is also recognized that there is a view held by some in the development community that continued protection of rights held by those in the developed world actually depresses local growth and development in developing countries –developing countries merely effect transfer payments to rights holders in the developed world while providing disincentives at home for innovation and growth of local high-tech industries.

Even in a market place dominated by "open source" and open systems, copyright and commercial concerns are still valid. In other words, open source systems still rely on copyright law to enforce the openness of open source systems.

The TRIPS Agreement provides national treatment, minimum standards and dispute resolution procedures. This international system, part of the WTO, protects rights to encourage foreign direct investment of hardware and software necessary for conducting e-commerce, preserves international standards, but would generally leave innovation and incentives with existing rights holders.

The new role of intellectual property rights advocated more and more within the development community still protects rights holders. However the reliance on open systems (including open source software) can reduce unit costs, allows for projects to be scaled to meet particular needs, allows development of local content and encourages innovation and entrepreneurship locally. A by-product of developing more content in local languages and more use locally is to slow "brain drain".

In the area of ADR, the focus is not on whether mediation is preferred to arbitration or whether ADR should be used as a matter of course as an alternative to the courts. Rather the focus is on whether the use of ADR to engage in non-adversarial resolution can create incentives for or encourage use of e-commerce.

Certain characteristics about ADR would indicate that it is susceptible to creating an incentive environment for resolving disputes. Among these attributes are that ADR can be non-adversarial; it can be flexible and scalable (smaller problems can be addressed through smaller, quicker procedures); it can be oriented towards a specific type of commonly recurring issue or to a particular industry issue; because it is more flexible, it permits the rapid introduction of best practices and related, relevant experiences into the dispute resolution process; and it can address situations not necessarily specifically dealt with in existing law (especially in civil law jurisdictions).

But in order for ADR to be a useful tool for creating incentives to use e-commerce. The procedures and institutions must be credible and transparent, and the results must be enforceable. Accordingly, national law should encourage ADR and provide for adequate enforcement measures.

6

Faces of Cyberspace

Information presentation in visual images, sound and natural language either as text or speech is gradually becoming the norm. The Internet is creating a global platform where a worldwide forum is evolving that is becoming vital to economic, social and political success. However, all these developments create problems. Examples of such problems are: access to much of the information may be available only to the computer literate and those who understand English. Also, due to the vast amount of information available, it is becoming hard to identify and select what is relevant that may satisfy a certain degree of credibility.

The development of interfaces and components that help users to identify relevant information and then present it to them in the most appropriate manner according to the information content and their cultural and linguistic backgrounds is still lagging behind the rate of information growth. Language engineering is an endeavor in which language technologies are integrated and embedded into language-enabled services and products to support business in a global context and to facilitate interpersonal communication across languages. The Role of Language Engineering Efforts now are concentrating in developing tools and standards that enable the creation of websites in several languages or in at least one non-Western language. Now an Internet standard (RFC 2070) based on Unicode supports HTML documents in practically every language.

In particular, some of the features dealt with are: Markup of bi-directional text, i.e. test where left-to-right and right-to-left scripts are mixed and control of cursive joining behavior in contexts where the default behavior is not appropriate. Also, the HTTP which is the hypertext transfer protocol in use since 1990 is being internationalized. The relevant aspects are character set labeling which ensures correct document interpretation and language negotiation which is used at a site to provide documents in the user's language of preference.Language technology will help in designing and implementing the systems needed to effectively deal with information and knowledge in a number of ways.

Speech recognition will help in interacting with a number of devices in our own native language. Also, information could be presented by generating speech. Understanding requests and browsing the vast amount of knowledge available is an essential component that can alleviate the problem of information overload and ensures that the relevant knowledge is accessed. It will also be possible to generate and present information in different languages through automated machine translation. Language engineering will be essential for supporting global business in general and electronic commerce in particular. The success of any business will depend on the quality of information about its customers, its competitors and the market in general. The needed information has to be identified, extracted and presented in natural language either as text or speech. In general, language engineering will deliver the right information at the right time and in the language of the recipient. Automated translation together with document management will improve the quality of service in a global marketplace. In general, success in globalization requires putting emphasis on localization.

Some companies interested in international markets organize their effort in a number of activities that could be summarized as follows:

1. Developers organize a product so that linguistic components can be modified easily (internationalization).
2. Translators make the product available in different target languages.
3. Editors review each version to ensure that culture-specific items are not missed.
4. Marketing division takes care of localization to adapt the product to the local market.

The Internet is dominated now by the English language. However, due to the near future possibilities of widespread use, it is becoming essential to consider its multilingual nature. Some efforts are being conducted in that respect - e.g. the Babel project which is a joint initiative between Alis Technologies and the Internet Society. They are considering the world's 20 main languages and are trying to study the actual distribution of languages on the Internet. Although the Internet penetration is not high at the moment in some regions, this is expected to change radically in the future. As an example, results of the Internet Domain Survey for Arab Countries is shown in Table 1 for January 1998. Efforts now are concentrating in developing tools and standards that enable the creation of websites in several languages or in at least one non-Western language. Now an Internet standard (RFC 2070) based on Unicode supports HTML documents in practically every language. In particular, some of the features dealt with are: Markup of bi-directional text, i.e. test where left-to-right and right-to-left scripts are mixed and control of cursive joining behavior in contexts where the default behavior is not appropriate. Also, the HTTP which is the hypertext transfer protocol in use since 1990 is being internationalized.

The relevant aspects are character set labeling which ensures correct document interpretation and language negotiation which is used at a site to provide documents in the user's language of preference.

Multilingual Machine Translation Issues

There are many situations in which multilingual translation is needed. Translation from many languages into a single language will be required by large information gathering and processing organizations. Translation from a single language into many languages will be required in the context of foreign trade when operation and other manuals for industrial equipment need to be translated into the language of the countries where the equipment is to be marketed.

Table 1 Internet Domain Survey Arab Countries, January 1998

Domain	Hosts	All Hosts	DuplicateNames	Level 2 Domain	Level 3 Domain
ku	4057	4749	692	9	2925
eg	2013	16930	14917	7	191
ae	1940	1955	15	8	56
lb	1134	1377	243	7	59
om	670	671	1	16	20
ma	431	463	32	5	339
bh	338	339	1	2	4
jo	249	249	0	5	13
qa	189	191	2	5	9
tn	69	69	0	10	68
sa	37	37	0	4	6
dz	16	17	1	1	16
ye	10	10	0	7	6
ly	1	2	1	1	1
sy, sd, iq	0				
	11154	27059			

Multilingual interlingual machine translation systems translate between a number of languages. In this approach, a universal language independent representation of text known as interlingua is developed. Therefore, the translation process is reduced to two phases: the analysis phase between the source language and the interlingua, and the generation phase from the interlingua to the target language. For successful machine translation, detailed knowledge of the languages is required at many levels: lexicon syntax, semantics and discourse. It is very difficult to provide such linguistic knowledge for an entire language. However, if we consider only language in a particular domain much of this knowledge could be obtained. The variety of language used in a given science or technology is not only much smaller than the whole language, but is also more clearly systematic in structure and meaning. Therefore linguists and computer scientists co-operate to study the properties of such specialized languages which are called sublanguages or controlled language. Each sublanguage has a distinctive grammar even though it is related to the grammar of the full standard language. Also, the theoretical problem of relating linguistic form to communicative function comes into sharper focus when individual sublanguages are examined.

Sometimes it is essential to distinguish between two translation activities. The first one is called localization (e.g. that used for computer manuals for end users) where it is important to adapt certain parts of the content and perhaps the style of presentation to a certain cultural and linguistic environment.

The second one is called diffusion translation where the objective content must be strictly rendered in another language without addition and omission. A brief outline will now be given for efforts related to Arabic/English translation. AppTek started an English-Arabic translator named TranSphere that uses Lexical Functional Grammar together with a general dictionary having 100,000 words. A number of domain-specific dictionaries have also been developed. This system could be either standalone or part of an integrated system.

Sakhr within Al-Alamiah Group [Sakhr, 1998] is also developing a translation scheme for Arabic-English and English-Arabic. It makes use of the available tools that have been developed before for morphological and syntactical analyzers, electronic dictionaries, semantic support together with a number of other development tools. It is also developing a general platform for dealing with Arabic computations. IBM Egypt is also developing Machine Aided Human Translation schemes. ALIS, Inc. offers a solution that integrates core language-handling technology and translation products. Electronics Research Institute in Egypt, in co-operation with the European Community is developing an English-Arabic and Arabic to English and German medical text translation.

This is done in the framework of CAT2 (Computer Assisted Translation) which uses an interlingua approach. Also, some work related to ambiguity in Arabic language processing is being studied. PRINCITRAN: In this system a large-scale lexicon is to be constructed for an interlingual machine translation system for Arabic, English, Korean and Spanish. For Arabic, the starting point was the use of the Alpnet bilingual Arabic-English online dictionary. Then automatic mappings between English glosses from Alpnet into LDOCE (Longman's Dictionary of Contemporary English) codes were performed. The codes were then converted into thematic grids which were then exhaustively hand-verified.

Electronic Commerce and Multilinguality

Global market opportunities are now increasing rapidly and is going to use heavily the facilities introduced by the Internet. Thus, the advent of global electronic commerce will add an economic dimension to cultural and linguistic issues. In international trade, companies that adopt a multilingual, multicultural approach are expected to gain a competitive advantage over their monolingual, monocultural competitors.

Regarding business-consumer relations, the following language issues could be stated: The seller of goods or services must be able to publish information in the language and cultural convention of the customers (multilingual electronic publishing). The buyer of goods or services must be able to find, understand and compare information in his own language (multilingual information retrieval). Both buyer and seller must be able to interact naturally and effectively in a common language or across different languages. There is a possibility that from the number of 5,000 to 6,000 languages spoken in the world today, only a few hundred will survive a century later.

The pressure on languages can take different forms: economic, social, cultural, etc.. Usually, people directly affected are minorities, but their languages represent the linguistic diversity that has developed over the course of human history. Some linguists argue that language endangerment is serious with great humanistic and scientific consequences. Can new developments in the information age help in preserving some of these languages and thus save language diversity. Information revolution is the global phenomenon that has an impact on all nations.

Nobody can stay out of the Information Society. That is why nowadays problems of ethical, cultural and social type has an increasing value. Only in resolving these problems the Information Society can achieve the declared goal of globalization: to promote quality of life and sustain a cohesive development. Due to the advent of the Information Society UNESCO faces new problems demanding to define its role in new world communication processes. That is why the UNESCO strategy should embrace the wide range of activities:

- concentration on key structures of the Information Society;
- ethic problems of the Information Society and the Cyberspace;
- elaboration of information policy;
- the impact of the globalization processes;
- specific education ;
- forming networks;
- fulfilling projects for the Information Society

These problems demand thorough considerations and constant attention. Textual information remains the main form of demanded information for majority of interstate or global international networks such as INTERNET. Due to the rapid success of communication technologies active use of spoken and visual information is foreseen in the nearest future.

Nowadays there are near 3000 spoken languages in the world and only 100 of them are written. Such a variety of languages under increased value of international contacts, high intensity of information flows of economic, political, scientific, technological and social types put forward as a priority task the development of human language technologies. Multilingualism is an inevitable historical attribute of the international communication process. The notion "multilingual information society " solidly occupies the place in the range of problems discussed by computer science specialists and predefined strategic directions of many international organizations and companies dealing with information distribution and processing.

Human language technologies obtained the valid political understanding and support. At the third UNESCO Congress on Informatics and Education held in Moscow, July 1996, more than 40 countries representatives confirmed their willingness to participate in the establishing multilingual telematics support for educational needs. The relevance of linguistic and cultural aspects of the Information Society in Europe has been stressed by the European Council meetings in Corfu. 24-25 June 1994, in Cannes, 26-27 June 1995 and on the G7 Conference of Ministers in Brussels, 25-26 February 1995. In May 1995 the European Commission has adopted the upcoming Fifth RTD Framework Programme which includes points devoted to developing human language technologies.

Technological Multilingualism

In the multilingualism problem there exists one important factor which usually slips out in discussions of this issue. The high level of technology of the modern civilization broadens the notion of multilingualism in information society including in it artificial intellectual electronic devices. This newly arisen complex communication structure forms the Cyberspace that is marked by extremely complex processes of control and self-development. In the Cyberspace the humanitarian multilingualism interacts with the technological multilingualism of communication protocols, computer interfaces, programming languages and data protection methods. Communication multilingualism of computing devices is to some extent being solved by introducing conventional technological standards regulating data exchange and transformation processes. Different computers in networks can transmit information using standard popular protocols TCP/IP (Transmission Control Protocol / Internet Protocol), IPX/SPX (Internetwork Packet Exchange / Sequenced Packet Exchange) or SNA (System Network Architecture). Such protocols as FTP (File Transfer Protocol), HTTP (Hyper Text Transfer Protocol), address standard URL (Uniform Resource Locator), standard sluice interface CGI are in active use in the INTERNET. High expressive possibilities of Web pages rely on implementations of HTML and Java languages.

For protecting information from different forms of eavesdropping cryptographic protocols SET (Secure Electronic Transfer) , SSL (Secure Sockets Layer) and some others have been elaborated. The "hardware multilingualism" aggravates the problem of the humanitarian multilingualism in the Cyberspace. It is interesting to note some resemblance in humanitarian and technical multilingualism. Communication multilingualism is stormy developing and to some extent repeats the dramatic way of human multilingualism. Here also numerous languages and dialects currently appear and die, conflicts of standards, programming languages and interfaces is an usual event.

Any technological innovation can lead to the chain, or may be it will be better to say "domino", reaction of expressive and communication means. The Cyberspace evolution is marked by constant attempts to resolve problems of humanitarian and technological multilingualism. The general common base for advances in these areas are backed by developing theory of semiotic systems, artificial intelligence, translation methods, algorithmic analyses, evolution of discourse, technologies sustaining lingual engineering.

Multilingualism Challenge

Historically formed present situation presupposes two general approaches for partial resolving the multinational communication problem. The first approach relies on the idea to adopt some universal unique well understanding language for invariant multilingual communication. The second approach lays on elaborating powerful technique for simulating expressive means of one language by expressive forms of another one. There are known three main variants in implementation of the first mentioned above approach.

- For some definite restricted knowledge areas to use specialized formalized languages such as Latin for medicine, language of formulas for mathematics, etc. This approach can be applied successfully only to very restricted object areas and cannot embrace cultural or social aspect of communication.
- To create one general artificial universal language which is neutral to national peculiarities of language communication. The most known language of this class is Esperanto. The less known is Sanskrit. The main drawback of this approach as in the previous case above is its impossibility to fill the communication gap in expressing national cultural potential.
- To conveniently adopt the use of one of national language. There is one well-known very strong candidate to play this role. Domination in the world processes (trade, science, technology, culture, etc.) of English speaking countries led to the huge spread of the English as a communication language. There are 1 billion and 400 millions of English speaking people

in the world. Only for 400 million of them this language is native. This means that for more than 1 billion of world population this language is the second or even the third one. And we are all witnesses that domination of the English as the communication tool in the Cyberspace is spreading with more and more increasing feedback link. The positive aspect of this event is extending for other nations the rich world of English speaking countries in all its appearances. The negative aspect is that such a global language invasion contradicts to natural eagerness of other nations to preserve local cultural achievements and adequate lingual means of their presentation. Even in the field of technological documentation complete relying on not native language information can affect the reliability of elaborating systems. Moreover, due to its internal evolution and rapid changing the fixed international English language can never be framed.

The second approach, which is simulating expressive means of one language by expressive forms of the other one, is traditionally reduced to the translation process. Before the computer era a bilingual or a multilingual interpreter was a man. Under computer expansion the language translation problem has obtained a new content - an automated language translation. In its full context this problem relates to the very complex problems of formalizing natural language understanding and cognitive context which are very far from the final decision. Nevertheless there are some recent evident successes in this area. The number of commercial systems for machine translation, as well as other types such as spell-checkers, multilingual mailers, dictionaries, etc. is rapidly growing.

During the last two years a few multilingual services available within Internet appeared. Multilingual Communication Corporation (USA) is offering its powerful WEB.TRANS service for global business. The two main browsers providers for WWW, companies Alis and Globalink, include the multilingual support in their products. The Tango, multilingual browser, using the Alis technologies, is a high performance Web tool that allows users to display Web pages authored in any of over 90 languages, select the languages of its interface, automatically retrieve these pages in the language version user prefers and input a text in a wide variety of languages. Alice Technologies has brought together several leading companies in the language industry to create Columbus - a suite of communication and translation tools and services designed to offer corporations the most comprehensive, convenient and cost-effective solutions on the market. There are other well-known companies offering a variety of multilingual solutions among them: ACCENT (Israel), Ajax Software Corp. (Russia), IBM, Intersol Brea, SYSTRAN (USA).

We can also concentrate on activity of BIT Software, Inc. (Russia), as well as ABBYY Company, formerly BIT Ukraine. These software companies are famous by their multi-lingual products like Stylus Gigant (powerul heuristic translator from five European languages to Russian and visa versa), Lingvo (large hyper-text interactive dictionary), WebTranSite (online "transparent" Internet translator), etc. There is one interesting frequently met feature of the multilingualism paradigm. Due to different historical reasons in one country (nation, popularity) there are two or several internal natural languages sharing the same information space. Such a situation exists in many NIS countries, Ireland, Canada,

India, Benelux countries and in many others. Ukraine is the bilingual country where the Ukrainian language has the state status. In this case specific domestic features could complicate the international multilingualism problem. Furthermore, problems become really global, e.g., after 7 years of official independence, Ukraine doesn't even have fully defined symbol code page (380), because four or five existing standards are already widespread and it's difficult to change any of them right now. Sometimes (as in Ireland) politics can influence the multilingualism decisions. Much attention is paid to the processes of creating computer supported information infrastructure in Ukraine.

The State program of informatization in Ukraine has been approved by the government. This program is backed by some legislative basis. There are three juridical laws concerning the informatization program. The first law defines the concept of the informatization in Ukraine. The second one defines objectives of the program. And the third law determines the content of the program. We would like to stress that the our Center is the leading organization in forming the concept and the governmental program of informatization in Ukraine.

International Research and Training Center of Information Technologies and Systems. In the organization we present here intensive research and technological works in language engineering are carried out. Let us mention briefly some of them.

- *Multilingual speech technology:* The technology of natural speech recognition and synthesis in a few foreign languages is developing by the specialists of our center for more than twenty years. In 1986 -1991 in frames of UNESCO contracts the multilingual (7 languages) speech dialogue system RECH-121 for CDS-ISIS Micro has been created. The works in the direction to create oral vocabularies-translators, dictating machines, machines simulating a human voice, individual speech passports, systems of multilingual speech interpreters are continued at present.

All these elaborations are based on the modeling of human intellectual activity and on the constructive analysis of digital information by means of its synthesis. The method that is used is recognized around the world.

- *Algorithmic analysis of the deep language structures:* Attempts to create systems of artificial intelligence demand the deep analyses of historical roots and evolution of language structures and human cognition processes. Such analysis has been done using new algorithmic methods. The kernel recursive structure of language sentences and literature constructions have been revealed. The algorithmic model of language constructions invariant to the natural languages has been suggested. The practical results of this research include applications to the authorship problem, psycholinguistics, associative expert systems, analyzes of myths, multilingual translators and some others.
- Automatic forming and translation of keywords in querying systems. In the navigating the multilingual Internet the problem of adequate translation of keywords is of great importance. The direçt translation of keywords from a language A to a language B is connected with high ambiguity and can complicate the search of necessary documents. More correct idea to the keywords translation is based on

the comparison of texts in the language A, which correspond to the given set of keywords, with texts in the language B which could be found by means of all variants of translations of the given key-word set. In the process of looking for similarity of keywords an neural network model could be used.

The neural network methodology for implementation of this method has been elaborated. The methodology was checked in the automatic detection of user's interests.

These principles formed the base for creating neural networks supporting processes of making decisions and pattern recognition. Particularly, works in handwritten symbols neural recognition have been started with the Japanese company WACOM and at present gives good results. The same results could be used in the multilingual Internet.

- *Multilingual Internet and Educational Problems:* Multilingual Internet is thus becoming a real need for the nearest future, and important and urgent efforts should be made to solve the global problem of bi-directional communication barriers on different levels, addressing different user groups, etc. At the same time, due to low experience of the new users in the language and telematics, additional measures should be undertaken to provide training and educational facilities for these users.

Ukraine (and some CIS countries) can be considered as a typical "country in transition" concerning production, dissemination and use of multilingual information on the global information highways. There is an urgent need to develop an effective infrastructure in the field and to adjust to international standards. On the other hand, it is ready for international co-operative projects, having know-how and qualified specialists in many fields, including computer science, linguistics, programming, education, etc. Currently the following directions are considered as a first priorities in the National Informatization Programme: Basics in Telematics (Internet), networking of information and educational resources and multilingual computer-based support in science, education and communication, creation of the distance education centre.

Our preliminary analysis shows that the CIS countries have serious needs in the field of multilingual telematics support. Russian and French-speaking users are very conscious that they waste too much time and loose essential context information when they read/write texts in another language, even if they are competent in it. To keep one language such as English as unique language of communication is not cost-effective. There is a strong desire to stay within own native languages, which does not of course except trying to learn a few others for personal communicational and cultural purposes. The following specific multilingual user's needs are:

- support of communication at the basic level (reading and writing) via e-mail;
- opprtunities to use the adequate e-mail packages to remove essential obstacles in the way of communication both in countries, and in international communication;
- analysis of the multilingual products and services in Internet;

- analysis of the machine translators (on-line and off-line), dictionaries (on-line, off-line), thesauruses, multilingual mailers, tools for multilingual WWW-pages design, etc,
- training in multilingual Internet services (free distant courses via e-mail, WWW-courses etc.);
- updated information about new tendencies and products in multilingual telematics support;
- resolve the problems of standardization for multilingual software for every site in CIS countries;
- organization of the multilingual support of users' sites and consultation services.

The problems related to supporting user and/or suppliers groups and standardization becoming more and more actual both for East users and West suppliers. To make all relevant information available to its potential users and to provide an information exchange between Internet-users from various professional fields and from different countries, relevant national sites must be equipped by tools which form friendly and comfortable environment, making communication attractive for users world-wide, developing their information needs, widening their horizons and motivating their creativity. To facilitate a world-wide exchange via Internet specific needs of the users from wide range of cultural settings should be analyzed and generalized to find an effective solution. The general goals of the multilingual telematic support for education and training are the following:

1. to provide basic language tools for effective information exchange between Internet users from all possible professional fields and different English/ French and Russian speaking countries;

2. to improve accessibility of the Internet-based information for non-English speaking users;
3. to facilitate utilization of educational and training materials available in English for the French- and Russian-speaking users as well as to ensure share of such materials available on the net of the French and Russian-speaking countries;
4. to ensure exchange of educational and training information within Russian- speaking users groups directly, without necessity to pass through English.

To achieve these goals, the interested in multilingual applications sites must be equipped with tools which form user-friendly and comfortable multilingual environment. Communication within Network must be made attractive for users world-wide, developing their information needs, widening their horizons and motivating their creativity and inter- communications. The necessity of linguistic support for multilingual communication, information search and acquisition requires the use of modern linguistic tools such as spelling and grammar checkers, dictionaries, thesauri, vocabularies, elements of automatic translation and, eventually, multimedia voice encoders and decoders. To achieve the main goals for CIS countries, the translation tools for English into Russian and Ukrainian will be used.

- Virtual University as the examples of the multilingual telematics support for education and training. The life-long education of the 21st century will be global from two perspectives: from a horizontal perspective, cultures are meeting each other on the surface of the globe, entering into creative encounters that will produce a international collective virtual educational environment; from a vertical perspective, they must maximise using the world knowledge's for organisation of international virtual educational environment in order to provide a stable and secure base for future development. on the national and international levels .

The general goals of the multilingual telematic support for education and training are the following:

1. to provide basic language tools for effective information exchange between Internet users from all possible professional fields and different English/ French and Russian speaking countries;
2. to improve accessibility of the Internet-based information for non-English speaking users;
3. to facilitate utilization of educational and training materials available in English for the French- and Russian-speaking users as well as to ensure share of such materials available on the net of the French and Russian-speaking countries;
4. to ensure exchange of educational and training information within Russian- speaking users groups directly, without necessity to pass through English.

These problems must be solved at local, regional, national and international levels. The global aims of the IVU "Ukraine" are the following:

1. to provide inter-cultural courses, accessible to students all over the world through distance learning methods.
2. to create multilingual learning environment for telematic-based education and training

3. to stimulate learning to creative candidates in order to form complete human beings with erudition.

The multilingual telematics support for education and training should be based on innovative ways for flexible integration of modern technologies into the new solutions directed to the development of multimedia learning environment, which in its turn will contribute to the introduction of innovative solutions and skills for telematics-based training in world society, promoting new opportunities for life-long distance education. To facilitate a world-wide exchange within the Network its local/national sites should analyse specific-needs of its users to find an effective solution within the Network.

One of this specific needs is the necessity of language support for multi-lingual communication and exchange of materials. To facilitate the use of samples and examples from different sources the Network should support a communication between teachers, as well as material translation into native language. This language service within local sites would not only promote the use of English-based materials outside English-speaking countries but also open the gates to teachers experience in other cultures and languages. The use of current machine translation tools, spell- and grammar-checkers, vocabularies would help to improve them making a necessary office tool, as text editor or word processor. Multilingual Internet support development. Main research direction is methods development for multilingual Internet technologies teaching to insure intencive use of the modern infornation resourses by the different groups of people.

Working in Internet multilingual environment create a large amount of the problems for non-English speakers.

Such users cannot to solve these problems allways self-sufficiently. Activity in this direction was initiated at Second International Congress UNESCO and was supported by the 42 counries round the world. Such developments are absent in Ukraine.

However, there is strong need to overcome language barriers and ensure certain translation or explanation of terms are selected by the user. Besides that, there isn't any materials about language barriers overcoming, in spite of existing such experience for English, Dutch and French languages. For Russian and Ukrainian languages we have only American translation off-line centers. So this problem is actual for Ukraine, that only tries to occupy certain place among leading countries in telecommunication issues. Object of investigation is ways of access to modern information Internet resourses with on-line and off-line electronic dictionaries and translators, and insuring flexible distance learning and providing measures, that will facilitate active use of the multilingual Internet environment.

Multilingualism: A Canadian Experience

Since its birth a generation ago, the Internet has been dominated by the English language and North American culture. In a 1998 survey conducted by the Internet research group, eMarketer, two-thirds (68 percent) of a little over 60 million Internet users worldwide reside in just two countries, the United States, with 37 million users, and Canada, which has just over 4 million. About 60 percent of the Internet host computers are located in the United States. Nine out of 10 Internet users today are English-speaking. No fewer than 82 percent of home pages (web sites) are in English, according to the Internet Society's survey of 60,000 computers with Internet addresses. Yet some foresee an end to this electronic hegemony.

The number of non-U.S. Internet users is about to outnumber those inside the country soon and increase by nine-fold over the next five years, from 16.4 million in 1997 to 143 million by the year 2002, representing an annual growth rate of 70 percent. In that case, the present practice of conducting business, presenting news and information, and performing discussion on the Internet will have to be drastically changed. The widespread use of English will eventually be contested and the Internet itself will become multicultural. This is already happening. A consortium of American computer companies has developed a universal digital code known as Unicode to allow computers to represent the letters and characters of virtually all the world's languages. Major search engines like Yahoo and Excite offer their services in multiple languages.

Netscape Communications in partnership with the leading Latin American Internet service, Star Media Network, provides a free Internet guide in Spanish and Portuguese. Internet services in languages other than English, like Star Media, are starting to provide world and regional news, weather, stock listings, e-mail, chat rooms, Internet access and more, all in the users' native language. Given such developments, optimists argue that far from ending diversity, the Internet will promote it by allowing even small groups of people to disseminate their messages worldwide. By overtaking the "middle range" languages, it may actually protect minority languages threatened with extinction. A wider range of languages on the Internet means at least in theory that a wider range of ideas will be exchanged in a cyberspace, the long-promised global village. Despite a tremendous influx of non-English languages in recent years, however, the Internet has a long way to go before it becomes a truly multilingual medium.

As long as English can be understood by the largest number of Internet users, the cyberspace will continue to be dominated by English as the primary language for international discourse and commerce, European languages as a tool for regional and specialized communication, and many other minor languages for local communication. At a glance there is an advantage to having one language dominant in the cyberspace. In a world of five to eight thousand different ethnic groups who reside in approximately 160 nation states speaking 5,000 distinct languages, some language must be the common language of the Internet.

Many people believe that English must be by default the standard language on the Internet, much as it is the international language of aviation. At present there are clear indications of English becoming a lingua franca in the cyberspace. The Internet, the network of networks, is most likely to be governed by the logic of the "Metcalfe's Law," the so-called magic of interconnections. Connect any number of machines, 'n', whether computers, phones or even cars, and you get 'n' squared in exponential value.

Simply put, the values of the interconnected entities increase exponentially. To expand this logic further, as English-speaking countries have happened to take the central role in world politics and economy in modern period (namely, Pax Britannica and Pax Americana), the

English language will deepen its hold on the world as more people go on line. As a recent British Council report shows, the evolution of the English language accelerates as it spreads beyond Anglo-Saxonism.

The critical mass of English amongst providers and users is likely to drive the usage inexorably towards monoglot English. Even the French, famously fastidious about guarding their language against dilution by foreign words and phrases, has been forced to surrender to American vernacular on Internet matters. As English continues to dominate the cyberspace with greater intensity and speed, global resistance to it accelerates with equal strength. Some countries already disgruntled by the encroachment of the American culture—from pop music, blue jeans, to videos—are worried that their cultures will be further eroded by an American dominance in the cyberspace. In their minds, English, by association, immediately evokes a negative image of colonial imperialism. They feel that it may threaten their cultures, their languages, even identities.

For this ideological reason, many people in the Third World countries are opposed to having English as the lingua franca for commerce and trade, crisis management, and scholarly and intellectual discourse on the Internet. While the Internet is awash in information, almost all of it flows in one direction, i.e., from the United Sates to the rest of the increasingly wired world. It brings home the age-old controversy regarding unbalanced and unidirectional flow of information from the world's richest countries to the Third World, an on-going controversy that prompted UNESCO to declare a New World Information Order (NWIO) on several occasions.

For the ideological as well as practical purposes, many countries have taken steps to protect the Internet from excessive American influence. The French government once filed a lawsuit against a Georgia Tech campus in Metz, France, whose web page did not translate its contents into French. Arab countries proposed creation of an Arab Intranet, a closed network in which indiscriminate access to pornography and political discussion could be blocked. Canadian content requirements are to be extended to the Internet to keep out the American "cultural vulture."

Multilingualism: A Korean Experience

American culture has continued to exert its influence in Korea, first through Christian missions, trade and Hollywood productions, and more recently via the Internet. Thanks to the Korean government's aggressive drive, an estimated 2.5 million Koreans are linked to the global medium. An equally large share of the credit for the phenomenal growth of the Internet goes to the media organizations in Korea, which have in recent years vigorously campaigned for introducing the "Net" to the school community through such programs as the KidNet (Chosun Ilbo) and Internet in Education (Joongang Ilbo).

In the vicissitudes of hopes and fears about the Internet, two isolated but interrelated events recently took place in Korea, all with a nationalistic overtone. One is the Microsoft's abortive attempt to buy out a local Korean software company in exchange for a multi-million dollar investment. The other has to do with a somewhat radical proposal by a Korean writer to adopt English as a common language on the Internet.

In the midst of currency crisis in Korea these days came the shocking announcement that the Hangul and Computer (H&C) Company, a Korean software company, had agreed with Microsoft to stop development of its popular Arae A Hangul word processor program in exchange for a $20 million capital investment. Apparently, what Microsoft hoped for in the deal was to secure a monopolistic right of its Korean language version of Windows and Word in the Korean market. When it first appeared in 1990, Arae A Hangul-- named after the Korean alphabet invented by King Sejong more than five centuries ago--was the only word processor based on hangul instead of Roman letters with the hangul mapping.

Arae A Hangul, "insanely great" in the words of Apple Computer's founder Steven Jobs, was multilingual at a time when DOS versions of Word and WordPerfect barely went beyond ASCII. This made it easy to develop a number of attractive fonts frequently used in displaying old Korean characters.

Media reports of the deal aroused anger and frustration among Korean computer users and non-users alike. Defenders of Hangul, who were opposed to the Microsoft's planned equity participation in H&C, quickly invoked the issue of Korean national pride to rally the public support for the program. A massive nationwide campaign saved Hangul at the eleventh hour from the threat of extinction as its developer, H&C, reversed its earlier decision to sell off the software, bowing to a nationwide campaign spearheaded by Korean scholarly community and venture capitalists. As hindsight, invoking Korean pride as a defense against predatory foreign companies appears to be too far-fetched and even xenophobic. On the other hand, Microsoft's aggressive marketing strategy to effectively terminate H&C's further development of Hangul can be viewed as too selfish and insensitive to the Korean nationalistic sentiment. Now that 2.5 millions of Koreans are linked up to form a global community, how will they communicate- Majority of Korean Internet users was found to use the global medium mainly for communication within the national boundary, according to an Internet user survey. To most of them the Internet remains largely an unexplored reservoir of knowledge and information due to language barrier.

Their grasp of English is quite rudimentary, sufficient only for processing basic information such as the weather, sports, and erotic visuals. Only a fraction of the Internet users can, to whatever degree, comprehend and produce written or spoken utterances in English. As a result, they are denied of the tremendous opportunities that the Internet has to offer, namely, in-depth information and more serious discussions with the netizens all around the world. To be an effective Internet user one has to be equipped with both receptive and productive abilities in English. Such an expectation, however, appears to be neither practical nor realistic as far as Korea is concerned.

Bok Koh-Ill, a professional Korean writer, thinks otherwise. He came up with a radical idea to make English as an official language of Korea along with Korean. Touching on the sensitive theme of Korean nationalism, Bok argued that "putting 'emotional' nationalism under control is not enough." "As the world is rapidly moving toward a Terrestrial Empire," he further asserted, "not only the political supranational organizations such as the WTO and IMF but also the communication tools like the Internet are increasingly integrated into one unity." Now comes his argument concerning English, the dominant language on the Internet. Bok observed that "the emergence of the universal language is interlocked with the enlargement of network." He predicted that "the Korean language will soon be little more than a museum piece as more nations will adopt a bilingual system in which their own languages coexist with English." His underlying perspective about language is that "language is a tool, and worshipping it as an idol is irrational."

Sensationalism notwithstanding, Bok's audacious proposal immediately touched off a flurry of verbal battle between the conservatives and liberals in Korea. In a wild exchange of high-pitched diatribes, Bok's opponents argued that English was not panacea and accepting his idea would wither Korea's unique traditions and hamstring the very cultural foundation.

Bok's supporters applauded accuracy of his observation that Koreans possess an excessive national pride, which Bok sees as the obstacle to the advancement of the Korean society. Bok even dared all his critics by asking, "If you had to choose between English and Korean for your child's native language, which one would you select? If you choose English, your child is sure to have faster access to cutting-edge technology and information. If the Korean language is your choice, your child is doomed to lag behind in competition with others." Whether he will succeed in his effort is far from certain. Bok says, "In our society, nationalism and national language are far too sensitive issues to be discussed with composure." Yet his other key point—that

Koreans are too sensitive to these kinds of issues—seems not that far from reality. A non-random online survey taken immediately after the verbal battle showed 58 percent of those polled were against Bok. Even more noteworthy is the fact that as high as 42 percent sided with Bok and his idea. The deepening dispute seems here to stay, at least for a while.

Multilingual Translation

For a truly multilingual Internet, the long-promised global village, to come of age, there are a host of difficult hurdles to overcome, including, among the many, technical difficulties of communicating in the majority of the world's languages and development of hardware and software for machine-aided translations. Some progress has been made, and more in sight, in the development of hardware and software for processing texts, from seven-bit ASCII to ISO-Latin, and more recently, to Unicode (ISO 10646), a coding scheme for characters of most of the world's scripts. Widely hailed as a significant breakthrough in electronic communication worldwide, Unicode character encoding, however, may not be the best one to use in our environment. For example, the Software Laboratory of Nippon Telegraph and Telephone Corporation (NTT) found that Chinese, Japanese, and Korean (CJK) ideographs share the same code space, when Unicode is used in a global search-engine context. Thus, if a Japanese searcher inputs a string for searching, it can equally match against Chinese and Korean counterparts.

Another major problem with Unicode for CJK users is that it doesn't contain enough code space to capture all ideographs. For the development of a perfect multilingual architecture, incorporating languages that build compound characters or right-to-left ordering needs further tests. Transmitting a message in a language of reader's preference is one thing; one's ability to comprehend it is quite another.

In order to send and receive a message, most readers will have to rely on human translators/interpreters. The Internet is home to many language translation sites that offer everything from simple online dictionaries to e-mailed translation services. From the desktop, one can request a translation by selecting to pay for human translation. The global nature of the Internet has proved a boon to translation services, such as TAR Communication in New York, which translated Web-based press releases into 28 languages during the Atlanta Olympic Games in 1996. Translation business via the Internet within the next five years is expected to account for 30 percent of their work.

Given the volume and variety of messages on the Internet, however, exclusive reliance on human translation appears to be an unrealistic proposition. It is too slow and costly to make it a sensible choice for maintaining multilingual websites. A viable alternative is machine-aided translation, which has been vigorously pursued mostly in Japan, Canada and Europe with somewhat mixed results. Systran, available on the French Minitel network since 1983 and Canada's Meteo system, which translates meteorological bulletins between French and English, are considered to be success stories.

In Korea there are several translation softwares capable of machine-translating foreign language texts into Korean. In an attempt to assess the quality of these softwares, the author had a wide variety of texts in Japanese and English translated into Korean by means of King Sejong, one of the most popular translation softwares in the market. To begin with a conclusion, the Japanese-Korean translation effort proved to be a resounding success, whereas the translated version of the English texts was dismally unsatisfactory.

In terms of the syntax and grammar both Korean and Japanese share a lot of things in common, whereas there is a mile of difference between Korean and English. It seemed as if the intercultural difference involved in the English-Korean translation were an insurmountable wall indeed. The English texts included Abraham Lincoln's Gettysburg address, a *USA Today* article headlined "White House Loses Round in Lindsey Case," a passage in Jean Baudrillard's La Pensee Radicale, excerpts from the novel Little Prince, and a paragraph in Nico Randeraad's article "Authority in Search of Liberty." This mini exercise yielded disconcertingly unsatisfactory results. The translated versions were totally unintelligible, and not good enough to be revisable even with the intervention of human editors. It appeared that the texts replete with sophisticated literary expressions—the Lincoln's address and Baudrillard's work in particular—simply defied machine-aided translation.

Of the five different kinds of the English texts, only the *USA Today* article—concerning a U. S. court's refusal of the White House appeal to block prosecutors from questioning a presidential aide about Monica Lewinsky--showed some sign of hope. Compared with the other texts, the news article revealed a relatively high level of fidelity in translation. Why did the newspaper article alone fare reasonably well, while other texts simply failed to be translated into Korean? The translator's familiarity with the subject matter, i.e. President Clinton's sex scandal, could be an important factor. A more plausible explanation lies in the journalistic style in which the article is written. Journalists are required to adhere to the journalistic principle of brevity and precision when they write about an issue or event.

All the important elements are to be clearly spelled without excessive literary ornamentation. Such a finding could have a practical implication for the information producers on the Internet. For the benefit of a large number of population worldwide they are strongly encouraged to provide a brief and concise abstract of the full text in a machine-friendly manner, so that the abstract can be translated into many languages without losing fidelity. Also useful in multilingual translation will be a two-step process now being implemented by several groups including the United Nations University in Tokyo. In the two-step process, a text is first thoroughly analyzed into component parts (title, paragraph, sentence), clarified when necessary and possible by a dialogue with the author, then translated into an intermediate, abstract representation—which is used to generate translations in different languages. In this way, readers who have no receptive ability in a foreign language could at least get the gist of the material in hand with the help of translation softwares.

Human-assisted Machine Translation

Given the low quality of machine translation and the expensive nature of human translation, the only logical option available to Korea--and for that matter to many countries in the world--appears to be human-assisted/ validated machine translation. Experts at numerous regional and international conferences have already addressed to the crucial importance of human-assisted translation. To briefly summarize their recommendations and suggestions:

1) it is vital that a human validator is used to correct automatic translation;
2) it is important to take cultural-specific notions into account when undertaking translations between culturally different linguistic areas;
3) human translations can benefit from processing of files against terminology databases to ensure that technical phrases are translated in a domain-specific way;
4) as keyword matching does not work across domains or across languages, searchable concept-based terminology resources and thesauri are needed;
5) it is important to integrate machine translation and domain-specific terminology sets with authoring tools to speed up translation services.

Technological solution to machine translation is one thing, financial difficulty associated with making machine translation services available through the Internet is another. Because these services take up too many CPU cycles, Information Service Providers would rather offer these services via specialist servers, not as a part of their mainstream operations. The question then arises as to who pays for such servers, and how. Also, the preponderance of English on the Web, with some estimates ranging as high as 95%, appears at odds with the huge investments in translation to be made by the software industry. Investments are likely to be made in the cost-effective European languages, but not in minor languages. Preparing for the multilingual Internet calls for a concerted effort by both public institutions and industry players that produce and utilize language services, tools, and systems.

Regional cooperation among nations that share cultural and linguistic similarities, such as Korea, Japan, and China, must be strongly encouraged not only by the governments concerned but also by regional and international organizations such as UNESCO. Through collaborative R&D arrangements, they can jointly develop multilingual translation tools and services in a much more cost-effective way. As personal computers become less expensive and user-friendlier, people outside North America and European countries are becoming increasingly linked.

In this atmosphere diversity of languages will further enrich the on-line environment by making it possible for people of different cultures and languages to engage themselves in more serious in-depth discussions with other people. There are many advantages of a multilingual Internet: it would allow much more effective and wide diffusion of information and knowledge than would otherwise be possible; common mistakes and misunderstandings resulting from language barrier will be curtailed; and it could be a crack in Americana hegemony over Internet culture.

Chapter 7

Emerging Challenges of E-governance

Mexico has taken the first step towards e-governance by facilitating the migration of certain governmental functions and services—namely, citizen participation, civil servant declarations, tramites (official solicitations and registrations), procurement, the registros publicos ("public registries"), and tax filings - to an expanding network of government operated websites. Reflecting the nascent state of e-government in Mexico, some of these websites have the look, feel, and functionality of static electronic brochures. Those sites that are not already interactive will undoubtedly become so, going forward, as the Mexican government comes under pressure to meet the demands of increasingly service- and performance-oriented citizens and investors. The ways in which the aforementioned governmental functions and services are amenable to the transformative influences of the Internet are discussed below.

Citizen Participation

Notwithstanding the fact that it has a governmental structure organically similar to that of the United States (i.e., a tripartite division premised on the notion of a separation of powers), Mexico has never had a strong tradition of citizen participation in government. Testifying before the House Committee on Small Business, noted Mexican scholar John Bailey characterized Mexico's political system as one "obsessed with central control, lacking a tradition of democracy and participation, and deeply skeptical about the uncertainties of risk taking inherent in democratic competition." Continuing, he noted: "Its basic instinct in confronting opposition is to co-opt, negotiate, and persuade; if these fail, its methods include divide, debilitate, denounce, and - as a last resort -repress."

The historic losses recently suffered by the PRI have profoundly impacted the legislative process in Mexico. Where the PRI's long-standing control of the congress facilitated a top-down, "metaconstitutional" approach to law making, the presently divided nature of Congress requires Mexican legislators to develop and deploy consensus and/or coalition building skills. As one trade publication relates, "Mexico is shaking off the authoritarian one-party state that has governed for most of this century and a more plural and democratic country is emerging. With it, too, a new culture is slowly forming, characterized for the first time by negotiation and persuasion and democratic give and take." The novel situation of shifting party alliances and legislative uncertainty produced by this change, coupled with the contemporaneous explosion of political awareness made possible by the rapid spread of information and communications technologies ("ICTs"), has opened up unprecedented opportunities for citizen participation in Mexico. In this context of real political competition, Mexico's elected officials are learning that legislative success comes to those who are most responsive to the input of an expanding range of increasingly organized constituents and interest groups. In recognition of the evolving political significance of the Mexican citizen, the Fox Administration has established a digital channel whereby individual citizens and civic groups can participate in the articulation of Mexico's National Development Plan (the "Consult a Ciudadana").

Based on the "E-Advocacy" and "Interactive Service" (G2C2G) models, the Consult a Ciudadana facilitates both the expression of opinion (Foro de Consult a) and the proactive presentation of legislative proposals (Buzon deConsultas). The creation of this channel is positive insofar as it enables more individuals and groups to gain admission to the law-making arena by removing the barriers of distance and political access. This is noteworthy given the fact that Mexico's laws have traditionally been made by Mexico City based elites with little first-hand knowledge of the social, economic, legal, and political interests and/or concerns of the people they govern. Going forward, the Consult a Ciudadana has the potential to serve as (1) an important conduit for the expression of fresh political thoughts, practices, and values, and (2) a mechanism for assuring that laws promulgated in the capital pragmatically relate to the reality of the subject matter they intend to regulate.

The emergence of digital spaces such as the Consult a Ciudadana, together with the promulgation of legislation designed to strengthen the participation of civil society, is additionally significant in that it opens the door to the disintermediation of politics in Mexico and the rise of a more "direct" form of democracy. Assuming the rectification of Mexico's substantial Internet access problem, and (2) the existence of the genuine political will to expand the substantive scope of the channel, the Consult a Ciudadana could help bring about a fundamental redefinition of the social contract underlying the citizen-government relationship. These ICT related developments could, in turn, contribute to the transformation of Mexican authority structures and facilitate the growth of self-regulatory practices.

Transparency

Mexico has a deeply entrenched history of non-transparency. The PRI's seven decade stranglehold on power, coupled with its careful control of information and self-serving manipulation of the canard of "national sovereignty," insulated Mexico from adverse scrutiny and, to a lesser degree, accountability. Considered in the context of Mexico's traditionally paternalistic and corporatist socio-political organization, this lack of transparency fostered rampant corruption and eroded economic, political, and legal certainty. Drawing on the successful experience of other Latin nations in using the Internet as a tool for overcoming the developmental impediments posed by non-transparency and corruption, the Fox administration has begun to use the E-Mexico program as a platform for capturing and recording the patrimonial information of public servants associated with the entities and dependencies of the federal public administration ("Declaranet"). Premised on the "Broadcasting/Wider Dissemination" model, this type of digital resource "opens up an alternate channel for people to access information as well as to validate information available form other sources." While Declaranet constitutes an important step in the direction of transparency, it may ultimately be of limited value in that the practices followed in valuing and accounting for the patrimony of a public servant are left to the absolute discretion of the government.

A further limitation entails the fact that article 40 of the LFRASP (not surprisingly) makes the subsequent publication of captured patrimonial information expressly contingent on the prior authorization of the individual public servant. The inescapable implication of this provision is that the ultimate utility of the Declaranet site as a publicly available anti-opacity/corruption tool will be a function of public servants' good will and, perhaps more accurately, confidence in the "cleanliness" of their personal affairs. Transparency in Mexico will likely be enhanced by the recent passage of landmark legislation involving the reporting of and access to information.

Conceptually and functionally a kin to the Freedom of Information Act ("FOIA") in the United States, Mexico's new Ley Federal de Transparenciay Acceso a la Informacion Publica Gubernamental promises to remedy information failure by (1) requiring the obligated subjects of the federal public administration to make structural and operating information (for example, regarding budgets, procurement contracts, licenses, concessions, etc.) available to the public via Internet and (2) creating an administrative mechanism by which citizens can proactively request and obtain information of a non-reserved character from all branches, entities, and dependencies of the federal government. Assuming the effective operation of the law's civilian oversight feature (i.e., the operationally autonomous Instituto Federal de Acceso a la Informacion Publica), Mexico's L.F.T.A .could function as a powerful tool for influencing governmental action and deterring corruption, facilitating the clarification and/or settlement of past controversies, strengthening the rights of Mexican citizens set forth in the Constitution and other international treaties to which it is a party, and assuring compliance with supreme court decisions. As was the case with the issue of Declaranet-related information disclosure, supra, the introduction of a mechanism for discovering information pertaining to government departments and personnel, coupled with an increased commitment to securing accountability, could result in the establishment of more stable developmental conditions in Mexico.

Electronic Tramites

One of the greatest obstacles to economic development faced by Mexico and Latin America involves the inefficient, formalistic, and corruption ridden process of soliciting and/or obtaining government permits, licenses, and or concessions (for example, in connection with incorporations, the registration of intellectual property, the issuance of powers of attorney, dissolutions, etc.). Faced with slow response times, high costs, complicated procedures, and uncertain results, citizens and foreign businesses frequently attempt to structure their affairs around the government. This practical hinders economic development to the extent that (1) informally operated small- and medium- sized companies are unable to title, insure, and leverage assets and/or avail themselves of potentially lucrative government programs and benefits (involving, for example, the obtainment of micro-credit, health care, export assistance, etc.) and (2) the government is unable to collect the tax revenue it needs to create and support infrastructure and industrial development projects, education and training programs, regulatory enforcement regimes, and social security services.

Cognizant of the obstacle posed to development by excessive and complicated registration and permit filing procedures, the Zedillo administration introduced a deregulation program designed to reduce "the bureaucratic red tape that stifles competitive markets and limits economic growth." Most recently, the Fox administration has sought to achieve further administrative and regulatory efficiency by making it possible for citizens and investors to realize certain filings online (Tramitanet). Borne of the Interactive Service (G2C2G) model, Tramitanet provides information pertaining to substantive and procedural filing requirements (for example, content, form, authentication, costs, etc.) and enables the electronic submission of a limited range of routine tramites and denouncements.

The legal viability of electronic filings made through the Tramitanet system is assured by the fact that Mexico's civil, commercial, and procedural codes, as reformed, expressly recognize the validity of electronically generated data messages and assure non-discrimination with respect to data messages as a form of proof Properly managed, this site could enhance economic growth and development in Mexico by (1) encouraging informally operated small- and medium-sized business entities to register with the government, (2) reducing opportunities for fraud and error, (3) saving citizens, investors and the government time and money, and (4) contributing to the formation of a robust and reliable database regarding economic and civic activity.

Electronic Government Procurement

Government procurement has traditionally been one of the most important drivers of economic activity in Latin America. In Mexico, it is estimated that 25% to 30% of the federal budget regularly goes to the purchase or lease of goods and/or services. Notwithstanding the substantial economic upside associated with this activity, government procurement in Mexico has long been a fertile breeding ground for inefficiency and corruption. Responding to the absence of clearly defined (and/or enforced) guidelines and the over-abundance of poorly paid intermediaries, private sector suppliers commonly assess up to a 20% surcharge on government sales so as to cover losses caused by bureaucratic inefficiency and bribes demanded by government purchasing officers. The net effect of this overcharging is to diminish the governmental resources available for the realization of development related projects such as schools, hospitals, and infrastructure.

As part of Mexico's attempt to promote development by reducing inefficiency and corruption, the Secretaria de Controloriay Desarollo Administrativo (SECODAM) has automated and disintermediated government procurement by launching the Compranet site. Representing a fully Interactive Service (G2C2G) model, Compranet is intended to simplify and modernize the procurement process by (1) making it easier for suppliers to discover government needs, (2) standardizing the procedures and documentation involved in procurement,

(3) minimizing the involvement of civil servants, (4) and providing for the electronic submission of bids. Each bid submitted must be authenticated by means of a digital signature.

As of October 1999, the Compranet site was accommodating more that 6,000 public sector tenders on a daily basis and had registered more than 20,000 service providing firms as regular users. The standardization, automation, and disintermediation of government procurement practices, considered in conjunction with the reduced cost of accessing the government's electronic procurement network, has improved economic transparency, increased citizen participation in the bidding process for public contracts, and enabled the government to curtail supplier surcharges.

More importantly, the expanded monitoring and auditing opportunities presented by Compranet's searchable archive of procurement records will make it easier to detect and punish civil servant fraud. In this regard, Mexico's recent experience with the "Towelgate" scandal clearly demonstrates the system's capacity to expose fraudulent violations of the public trust. Finally, by reducing opportunities for corruption, Compranet permits Mexico to more fully comply with its obligations under the OECD's Convention on Combating Bribery of Foreign Public Officials and the OAS' Inter-American Convention Against Corruption.

Electronic Public Registries of Commerce and Property

The unavailability of commercial credit that Mexico has experienced since 1993 has created a significant drag on the country's economic growth and development. While many factors account for this reality, one of the most important involves the non-existence of a functional and reliable system of secured financing. Referring to the "defective" form in which property is documented and held in many Latin nations (including Mexico), Hernando De Soto notes: "assets cannot readily be turned into capital, cannot be traced outside of narrow local circles where people know and trust each other, cannot be used as collateral for a loan, and cannot be used as a share against an investment." The underproductive nature of the majority of Latin America's capital constitutes a fundamental obstacle to the region's sustained development.

Consistent with its efforts to transform the country's moribund financial system into an engine of economic productivity, the Mexican government recently announced its intent to join forces with the states in integrating and automating Mexico's antiquated network of public registries of commerce and property (the SIGER network). Conforming to the Interactive Service (G2C2G) model, the completed system will respond to the requirements of art. 20 of the Codigo de Comercio, as reformed, by providing an Internet based means of interfacing with Mexico's registries. Considered from the perspective of secured financing, the SIGER will facilitate the conduction of registry searches and the registration of liens (and/or related mercantile acts). As was the case with the Tramitanet system, the juridical security of electronic filings in the public registries of commerce and property is assured by the recent reforms to Mexico's Codigo de Comercio, Codigo Civil, and Codigo Federal de Procedimientos Civiles.

The launching of the SIGER will improve Mexico's registry systems by reducing the likelihood of fraud and error, expediting the process for ascertaining the existence of specific filings (for example, a lien), and enabling the establishment of an integrated database of encumbered property. Assuming the establishment of meaningful degree of Internet access, these improvements will facilitate economic growth and development by providing merchants with the transactional certainty necessary for entering into an increased number of deals with an expanded range of business partners.

Electronic tax filings

The massive privatization program carried out in the 1990s, combined with the implementation of economic policies designed to reduce Mexico's dependence on revenues generated by the sale of oil, the continued loss of human capital in the form of the temporary or permanent migration to the United States, and generally weakened levels of in bound tourism has resulted in the elimination and/or circumscription of traditionally lucrative sources of budget revenue and underscored the need for diversifying government income. Lacking the funds to simultaneously service its foreign debt and operate the government in a way that adequately meets the needs of its citizens, Mexico has undertaken a program of fiscal reform designed to shut down loopholes, expand the tax base, and increase the federal budget.

Noting the success that other Latin nations have encountered in using the Internet to maximize tax revenue, Mexico recently expanded its e-government program to provide for the electronic presentation of declarations and payment of taxes (through the Servicio de Administracion Tributaria, or "SAT"). Constituting an Interactive Service (G2C2G) model, the SAT site (either independently or in conjunction with private sector financial institutions) permits inscribed users to file tax statements, make payments (realized via an electronic transfer of funds from the tax payer's bank to the Tesoreria de la Federacion), confirm receipt of payment, and review prior tax transactions.

Security for this system is accomplished through the use of a "security key" (i.e., a private key) bound by the "Modulo de Atencion Fiscal de la Adminsitracion Local de Recaudacion" corresponding to the tax payer's domicile (the corresponding digital certificate required to use the system is subsequently sent by e-mail). Similar online tax filing and payment systems have been set up by different state governments in Mexico. Again assuming adequate Internet access, the SAT system can help the Mexican government maximize tax revenue by (1) contributing to the preservation of scarce government resources (via the dissemination of tax filing information and instructions in a more cost effective manner); (2) removing distance as a barrier to tax filing; (3) minimizing the opportunity for fraud and error; (4) expediting processing time; (5) enabling the establishment of a reliable taxpayer database; and (6) facilitating the prosecution of tax evaders. These developments could, to the extent they expand the base of government resources, help avert a reduction in foreign investment occasioned by the perception that the weakened state of Mexico's public finances effectively precludes the realization of large scale infrastructure projects. The expansion of Mexico's tax base, on the other hand, could be accomplished by making the SAT's online tax filing and payment services available to all Mexican citizens.

Recognizing the power of the Internet to fundamentally improve traditional political and economic systems, Mexico has aggressively initiated the process of moving official functions and services online. As a result of these efforts, Mexico's citizens are better able to claim a stake in a more transparent and potentially less corrupt government. The communications and operational efficiencies associated with the Internet have, moreover, resulted in both increased revenues and substantial savings in terms of time and resources.

These developments, in aggregate, have justifiably improved the confidence of citizens and investors in exico. More can and must be done, however, if Mexico is to fully realize the developmental opportunities associated with the Internet. The adoption of the following policy recommendations will further strengthen democratic governance, economic development, and the rule of law in Mexico:

Expand the E-mexico Programme to include electronic Voting and the administration of Justice While significant advances have been made in bringing the Mexican government into the digital age, the issues of voting and the administration of justice have remained largely outside the scope of the E-Mexico program. The subsequent sections identify and explore the benefits that would flow from the digitalization of these historically inefficient areas of public administration.

Electronic voting

Elections have long been problematic in Mexico.

Notwithstanding the creation of an independent Federal Electoral Institute, the presence of international observers, the dramatic rise to power of non-PRI candidates and parties, reports of missing and/or overstuffed ballot boxes (the latter tactic is known as the "taco"), unclear voting station procedures (a tactic known as the "raton loco," or crazy rat), identification fraud (tactics involving the fraudulent manipulation of voter lists are locally known as the "cambio de panal," or diaper change), vote buying, intimidation tactics, and questionable tabulation techniques persist.

The degree to which Mexican elections accurately reflect the will of the people is further reduced by the large number of voters who, for reasons of age, health, or distance, do not vote. Particularly significant in this regard is the increasing number of Mexicans that live, either permanently or temporarily, outside the country. The experience of other Latin nations indicates that the conduction of electronic elections can save scarce government resources (by minimizing the need for the deployment of large numbers of election personnel and reducing the volume of paperwork involved in the process), improve voter turn out (by eliminating the obstacles posed to rural inhabitants and expatriates by poor travel infrastructure and/or distance), counter the effects of illiteracy (by using photographic images in a touch screen format), and produce more objective, error-free, and timely tabulations.

Assuming the existence of the political will and the implementation of the appropriate authentication and/or security procedures, the introduction of an IFE managed interactive system of electronic voting could reduce the frequency with which the legitimacy of elected officials becomes controverted and mitigate lingering notions of disenfranchisement (i.e., on the part of those individuals and/or groups which claim to have been victimized by electoral fraud). These results could, in turn, help free up the Amparo dockets and enhance the overall perception of Mexico's stability in the eyes of both citizens and investors.

The Administration of justice

Latin America's political and economic development has been increasingly linked to the rule of law. As military dictatorships have given way to civilian rule and free trade in competitive markets has displaced trade protectionism (for example, import substitution), nations throughout the region have discovered that cosmetic changes in the law, unaccompanied by changes in the underlying culture and values of legal and political institutions, will not produce the certainty necessary for the growth and development of free markets and societies. Speaking to the economic aspect of this equation, noted constitutional scholar Lawrence Lessig states "if anything makes an economy work, it is a stable political environment governed by the rule of law." Focusing, in turn, on the political component of this equation, the President of Mexico's Supreme Court asserts "there can be no solid democracy [in Mexico] without a strong and independent federal judicial power."

Having determined that a greater level of legal certainty is critical to both the country's internal development and participation in the global economy, Mexico has, over the course of the last decade, undertaken the reform of its notoriously slow, corrupt, and costly system of judicial administration. In this connection, Mexico has identified - though not yet coherently developed - a central role for the Internet (premised on both the Broadcast/Wider Dissemination and Interactive Service models) in the process of strengthening the country's legal system. For example, Federal and state judicial authorities have recently begun to use the Internet for the dissemination of legal content, (laws, initiatives, jurisprudencia, teses, boletines, and other official publications) and the delivery of ADR services. While these developments undoubtedly make the administration of justice more efficient, there is significant room for improvement.

The federal and state legal databases available online are frequently uneven in terms of coverage depth and quality. Reglamentos—the critical regulations which accompany and flesh out primary Mexican legislation - are often not presented. In a related vein, the online version of the Diario Official is of limited value in that its coverage extends back only as far as 2000. The utility of the Mexican Supreme Court's database of jurisprudencia is, on the other hand, diminished by the sub-par functionality of the site's search feature. Finally, online notification systems (i.e., electronic boletines oficiales) - where the service is even available - tend to be primitive in terms of scope and execution.

Going forward, Mexico should consider bringing the administrative infrastructures of the federal and state judicial systems under the technical umbrella of the E-Mexico program. In networking these systems, Mexico would be able to (1) centralize and standardize legal content; thereby improving the functionality of the government's law-oriented websites; (2) improve the quality and timeliness of legal information disseminated online; (3) facilitate the use of online ADR services; and (4) expand the ability of parties to file certain pleadings and documents online (assuming the use of security measures to protect the content of filings), send and receive notifications electronically, and use information technology in the conduction of hearings (offering, for example, testimony by means of video-conference or video-deposition).

These developments could, in turn, strengthen the penetration of laws and jurisprudencia, expedite legal proceedings, clear dockets, improve judicial record keeping practices, eliminate sources of corruption, and decrease the cost of litigation. The ultimate beneficiary of a more efficient and equitable judicial system would, of course, be citizens and investors. Having increased faith in the ability of Mexican courts to resolve disputes in a swift, impartial, and cost effective manner, individuals and entities - national and foreign alike - would be less inclined to structure their affairs outside the court system and/or restrict their dealings to parties with whom they have established relationships. This certainty driven rise in the number of market participants would, to the extent it translated into enhanced levels of deal flow, promote economic growth and development.

Improve internet access

If Mexico's fledgling E-government program is to develop in accordance with its potential, Internet access must be improved. It is estimated that Mexico currently has 2.2 computers for every 100 people. Stated in terms of population, this signifies that only 1.5 million of Mexico's 96 million citizens (i.e., between 1-2% of the population) have access to the Internet. While these numbers are slowly increasing, the developmental benefits to be derived from moving governmental functions and services online will remain illusory pending the rectification of the access issue and the establishment of a functional "critical mass" of users.

The Internet may be growing exponentially, but it is only very slowly representing a more democratic cross-section of our society." Mindful of the obstacles posed to Internet access by relatively low PC penetration rates, high service and connection costs (i.e., telephone, ISP), and the poor quality of transmission signals caused by the country's weak telecommunications infrastructure, the government and private sector are working to raise the number of Internet users in Mexico. To this end, secretariats, institutions, and corporations such as the SCT, COFETEL, SEDESOL, SEP, the ITESM, and TELMEX, inter alia, have undertaken projects to boost teledensity (for example, by integrating the countries fixed and wireless communications networks) and increase Internet connectivity (by enhancing access to the necessary equipment and connections).

In the same vein, private sector entities are pursuing large-scale projects designed to bring Internet access, e-mail content, and multimedia capabilities to public places (for example, airports, bus terminals, hospitals, shopping centers, etc.).These endeavors have been supplemented by the introduction of alternative, less costly means of accessing the Internet (for example, via PDA, web phone, smart phone, cable set top box equipped with bidirectional modem, etc.).

The success of Mexico's e-government program will ultimately depend on its ability to create and assure infrastructure, investment, and regulatory conditions conducive to the realization of projects geared toward increasing Internet connectivity. In this connection, Mexico must take steps to enhance competition in the telecommunications and IT sectors by curtailing the monopoly power of TELMEX and vesting COFETEL with meaningful regulatory authority. Presuming such optimal developmental conditions, it is reasonable to think that Mexico will accomplish its goal of connecting approximately 2,500 municipalities to the Internet by the end of 2001 and 10,000 by the end of the Fox administration (2006).

Increase Information Technology Training and Support for Government Officials and Citizens

Another impediment to the successful development of the E-Mexico program involves the relatively limited technological skills and knowledge of Mexico's government officials and citizenry. Facing what one Mexican government official describes as "profound computer illiteracy," it is crucial that Mexico take steps to increase training and support with regard to new technology (for example, the use of electronic signatures, digital certificates, database management, etc.). Failure in this regard would undermine the communications and operational benefits of the E-Mexico program insofar as technologically unsophisticated government officials and citizens would be required to continue interacting pursuant to traditional paper based methods.

One way of avoiding this outcome would be for the Mexican government to establish "in house" training programs tailored to the specific needs and functions of each branch of government (as well as their assorted dependencies). Alternatively, the Mexican government could require key officials to attend the OAS-IACD sponsored "E-Government Academy." On another level, the provision of more detailed (yet nonetheless "user friendly") online instructions and expanded telephonic assistance could help Mexico's citizens master applications and programs with respect to which they have had no prior experience.

A good example in this connection involves the way Declaranet provides civil servants electing to file electronic declarations with training courses, technical assistance (via e-mail or telephone consultation), and comprehensive download instructions. An important corollary to the aforementioned endeavors involves the strengthening of information technology training programs at academic institutions and private sector corporations. While universities such as the ITESM and ITAM have recently launched graduate level IT programs for the benefit of citizens in major population centers, there are significantly fewer training opportunities available to citizens in other areas.

As virtual universities and other online training and learning centers become better established, however, it will be possible for a larger, more geographically diverse groups of citizens to obtain IT training. Corporations (particularly medium- to large-sized entities), on the other hand, are increasingly training employees to operate basic hardware and applications. In some cases, employee training has even extended to programming and software development. By acting to provide basic training for today's population - 40% of which is under age 15 - Mexico will assure the technological proficiency of the E-Mexico program's future users.

Ensure Citizen Privacy and Transactional Security

The final policy recommendation this paper makes focuses on the necessity of ensuring the privacy and security of electronically realized citizen-government transactions. Mexicans have in the past been unwilling to express their true thoughts and beliefs for fear of political and/or economic retaliation by local and/or regional political leaders. Despite the fact that the citizenry's susceptibility to this sort of pressure is gradually dissipating with the emergence of real competition amongst the country's political parties, many Mexicans - especially the rural poor - continue to keep their political views and actions closely guarded. As noted Mexican historian Enrique Krauze notes in this regard, the political process in Mexico is marked by a "culture of secrecy and private decision." If Mexico's citizens are to embrace the enhanced participation opportunities made possible by the E-Mexico program, it is imperative that their rights of privacy and anonymity be assured and strictly upheld.

An analogous issue exists with respect to the citizenry's willingness to entrust personal or commercial data in digitalized form to public officials and/or third party intermediaries (for example, banks or ISPs). Absent the introduction of adequate security measures, many Mexicans may be inclined to reject Internet based methods of filing tax returns, procuring government contracts, and registering assets. Consistent with the recommendation of the AMITI and other groups, Mexico has, over the course of the last two years, taken legislative steps to strengthen citizen privacy and transactional security on the Internet. Mexico's Federal

Consumer Protection Law, as reformed, sanctions the failure of a "provider" (for example, an ISP or other intermediary) to keep consumer-citizen information confidential.

Citizen privacy and security stand to be further strengthened by the terms of the March 22, 2000 initiative regarding information crimes. In its current form, the bill criminalizes (1) the interruption of communications on public networks, (2) the opening or accessing of written electronic communications directed to others, (3) the use of electronic data to fraudulently obtain, transfer, or acquire the property of another, (4) the unauthorized alteration, use, and/or modification of personal, financial, or commercial data registered in programs or codes, and (5) the unauthorized disclosure of the data mentioned in item "4," supra. Supplementing these steps, in turn, are the terms of the currently pending Ley Federal de Proteccion de Datos Personales.

Modeled largely after the Habeas Data action otherwise available in Latin America, the terms of this bill are intended to assure the integrity and privacy of personal information and data. Last, recently enacted NOM 151-SCFI-2002 bolsters transactional certainty in the online environment by elaborating the procedures to be followed in connection with the archiving of data messages. While these legislative endeavors appear to bode well for the E-Mexico program, it is too early to determine either the degree to which they will be enforced (assuming, in the case of the bills, that they are ultimately enacted) or the impact they will have on citizen confidence. Mexico could re-enforce online privacy and security by formally adopting the OECD Guidelines on the Protection of Privacy and Transborder

Flows of Personal Data and/or expanding the scope of art. 16 of the Constitution (regarding the inviolability of private communications) to expressly include data messages generated by electronic media. The fall of communism in 1989, coupled with the rapid evolution of global communications capabilities, resulted in the rejection of the state-oriented CEPAL agenda and the validation of developmental strategies premised on neoliberal economic policy and democratic governance.

In the case of Mexico, it was specifically hoped that liberalization would help overcome the economic setbacks of the 1980s (i.e., the "lost" decade Mexico experienced as a consequence of the enactment of high-risk and short-sighted policies) and plant the seeds of meaningful political and social transformation. While some positive economic and political outcomes have flowed from the implementation of these strategies, a review of Mexico's developmental record over the course of the last decade indicates that the hoped for recuperation and transformation have, on balance, yet to occur.

Ten years of neoliberal reform—as embodied by extensive privatizations, the NAFTA, and Mexico's insertion into the global economy - have yet to improve the living and economic conditions experienced by the majority of Mexicans. Pointing to decreased levels of government social spending, the diminished salaries and purchasing power of citizens, elevated rates of loan default and bankruptcy (particularly amongst small- to medium-sized entities), the disappearance of domestically controlled commercial entities (inciting, in turn, a nationalism-tinged resentment amongst Mexicans that they are no longer the masters of their own destiny), rising unemployment figures, unbridled child labour abuses, declining health, sanitation, and education standards, heavy flows of out-migration (commonly to the U.S.), and an increasingly unstable social situation (characterized by heightened levels of crime and drug cartel activity), many citizens now claim that Mexico's adherence to the neoliberal concept of withstanding economic "pain" before the "gain" has been excessive.

Mexico's experience with neoliberal economic policy appears, moreover, to have perpetuated the gulf between the nation's wealthy and poor. According to the recent "Human Development Study" conducted by the United Nations Development Fund, the "richest 20% of [Mexico's] population gets 57% of the country's income, which is 14 times what the poorest 20% get." These findings are corroborated by Nobel Prize winning economist Joseph Stiglitz's observation that, in the case of Mexico, the primary beneficiaries of the liberal economic policies encompassed by the so-called "Washington Consensus" have been the upper thirty percent of the population (with an even more marked concentration of benefits occurring within the top ten percent). Conversely,

Stiglitz goes on to note, "those at the bottom have gained little; many are even worse off." Given such negative results, it should come as no surprise that a Reforma poll found that (1) almost 60% of respondents thought Mexico had not benefited from NAFTA, and (2) approximately 90% of respondents thought NAFTA had produced increased levels of unemployment in Mexico. The current reduction in the level of U.S. FDI, coupled with the recent drop in industrial output occasioned by a weakening U.S.demand for Mexican exports, will only exacerbate Mexico's precarious economic situation. It is unlikely that Mexico will be able to pick up this economic slack by relying on its web of FTAs given the global nature of the present downturn.

Compounding the negative record of neoliberalism is the fact that the values and practices of the country's political and legal classes have failed, for the most part, to evolve in a way that engender greater citizen confidence in the operation and integrity of government and the rule of law. Notwithstanding the dramatic electoral accomplishments of the past four years, political and legal processes in Mexico continue to be characterized by corruption, inefficiency, and impunity. In the words of one high-ranking former Mexican official, the country's politicians are still "faced with the temptation to disregard their mandate and to govern in their own interests, or on behalf of the interest groups with whom they are allied." Because of this propensity on the part of Mexico's political leadership, "it is imperative to establish control mechanisms to ensure that elected officials, especially those in the executive branch, will perform their duties honestly and efficiently."

Focusing on the present administration, another Mexican commentator underscores the fundamental lack of real change by noting: "A year after his formal assumption of power, Fox appears more and more like the representatives of the regime he criticized so much during his presidential campaign. The crimes of the PRI regime - ranging from an abusive exercise of discretion with respect to public resources to violations of human, political, and labour rights - continue unpunished."

The cynicism and disillusionment which this situation incites within Mexico's citizens directly undermines the development of democratic and pluralistic institutions. Against this backdrop of discontent has emerged a growing rejection of U.S. inspired economic policies and political practices. Addressing the global manifestations of this backlash, Michael J. Mazaar of the Center for Strategic and International Studies (CSIS) observes: "Economic and social reform and democracy have swept the region, sparking alienation and exacerbated economic inequalities. Cultural and ideological reactions to capitalism are gaining strength.

The great expectations that accompanied reforms in Argentina, Brazil, Mexico, and Chile have given way to widespread disaffection with reform." While governments throughout the hemisphere have adopted the Inter-American Democratic Charter, the annual Latinobarometro survey reveals that the number of Mexicans which believe democracy to be preferable to any other kind of government is dropping. Even more alarming, however, is the survey's finding of a growing tolerance on the part of Mexicans for "dictatorship." Consistent with this finding, one Mexican publication recently stated: "the miseries of our democracy incite within many citizens a longing for the return of dictatorship."

Another Mexican commentator echoes this sentiment when he observes that democracy in Mexico - which has yet to be consolidated - "could still fail, creating a vacuum that could engender conflict and violence." Reflecting the dissatisfaction of the times, Mexico has, since 1994, witnessed increased levels of civil disobedience and guerilla activity - as well as the corresponding militarization (involving the deployment of both official and private paramilitary forces) of the domestic sphere. This is consistent with the observation that "many governments in the face of economic hardships and social dislocations caused by neoliberal restructuring have adopted authoritarian measures and bolstered the state's capacity for repression."

The economic and political stagnation underlying this backlash is contrary to U.S. interests insofar as it (1) diminishes the prestige of American developmental initiatives and strategies, (2) complicates a U.S.-Mexico relationship already strained by issues of drugs, immigration, terrorism, and water, (3) makes hemispheric economic and trade integration less attractive to the other Latin nations, and (4) strengthens the hand of America's Asian and European competitors in the region. The aforementioned developments are, alternatively, contrary to Mexico's interests to the extent that such expressions of social, political, economic, and legal instability run the risk of diminishing the country's overall competitive advantage in the global order, thereby leading foreign investors to locate their commercial activities elsewhere.

The recent entry of China and Taiwan into the WTO could, in this connection, adversely impact Mexico's ability to attract and retain desperately needed foreign investment. The E-Mexico program, in tandem with the broad range of economic, social, political, and legal reforms undertaken over the past twenty years, presents an unique opportunity to overcome the systemic formalism, inefficiency, fraud, mistrust, and impunity that have long operated to preclude sustainable economic and substantive political development in Mexico. Assuming a timely and meaningful implementation, the E-Mexico program could improve the efficiency and certainty of commercial and governmental dealings and bolster Mexico's diminished faith in free markets and liberal democratic values. The accomplishment of these advances could, moreover, confirm Mexico's commitment to confronting the technological challenges of the future and protect its place in an increasingly competitive global economy. This progression, viewed from a long-term perspective, would be optimal insofar as history teaches that the strongest democracies are not those accomplished by fiat, but, rather, those that represent organic out growths of development.

Mexico's failure to take advantage of the developmental opportunities made possible by the Internet, considered in light of the cyclical nature of history in Latin America and the immediacy of the economic crisis produced by the terrorist attacks of September 11, 2001, will likely facilitate either a perpetuation of the status quo associated with the country's currently incomplete economic, political, and legal transformation or, in the worst case scenario, a partial or full return to previously discredited policies and perspectives.

E-Readiness: Challenges in Southern African Development Community (SADC)

ICT is a key weapon in the war against world poverty. When used properly, it offers huge potential to empower people in developing countries to overcome development obstacles, to address the most important social problems they face and to strengthen communities, democratic institutions, a free press and local economies. Yet, the reality of the digital divide is that a gulf exists between the potential of ICT and the actual levels of ICT use in developing countries.

World leaders in government, business and civil society are considering how best to harness the power of information and communications technology (ICT) for development. Current thinking on the topic often frames the discussion in terms of "e-readiness", or how ready a country is to gain the benefits offered by ICT generally in terms of policy, infrastructure and ground-level initiatives.

Three key factors motivate developing country decision-makers to improve e-readiness and promote the adoption of ICT in their countries:

— ICT promises enormous benefits as part of the solution to economic and social problems by empowering people in developing countries to help themselves.

— Countries face the threat of being left further behind if they do not address the growing digital divides both between and within countries. It is increasingly clear that ICT alone is notenough to solve long-standing imbalances, and can exacerbate existing inequalities if not appliedwisely.

— International leaders, foreign donors and lending agencies are increasingly requiring recipients to integrate ICT into their development and aid programmes.

Often developing country governments tackle e-readiness by focusing on either the need to improve the e-commerce capacity of the business sector or the need to improve access to ICT in disadvantaged communities. However, economic and social goals are interdependent and the relationship between them is complex. For example, social goals must incorporate business growth and the use of ICT as part of a larger vision, towards broader benefits for people.

However it is measured or approached, the broad range of factors that influence e-readiness are interconnected and the relationship between policy, infrastructure and ground-level initiatives are inextricable. Education is an excellent example of an issue that affects all areas. Education is central to the development of e-ready human capital, which is in turn an integral part of the growth of the local business sector and the implementation of programmes at ground-level. It is also a critical factor at the macroeconomic level, for instance where it influences foreign direct investment (FDI) decisions in developing countries.

Many developing country leaders are convinced that ICT use can be an engine for growth and development that will help their nations, and they are ready to drive the necessary changes to make that happen. However, translating a grand vision into practical steps that fit their local context is not a simple matter. They need to have a realistic appreciation for what ICT can - and cannot - do for their countries, and they must lead effectively and bolster public confidence in the path they take.

An e-readiness process based on an objective assessment that leads to sound e-strategies can offer a path for converting good intentions into planned action that brings real changes to people's lives.

E-Readiness in SADC Countries

There is no uniform level of e-readiness or economic and

social development within the SADC. Each SADC member state, and the region as a whole, must take its own path towards e-readiness, and any attempts to impose a single model would prove ineffective. Laws need to be tailor-made to address the unique policy, infrastructure and ground-level realities reflected within each state and the broader regional goals.

While most developed countries are regularly assessed, many developing countries, including some SADC countries, have had minimal or no assessment. Only eight of the SADC member states have been assessed. Most of these assessments are limited in content as they have been conducted through a short summary questionnaire or are merely comprised of non-explanatory statistical data.

South Africa has had six assessments, while Mauritius, Mozambique, Tanzania, and Zimbabwe have each been assessed twice. Botswana, the Democratic Republic f Congo (DRC) and Namibia have had only one assessment each, while Angola, Lesotho, Malawi, the Seychelles, Swaziland and Zambia have yet to be assessed.

Policy environment

There seems to be unanimous understanding among SADC governments about the benefits that telecommunications deregulation and liberalization can bring to the ICT industry, and the need for policy and market reforms. ICT policy reform processes have begun in almost all SADC member countries, but have not yet reached the implementation stage in all. Policy reforms to end monopolies in telecommunications are advanced in

Botswana, Lesotho, Mauritius, South Africa and Zambia.

Although an independent national regulator for telecommunications is still needed in the Seychelles, the telecoms network is fully privatized. For example, the second national operator is 51% foreign owned and has recently been licensed to provide fixed and mobile services.

The finance and banking sectors in most SADC countries are underdeveloped. Botswana, Mauritius, the Seychelles and South Africa, however, have advanced financial sectors, though these are also biased towards urban areas. Civil strife in Angola and the DRC continues to inhibit development in policy, infrastructure and ground-level projects.

Infrastructure development

SADC countries have unequal levels of infrastructure development. Overall, the existing ICT infrastructure is more developed in urban areas. Some countries, such as the DRC, have outdated and costly telecommunications infrastructure inherited from colonial times.

Aggressive infrastructure development is unfolding in Mauritius while Lesotho remains largely dependent on South Africa for electricity supply and transportation infrastructure. Transport infrastructure (roads, railways, harbours) development is uneven and the majority of rural highways are unpaved in most of the region. Large parts of the Angolan railway network are unusable due to landmines.

Ground-level projects

There are a number of initiatives under way at the ground level throughout the SADC region. World Links is working to train teachers and students in the use of technology to improve teaching and learning in South Africa, Mozambique, Botswana and Zimbabwe, with expansion to Swaziland and Tanzania anticipated in 2002.

A number of ICT access projects are run throughout the region by external development agencies such as the United States Agency for International Development (USAID), the World Bank and the Canadian International Development Agency (CIDA), as well as the public sector, such as the Microsoft Digital Villages initiative.

Projects to establish telecentres and other ICT access points are in place in most SADC countries. These efforts complement the initiatives launched by entrepreneurs and other market actors, providing goods and services on a commercial basis to thousands of subscribers.

The Southern Africa Regional Telecommunications Restructuring (SARTR) Project to help member states draft ICT policy reforms is in progress and significant advances have been made in Mauritius, South Africa and Swaziland.

Regional initiatives

Although each country has a unique development path to follow, broader initiatives have also been initiated at the regional level within the SADC. Organizations leading regional efforts in the SADC include Africa Connection, the coalition of Ministers of Communications in Africa, various NGOs and international bodies such as USAID and the International Development Research Center (IDRC).

In particular, a number of regional policy-making efforts are being launched, are under way, and have been completed with the aim to create a harmonized and coordinated approach to ICT policy reform. However, there are low levels of implementation at the national level to put regional agreements into effect. Moreover, some efforts are duplicative.

Regional agreements should be coordinated to ensure they do not duplicate efforts, and they should be implemented at the national level, their effectiveness evaluated, and the best practice lessons recorded for application in other developing countries.

Examples include:

— The SADC Human Resources Sector developed the SADC Protocol on Education and Training, signed in 1997. It promotes curriculum development and training, and coordinates policies, strategies and programmes promoting science and technology.

— The Southern African Transport and Telecommunications Commission (SATCC) formulated the Model Regulatory Framework for Telecommunications in 1998. Of the 14 member states 11 have established and have operating policies and autonomous regulatory authorities. Human resource development in this new field of regulation is a priority for the Telecommunications Regulatory Authority of Southern Africa (TRASA). In the remaining countries, progress in the application of the frameworks is in an advanced stage.

— The Southern African Telecommunications Association (SATA) obtained agreement on the GSM standard for SADC countries . SATA handles issues such as: technical standards, tariffs, sub-regional information infrastructure (SRII), cross-border investment (satellite technology) and public/private partnerships.

— TRASA has developed the Model Telecommunications Bill as well as regional guidelines on interconnection,tariffs and the frequency band plan. TRASA has also produced draft guidelines on universal access and services, licensing policy and implementation strategy in the SADC.

— TRASA has commissioned a project with the SADC and the Development Bank of Southern Africa (DBSA) to establish a database within the region. Information and performance indicators collated on a national level will be fed through to the SADC level to promote informed decision-making.

— Twelve .SADC governments have signed the SADC Protocol on Transport, Communication and Meteorology, published in March 1998. It details the need for a regional telecommunications policy and provides guidelines on issues from universal service, to technical standardization.

— The SADC drafted and adopted the Lusaka 1999 Theme Document: The Challenges and Opportunities of IT for SADC in the New Millennium, at the biannual Ministers meeting.

— The Common Market for Eastern and Southern Africa (COMESA) has drafted a Model Telecommunications Bill.

— Eight of the twenty-one COMESA member states hold dual membership in COMESA and SADC.

— SADC member countries have adopted at presidential level the policy guidelines on Making ICT a priority in turning SADC into an Information-Based Economy produced by SATCC.

SADC countries have three powerful means of directly improving e-readiness and harnessing ICT for social and economic advancement within the SADC region:

(1) establishing the policy framework for action,

(2) building the necessary infrastructure, and

(3) undertaking ground-level projects. Beyond direct interventions itself, the government can also act indirectly by creating a favourable environment for the private sector and NGOs to engage.

SADC governments are urged to promote ICT through dialogue with all stakeholders, and by setting a leadership example through e-government initiatives.A sound ICT policy framework creates a reliable environment within which business and social programmes can thrive.Key issues include: trade agreements and tariff standardization, enterprise and entrepreneurship development, e-commerce promotion and telecommunication liberalization.

ICT infrastructure is the broad foundation upon which business and social programmes are built.It includes basic infrastructure like electricity and transportation, and technical infrastructure like network connections and hardware. Key issues include: physical access to ICT, standards setting and interoperability, and country code top-level domains.Ground level initiatives spread the benefits of technology throughout society and provide a critical connection between policy considerations and the grassroots community.Ground-level initiatives are often driven by national policies, such as in the fields of education, entrepreneurship and healthcare. Key issues include: public access to ICT in disadvantaged and/or rural communities, e-government services, and local economic and enterprise development.

Policy Framework

Actions to promote e-readiness are affected by nearly all aspects of policy extending beyond specific ICT policy considerations, and ranging from digital signatures to collective bargaining to general macroeconomic policies. The relevant fields of policy to be considered can be generally grouped as follows:

— *Macroeconomic policies:* Fiscal stability, international coordination, customs standardization, tariffs and trade barriers, foreign direct investment, etc.

— *General industrial policies*: competition policy, taxation, defragmentation and free market considerations, labour policies, professional/vocational training, economic empowerment, collective bargaining and brain drain counter-measures

— *Sector specific policies*: e-commerce legislation, banking and financial sector structures, standards setting, telecommunications liberalization.

Macroeconomic policy issue: Trade agreements and tariffs standardization

(a) *Widely agreed policy recommendation*: Views on free trade agreements and tariff standardization vary depending on the economic context within which standardization is considered. Most countries generally perceive that standardization strengthens cooperation and unity of member states in trade areas; promotes the flow of trade and investments; protects members against unfair deals and exploitation by non-members in trade; and prevents competition between member states to avoid weakening the development community.

(b) *Key proponents of this recommendation*: ICT business community, Global Business Dialogue on e-commerce (GBDe), Organisation for Economic Co-operation and Development (OECD), World Bank, Telecommunication Service Providers, General Agreement on Trade and Tariffs (GATT), WTO (World Trade Organization).

(c) *Issues affecting application in developing countries*: By definition, tariff standardization will enable greater cooperation between SADC states. However, differences in local economic development levels and individual trade arrangements do not create an environment conducive to tariff standardization. Standardizing existing tariff agreements between South Africa and the European Union to include non-signatories of the agreement may be economically detrimental to the non-beneficiaries or smaller SADC members. Tariff standardization in regions of unequal economic development tends to favour the economically stronger states without fostering domestic growth in the economically weaker states in the region.

(d) *Recommended way forward*: Applying standard tariffs between unequal players tends to exacerbate existing inequalities and is unlikely to produce equitable outcomes. Emphasis should be placed on establishing coordinated political and economic fundamentals before applying standardized tariffs ultimately resulting in longer-term regional integration (as in the EU harmonization process). The SADC is struggling to establish and enforce acceptable political and economic basics among its members (political and/or economic turmoil in Angola, the DRC and Zimbabwe are examples). Tariff standardization should only be applied when common minimum levels of development are reached (these criteria should be debated and agreed upon by SADC states).

General industrial policy issue: Enterprise/ entrepreneur-ship development

(a) *Widely agreed policy recommendation*: The general view is that governments should promote a free enterprise economy, liberalize markets and pass supporting legislation that encourages the development of small, medium and micro enterprises (SMMEs). This is because fostering entrepreneurial activity helps boost economic development and sustainable job creation, and empowers local communities. Supporting training and skills development is required to ensure the sustainability and success of the entrepreneurial projects.

(b) *Key proponents of this recommendation*: Regional bodies (e.g. the SADC), international forums (e.g. World Economic Forum), private sector (e.g. Accenture) and academia (e.g. London Business School and University of Cape Town's Graduate School of Business).

(c) *Issues affecting application in developing countries*: Entrepreneurial activities in developing countries are hampered by high levels of unemployment and illiteracy, and an overall lack of basic skills, accompanied by a shortage of entrepreneurship support and capital. There is international expertise to be shared, but there are few linkages with communities and efforts at ground level to disseminate information in developing countries.

(d) *Recommended way forward*: Enterprise and entrepreneurship development programmes should be implemented to help advance ICT, to make ICT access and services affordable, provide employment and reduce poverty. Projects should run in conjunction with skills development programmes and public-private partnerships. Linkages should be established between policy-making and people at the grassroots level. Governments should create a favourable environment for the private sector, for instance by establishing well-designed ICT training and other projects, and introducing open standards for interoperability. Youth entrepreneurship and economic empowerment projects should be priorities.

Sector specific policy issue: Telecommunications liberalization

(a) *Widely agreed policy recommendation*: Telecom liberalization is widely accepted as the best way to reduce ICT prices and drive the widespread use of ICT for society's general benefit. This focuses on privatizing state-owned telecom agencies and making the transition to pro-competitive regulation that encourages new entrants to offer both basic and value added telecom services.

(b) *Key proponents of this recommendation*: ICT business community, GBDe, OECD, World Bank, telecommunication service providers, consumers of telecommunication services.

(c) *Issues affecting application in developing countries*: Telecom workers in developing countries whose jobs are threatened fail to see the longer-term benefits, so they support the telecommunications labour unions that oppose the liberalization of the sector. Governments are faced with the conflicting objectives of satisfying taxpayer (predominantly business community) demands on the one hand, and the demands of the voting majority and trade unions concerned with job security on the other hand. It is important to be aware of the depth of this issue within the national psyche, as many people in developing countries genuinely feel that natural resources (including things like telecommunications infrastructure) belong to the nation.

(d) *Recommended way forward*: Focus should be placed on overall employment gains through deregulation (within telecom services and in the broader ICT and

Internet sectors), to allay union concerns of job security. Retraining programmes are critical to ensure that workers are re-skilled for employment elsewhere. Governments further need to build widespread support for liberalization through public awareness campaigns to impart the positive impact of technology on people's lives.

Sector specific policy issue: E-commerce promotion

(a) *Widely agreed policy recommendation*: There are differing approaches to e-commerce policy with no general consensus, including on issues related to privacy, data protection, authentication, intellectual property, copyright, computer crime and security. One view generally supports regulation and enforcement by government; another view generally holds that the industry should self-regulate. An amalgamated third view is the preference for co-regulation over the two extremes of industry self-regulations and government-imposed regulation.

(b) *Key proponents of this recommendation*: Generally the US view supports the regulation of e-commerce related matters on a sector-by-sector basis, with sector-specific legal protections adopted solely in response to demonstrated cases of market failure. The EU view generally supports strong horizontal rules to prevent abuses and create a predictable legal and regulatory environment for electronic transactions. The amalgamation of these two views shows the recent tendency for government and the private sector to work together to come up with legislation that is both business-friendly and protects consumers, and is increasingly supported by international business and political leaders.

(c) *Issues affecting application in developing countries*: There is a real and perceived lack of trust by local populations towards government due to previous abuses of power and corruption. Concerns exist about government ability to safeguard electronic transactions. The AIDS crisis, for example, heightens fears of data insecurity and risks to personal privacy where medical records might be stored or exchanged electronically.

(d) *Recommended way forward*: Public discourse and broad consultation is needed to build trust. At this stage however, the key point for SADC countries is less about the choice between self-regulation and strict government regulation, than it is about the need to simply have a policy that is clear and enforceable. The adoption of either approach will improve the development of e-commerce. The task for developing country governments is to create an effective policy environment and dispel the uncertainty and lack of trust that is the biggest impediment to e-commerce and citizen use of electronic transactions. In the longer-term, the potential benefits to be had in co-regulation should be revisited.

Sector specific policy issue:Banking and financial sector development

(a) *Widely agreed policy recommendation:* A trusted and stable banking sector is necessary for participation in the e-economy, capable of providing reliable, secure and widely accessible payment systems and lines of credit for entrepreneurial ventures, both in the developing and developed world.

(b) *Key proponents of this recommendation*: International bodies such as the United Nations Commission on International Trade Law (UNCITRAL), the Bank for International Settlements (BIS), the International Chamber of Commerce (ICC), the WTO, business forums, finance departments, banks, financial sector companies.

(c) *Issues affecting application in developing countries*: Electronic transactions have speeded up the process but have brought the added dimension of cybercrime to the table. Developing countries need to be aware of the risks and precautions that go hand in hand with the advantages. In general, there are inadequate payment methods in the region by world standards. And SADC countries have the additional disadvantage that they face a lack of trust in the commercial sector, due to a strong perception that unaccountability and corruption exists in the region at higher levels than in the developed world, when this is plainly not the case.

(d) *Recommended way forward*: It is paramount that developing countries develop trusted and stable banking and financial sectors in order to fully participate in the international economy. Guidance should be sought from the international banking sectors on how to establish stronger local banking sectors, and governments should promote stringent and transparent financial sector guidelines drawn from international best practice and adapted to local conditions. Governments should also promote banking and other innovative initiatives to introduce payment products and options.

Infrastructure

Efforts to build infrastructure in the developing world, both by governments and development agencies, have focused predominantly on providing computer hardware, satellite connections and fibre-optic cabling. While these programmes are necessary, they must be supported by enabling infrastructure, such as adequate banking and transport facilities to enable growth and a continued development of basic infrastructure.

Affordable access to basic technology that is appropriate to local conditions best suits the developing world. Many of these substantive infrastructure considerations are affected by government policy and are influenced by policy prescriptions. Beyond the basic provision of telecommunications infrastructure, there are a number of complementary businesses and processes that need to be in place to allow the ICT sector to grow and to impact the rest of the economy. Governments must recognize that they are dealing with a complex system, and that they have to work in a broad fashion to support all of the actors that are involved in developing, using and exploiting ICT.

The relevant fields of infrastructure to be considered can be generally grouped as follows:

— *Availability of basic infrastructure*:Issues include the distribution of infrastructure along the rural-urban divide (using gross domestic product and poverty levels as indicators), basic electrification, transportation (e.g. road, rail, post), telephony and teledensity levels, universal access projects to ensure basic community access, computer density and available bandwidth.

— *Availability of technical infrastructure*:Issues include physical access and connecting infrastructure (e.g. T-1 lines, broadband access, satellite), hardware (e.g. personal computers, servers, routers), software (e.g. operating systems, applications), other (e.g. radio, television, handheld devices).

— *Access to enabling infrastructure*:Issues include the quality and diversity of service, the number of telecommunication operators, Internet service providers and Internet exchange points. It is unrealistic to expect that development aid, philanthropy or government subsidies will be enough to sustain infrastructure development, whether it comes in the form of donated computers or projects expanding telecommunications networks. At best, these projects can build constituencies for pro-competitive, market-opening policies in key areas (telecom regulation, foreign direct investment, etc.) and build critical mass for demand to support sustainable investment in ICT infrastructure. The implementation work may be undertaken by the public or private sectors or through combined public-private partnerships.

Basic infrastructure issue:Access to ICT

(a) *Widely agreed policy recommendation*:Increased globalization and the international information economy require ready access to ICT and global networks for information transfer and trade. In the developing world, mobile communication devices are regarded as a significant means to extend the information community.

(b) *Key proponents of this recommendation*:International business community, computer hardware and software providers, development agencies.

(c) *Issues affecting application in developing countries*:Given the impact of poverty and infrastructure limitations in rural settings, high computer penetration levels are often not feasible. Further, the whole process of introducing new technology and its cost in the context of social, cultural and technical aspects needs to be taken into account. In this regard, the developing world has shown a great affinity to the uptake of mobile ICT devices.

(d) *Recommended way forward*:Within disadvantaged communities, community-based access to computer resources is more realistic than individual access. Community access points providing desktop computing need to be supported by appropriate training programmes and relevant materials. Greater emphasis should be placed on mobile ICT devices that are increasingly more advanced and ubiquitous in terms of bandwidth, reach and utility. Research should be conducted to look at the potential of mobile devices to leapfrog preceding technologies. Projects to develop and deliver content via wireless applications should run concurrently.

Technical infrastructure issue:Standards setting and interoperability

(a) *Widely agreed policy recommendation*:The adoption of open ICT-related standards, as opposed to set standards, helps ensure the ease of communications and business transactions between countries, without tying countries to a particular solution. The openness and pace of change within the ICT sector mitigates against the effectiveness of set standard.

(b) *Key proponents of this recommendation*:ICT business community, international bodies (e.g. International Telecommunications Union and World Bank), users forums (e.g. International Telecommunications Users Group - INTUG), business forums (e.g. the Alliance for Global Business -AGB), commercial software and hardware providers.

(c) *Issues affecting application in developing countries*:Some view the implementation of a set standard as potentially costly and tightly controlled by developed world countries. Further, internationally accepted standards may exclude the needs of developing countries, as does the current "shortage" of Internet addresses. Others support the view that the adoption of standards can build and increase a common market for a specific technology in a developing country, allowing local or foreign producers to achieve the benefits of network effects and economies of scale in manufacturing.

(d) *Recommended way forward*:Standards setting and interoperability allow for ease of communications and participation in the international e-economy. In practice, however, very few standards exist. Emphasis should be placed on ensuring that technology is interoperable and that the preferred standard is open at least to the extent that it allows different networks/devices/technologies to work with each other. Regarding the "shortage" of Internet addresses, it is recommended that the African Regional Networking Centre (AFRINIC) be supported as the Regional Internet Registry. The Internet Protocol version 6 (IPv6) developed by the International Engineering Task Force (IETF) should be promoted. The strongly focused education of people in standards setting organizations and informed lobbying will ensure that the most optimal standards are adopted. The training of government officials making representations in the ITU is further recommended.

Technical infrastructure issue:Country code top-level domains

(a) *Widely agreed policy recommendation*:The efficient management and functioning of country code top-level domains (ccTLDs) support the adoption of growth of the Internet, bringing economic and social benefits to the region.

(b) *Key proponents of this recommendation*:ICANN, Internet Assigned Numbers Authority (IANA), Internet Society (ISOC), top level domain (TLD) administrators.

(c) *Issues affecting application in developing countries*:A significant percentage of ccTLDs are dysfunctional or non-functioning within Africa, hampering the growth of the Internet. The lack of sufficient data capturing techniques results in incorrect or missing service and information details in the IANA database. Developing countries also have to contend with the lack of an accepted standard for the appointment of TLD managers, and the degree of involvement of government agencies. Even in areas where the Internet is well established, the process of formalizing policy with regard to ccTLD administrations is not transparent or is incomplete.

(d) *Recommended way forward*: Research is required in the areas of ccTLD management. Developing countries must have ownership and manage their own domain names. There is potential for extending the lessons learned in the successful Kenyan ccTLD administration process to other developing countries. The DOT Force project has a focus point of assigning resources to people. It fosters people's participation in fora such as the Internet Corporation for Assigned Names and Numbers (ICANN). This project should be promoted, encouraged and expanded in the SADC region.

Ground-level Initiatives

While a supportive policy environment is essential, and infrastructure provides the necessary foundation for a country's use of technology, ICT must be applied on the ground for the country to realize its benefits in addressing traditional development concerns. Citizens must understand the value of ICT for their lives and be intrinsically aware of the potential for ICT to improve their lives. They must be involved in policy-making and development processes if their support for government reforms that may seem controversial is to be ensured. This will ensure the wide-scale economic and social advancement of the country. The approaches taken to improving e-readiness through ground-level initiatives are about as varied as the perspectives on the problem itself. A wide range of ground-level projects - both current and planned - aim at applying technology to the specific needs of people, from the provision of infrastructure to improving healthcare. The following broad categories represent the kinds of on-the-ground initiatives that should be considered:

— E-government initiatives

— Physical access providers

— Training programmes and e-awareness campaigns

— School computer learning programmes

— Distance education

— ICT support of basic education

— Locally relevant content generation

— Healthcare, particularly telemedicine and HIV/AIDs information dissemination

— Agriculture and sustainable development

Ground-level issue:Public access to ICT in disadvantaged and rural areas

(a) *Widely agreed action*:Experience in this field has shown the increasing necessity of having such access mechanisms made available to underserved communities, and that these services be financially sustainable.

(b) *Key proponents of this recommendation*:International organizations (e.g. ITU, UNESCO, World Bank), international donor organizations (e.g. IDRC), governments and private enterprises.

(c) *Issues affecting application in developing countries*:The sharp uptake of cellular telephone services in

Southern Africa is evidence of a strong desire for developing world societies to participate in the communication revolution. Further, cultures in rural settings are not adapted to the use of explicit, codified information. Programmes and pricing have to be adapted to reflect the usage and content realities of developing countries.

(d) *Recommended way forward*:Emphasis should be placed on sustainable development that will improve the communities ability to afford the services and ensure the viability of the initiative once the donor funding cycle ends. Interest in the services has already been seen. The provision of useful content in these centres will also ensure the higher prioritization of spending on communication services. This coupled with income generating information will help break the lack of sustainability cycle.

Ground-level issue: E-government services

(a) *Widely agreed action*:Best practice has shown that a citizen centric online government presence improves government efficiency and accountability to the population it serves.

(b) *Key proponents of this recommendation*:International organizations (e.g. UNCTAD) and civil society initiatives (e.g. Institute for Democracy in South Africa) support the introduction of government e-initiatives. Governments themselves are increasingly seeing e-government as a means to reach outlying communities.

(c) *Issues affecting application in developing countries*:A lack of existing infrastructure and levels of government corruption do not foster a general will towards e-initiatives. There is insufficient interaction between many of the smaller successful initiatives that take place at the subnational (municipal, state, region) level.

(d) *Recommended way forward*:E-government initiatives should be undertaken in conjunction with general government reforms and accountability initiatives in Southern Africa. Furthermore, e-government stands to make a greater impact in the developing world due to outlying and rural communities that will be reached. National policies should foster and integrate domestic initiatives, and provide them with standardized software only for those functions that are not already being successfully provided locally. Exchange of best practices and lessons learned should be promoted locally, regionally and internationally.

Ground-level issue: Local economic and enterprise development

(a) *Widely agreed action*:Private enterprise plays an important role in developing ICT capabilities and enabling economic and social growth. Access to finance and credit is fundamental for the creation of new enterprise, and the survival as well as growth of the existing ones. A fair and appropriate commercial law and property rights system encourages a trading environment and local wealth-creation. Other important enabling conditions are fair tax regimes, access to ICT products/services, and access to local, regional and global markets.

(b) *Key proponents of this recommendation*:International bodies (e.g. UNCITRAL, BIS, WTO), business forums (e.g. ICC), private sector (e.g. Accenture), finance departments, banks, financial sector companies.

(c) *Issues affecting application in developing countries*:A general view against this argument would come from the proponents of social welfare ideology who believe that service and access provision is a state responsibility.

(d) *Recommended way forward*:E-readiness development initiatives should be accompanied by entrepreneurship development, enterprise development policies and empowerment projects if they are to be sustainable. While it is widely agreed that service and access provision cannot in the long run be a state responsibility, renouncing all state stewardship of the process is equally untenable. Seed efforts (through measures such as fiscal incentives, terms of concessions in privatizations, etc.) have proven to be key components.

Delivering e-Readiness

Having outlined the specific recommendations without outlining a process for implementation would result in another e-readiness report, with concrete suggestions, that failed to effect changes in the lives of the people it sets out to help. This section outlines the practical "how to" process to be followed to implement actions based on locally specific e-readiness strategies. Most countries within the SADC have started along this path, while some still require an initial internal assessment and e-strategy development.

The process of moving from e-readiness to e-strategies to e-actions is harder and subtler than the highly publicized first (and often only) step of making the assessments. For most countries this process is well under way, including the World Economic Forum's broad-based international consultation that provides a forum for the exchange of expertise between and among members of the international community and the developing world.

First step: Do some homework (clarify goals, conduct an appropriate assessment)

Determining which e-readiness assessment tool is appropriate depends on the country's goals for ICT integration, so it is critical that the process begins with a clear understanding of where the country wants to go. There is no objective measure for e-readiness, and all assessment tools have an underlying standard of e-readiness that will necessarily shape the results. Comparisons between countries with analogous political, social and economic landscapes can provide useful benchmarks and clues for how to set appropriate goals. Plans that set unrealistic goals, or make unrealistic comparisons, are doomed to failure from the outset.

Second step:Draft a strategy

The action plan must outline concrete steps toward ICT integration goals, including specific policy measures, business initiatives and development programmes that are to be undertaken. It must consider who can implement them and how to engage the appropriate participants. It should also set a time frame for implementation, and determine the oversight and evaluation processes. It must include specific actions to address the needs and views of the relevant constituencies in a balanced way, such as consumer rights, business and labour. Critical success factors need to be clearly outlined, as well as checkpoints for measuring advances and making further informed decisions.

Third step:Implement your strategy with concrete actions

The implementation process is by far the most difficult step, and is also where the most help is needed, both in establishing the process and creating awareness. Yet there are relatively few resources offering advice and expertise to assist governments. While there is no universal method for achieving e-readiness, a few general principles and best practices are emerging that can help countries focus their efforts and effectively harness ICT in the long term.

Practices for achieving e-readiness

1 *Catalyse action throughout society.* Governments should realize that they do not have to carry the burden alone. Government has the unique ability to lead the way while facilitating others to expand the scope of activity and become involved in the process. Stakeholders in the private sector, academia, community organizations and in local government should be encouraged to get involved in the process

and start their own initiatives within the context of the national e-strategy, drawing on their own expertise and perspectives. Critical bottlenecks can be identified allowing for concerted and urgent action to remove them. If government, business and societal leaders champion the cause, their support can be cascaded down through the various levels beneath them. But to achieve this, these same individuals must fully understand the benefits and opportunities that ICT can offer.

2. *Seek public support for the e-readiness plan by helping citizens understand the potential benefits of ICT for their daily lives,and by involving the private sector.* Ground-level pilot projects can be used to explore the options for improving e-readiness, while demonstrating the value of ICT to citizens, winning public buy-in and gaining the participation of all stakeholders. It is important to establish relationships between the various groups that will foster technology use, facilitate productive local use of technology to generate demand for content and services developed and delivered through technology, and demonstrate this demand to the public and private sectors to cultivate a self-sustaining economic environment. Only with broad consultation can all levels of society benefit from the introduction of ICT. This will also ensure that the private sector is involved in addressing the digital opportunities presented, and involvement at the grassroots level will ensure public support for government policies.

3. *Establish links between on-the-ground efforts and policy-making processes.* Both ground-level initiatives and policy reform are necessary, and information flow

between them will make both approaches more effective. Many ground-level programmes are limited by the lack of a supportive legal and policy framework. Most policy-making processes related to ICT issues would benefit from a clearer understanding of how policy affects the technology end user at ground level. Unfortunately, there are few models that effectively bring the two together. Government, business, society and technology users must understand and acknowledge each other's position and responsibilities.

4. *Establish and continue a feedback process throughout implementation.* There must be an independent review of the process, and a continued dialogue between the various stakeholders to make sure their needs are being taken into account. Clear critical success factors and checkpoints identified in the e-strategy to measure advances will provide these feedback mechanisms.

5. *Coordinate and avoid duplication of efforts.* Efforts to improve e-readiness and narrow the divide must be coordinated nationally and internationally. It is difficult to estimate the number of governments, businesses and non-governmental organizations (NGOs) that are involved in these initiatives. The majority are involved unilaterally, and as a result there is duplication of effort and scarce resources are wasted. It is important to assess the picture as a whole and identify actions that will have a catalytic effect and greater spin-offs. Consider how elements interact with each other and focus on the initiatives with the greatest impact on transformation. For example, within Southern Africa, the great uptake of

mobile communications means that mobile initiatives will have a larger impact.

6. *Establish national vision and leadership at the highest levels of government.* This requires identification, through consultation between the government, industry, civil societies, communities and other stakeholders, of local and national priority areas of development, followed by a programme of action and clear plans on implementation (and delivery timetables), as well as evaluation and enforcement mechanisms.

7. *Identify levels of priority for urgent and longer-term actions.* On the basis of unequal resources and levels of development in each member state, it would be unrealistic if not imprudent for all countries to aim for a quantitatively uniform set of goals in a uniform space of time. Country-specific short-term, medium-term and long-term achievable goals should be identified. Programmes of action with enforcements and the regular evaluation of progress should be drawn up and carried out. Countries should adhere to the plan of action unless it needs improvement or revision.

8. *Strengthen institutional capacity.* This refers to state, business and private institutions. A stable political environment and the rule of law are the building blocks upon which institutional capacity can be built. Enabling commercial laws and economic policies (including tax, tariffs, import and export laws) are crucial for the success of business institutions. When e-assessments are conducted in the SADC, countries have rated low on human capital, which is significant for institutional capacity. Policy on and a culture of

regular training for employees and ICT professionals in institutions is needed. Regular research programmes on updating institutional capacity to modern innovations should become the norm.

9. *Collaborate regionally and harmonize regional policies especially in telecommunications infrastructure.* Without implying the application of model laws, member states should harmonize economic and trading policies, as well as minimum ICT development levels if they are to develop as a regional force. Bilateral agreements between countries can supplement SADC guidelines towards this end. Member states should also participate in efforts to share information, for example by participating in the TRASA project to develop a data bank for the SADC to support informed decision-making. If all states contributed regularly, the levels of policy implementation could be recorded and tracked in a dynamic manner that enhanced further regional cooperation. The SADC has the opportunity to draw upon lessons and expertise garnered in the developed countries. But it is paramount that these international developments are tailored to apply to domestic circumstances.

10. *Simultaneously address traditional development and e-readiness issues.* Traditional development initiatives and e-readiness can no longer be separated as an either-or situation. Both are required to ensure equitable and sustainable development in Southern Africa. Further, if harnessed effectively, ICT can bridge pre-existing divides along cultural, racial, gender and socio-economic lines. Emphasis on traditional development concerns of rural electrification, basic education, primary healthcare, access to transport routes and basic telephony will

ensure that governments do not attempt to create an e-ready society in a vacuum. It will help ensure that the developments are taken side by side. Attempts to create an e-ready society will be fruitless and ineffective otherwise.

11. *Form partnerships*. Broad consultation and cooperation between the public and private sectors and the formation of Public-Private Partnerships (PPPs) allows governments to take advantage of private sector skills and know-how, improve the efficiency of service delivery and gain access to finance for new investments. If well designed, PPPs can bring improvements in the quality, availability and cost effectiveness of services. Various successful public-private partnerships have already been instituted within the SADC to address substantive concerns within policy, infrastructure and ground-level initiatives, including:
    — SADC plans for regional economic development and integration stress strategies such as export-oriented industrialization and Spatial Development Initiatives (SDI). The SDI is a programme initiated in 1995 by the South African Department of Transport and Trade and Industry
    — A key to the implementation of SDIs is the formation of PPPs in order to finance infrastructure development. A most prominent example of such a PPP in the region took place in the Maputo Development Corridor (MDC). The MDC, with the MOZAL Project, a Mozambican PPP initiative to stimulate local economic development, is the most advanced SDI in Southern Africa. Lessons learned from this SDI are expected to lead the way and set

the tone for socio-economic development in Southern Africa and the African continent.

- A number of SADC states have started initiatives towards PPPs. This has been set against a backdrop of past policies that severely restricted the use of private sector resources, and many prejudices and misconceptions remain.
- In January 2001, the South African Department of Finance produced a Strategic Framework for Delivering Public Services through Public-Private Partnerships , set up a PPP Unit in the National Treasury and spearheaded a number of projects. On a national level, partnerships have included the Dolphin coast water concession and the building of national toll routes.
- The World Bank has published "Toolkits" intended to assist a state with preparation for PPPs.

12. *E-readiness is about more than adopting model laws.* Model laws are not enough - there is a need for local solutions, that a country will buy into and that meet local needs. Model laws are often instituted with the good intention of addressing a common problem faced by both the developed and developing world, or a problem specific to the developing world context. However, these are often inadequate because they simply are not aware of the existing laws, political tensions and economic environment of the country. Instead of model laws, guiding criteria for drafting tailor-made policies, including international best practices, and a clear path for implementing these policies will help meet the goals of delivering economic and social advancement.

Vision to Implementation

On Tuesday, June 18, 2002, the World Bank hosted a workshop on E-Government, focusing on implementation challenges. Several officials responsible for Canada's - well-known Government On-Line (GOL) initiative shared their practical experiences and insights, along with Bank staff and select representatives from IT companies working on e-government projects in developing countries. The workshop examined the characteristics of successful e-government applications (and identified potential pitfalls) for improving governance, service delivery, and economic competitiveness. The workshop was organized in partnership with The Knowledge Centre, E-Government Services Sector of Public Works and Government Services Canada. Synthesizes the lessons learned from the Canadian government experience and how these lessons relate to and differ from the experiences of developing countries.

Strategy for Online Government

The Canadian government embarked on e-government with an aim to improve public service for Canadian citizens. The Canadian government sought to enhance public services so that they could offer similar types of quality and efficiency that the private sector in Canada provide to Canadian citizens. The aim was to provide Canadian citizens with an additional avenue by which to interact with government at the time and place of their choosing and in the language of their choice - French or English. There are two targets are identified.

— The government seeks to put the most frequently used services online by 2005.

— The government aims to achieve a tén percent increase in service improvement and customer satisfaction by 2005.

While embarking on this action plan, the Canadian government assessed whether the government and the country was ready for such ambitious targets. The Canadian Government found that there a number of activities and policy frameworks that need to be in place to enable e-government. At a minimum, government should consider the following:

> Setting the course and establishing objectives: In the case of Canada, the objective was to improve citizen service and provide citizens with another channel in which to interact with the government. This differs substantially from other e-government goals, that primarily focus on cost savings.

Determining the state of readiness: The government found that while it needed to invest significantly in the government's ability to provide services online in terms of infrastructure, legal framework, and process re-engineering, the country was ready in terms of the network infrastructure to access services online. Canada is a highly networked country. Low cost telecommunications services has enabled the population to access Internet at an inexpensive cost relative to other countries, where costs have hindered the growth of ICT.

To be able to roll out e-government services, the Canadian prioritized its IT strategy to work on the following areas:

1. Common Secure infrastructure

2. PKI, privacy, and legal framework
3. Information policy that allows accessibility
4. Accountability mechanisms
5. Pathfinder Projects

Up front investment

The government has already invested about $ 280 million (Canadian Dollars) into government online projects with an additional $600 million planned expenditures by 2005 in creating a common infrastructure. The Canadian government spent $65 million on PKI infrastructure and creating a certification authority.

The Government of Canada was able to obtain political buy-in at the highest level. With the Prime Minister's support, the government was able to mobilize political leadership within the government, bring internal stakeholders together and select champions within the government that would raise awareness, sustain commitment, and help government accomplish its target.

Establishing the boundaries

The government delineated its target environment and decided to roll out e-government services at the national level with a national geographic reach. E-Government would not supplement existing capabilities, rather, it would complement them. The government also decided to structure is services around the services for Canadians, Canadian businesses and for non-Canadians needs. Organizing services through the lens of business and citizen needs would force agencies coordinate to provide services together. It would also require the government to think about how to join-up government from different jurisdictions and levels of government. Often, different services are provided by the national, provincial or local government, and it is up to the citizen to research which departments to contact.

The government proposed a government-wide business and technical architecture. They urged agencies to migrate to a common e-government infrastructure where possible. Agencies were encouraged to share networks and host common applications and incentives such as funding, were provided for joint application development and pilot projects. Shared management of the e-service was also encouraged. The government encouraged horizontal collaboration among stakeholders. Each agency was encouraged to build and govern web content using common look and feel standards. Each web area was assigned a champion. To sustain the culture of change, initiatives were rewarded and those affected by the change were protected. To receive feedback and review, stakeholders were consistently engaged in the process. Citizens were surveyed through focus groups to improve or change the service.

The government set up a new management framework to ensure that these processes were followed. Management working groups were set up according to the following hierarchical structures:

Policy Frameworks and Tools

The Canadian Government came up with the policy frameworks in various areas, including: Privacy, security, information management, service quality, and procurement. Tool kits for government agencies were also developed to provide guidance on common look and feel standards, business transformation, human resources, privacy impact assessment, GOL supply arrangement, and common measurement tool. A frequently used tool kit that has to be followed by all agencies is the Privacy Impact Assessment Policy (PIA): The PIA provides a consistent framework to identify and resolve privacy issues during design of redesign of programs and services. The PIAs are made publicly available. The government requires that an agency or department conduct a PIA in the following cases:

- Increased collection, use or disclosure of personal information
- Broadening of client populations
- Shift from direct to indirect collection of personal information
- New data matching or increased reuse or sharing of personal information

Public Private Partnerships

Government Telecommunications and Informatics Services (GTIS) Branch of Public Works and Government Services Canada (PWGSC), in collaboration with federal institutions have contracted with a large consortium primed by Bell Nexxia to complete the architecture, design and construction of the Government of Canada Secure Channel. Strategic direction and funding for the project is being provided by the CIO Branch of Treasury Board Secretariat (CIOB).

As delivery agent, PWGS is responsible for developing and implementing the Secure Channel. PWGSC will manage the contract with Team BCE, for the Secure Channel, and work cooperatively with them on its architecture development, design and implementation. Key early lessons learned to date for Secure Channel procurement between the public and private sector reflect many of the key successes and challenges in undertaking the management, communications, implementation and evaluation of this important initiative. Some of these lessons learned include the necessity for:

— strong leadership with a shared accountability framework for success of the initiative as a whole with a clear and consistent vision;

— an effective and multi-tiered governance framework, with understanding and trust between the parties, as an essential element during procurement which must be clearly set and planned so that the initiative is implemented efficiently and effectively;

— a business case and policy framework to guide strategic procurements and strategic initiatives

— designing and managing the procurement around clear and tangible outcomes and benefits to be achieved among government and industry;

— contracting at the tactical level which is both flexible and reflects tactical outcomes as success ultimately lies in satisfying tactical needs.

Key Lessons

The government found that clustering services to fit the needs of citizens and business was the appropriate starting point. This created a momentum and allowed for the creation of a culture of change. More importantly, the strategy faced process re-engineering issues head on and challenges dealing with providing integrated services were brought to the table. Many issues such as governance, partnerships, content management, service standards were addressed early on in the planning process. The government found that it is more important to spend time and money on developing back-end infrastructure before embarking on front-end services.

The Canadian government created a common measurement tool to evaluate service improvement. The Canadian government opted to employ public polling firms that would conduct surveys. The firms used a common baseline to measure public services by comparing them to services offered by banks or phone companies and the private sector in general. The government has not currently invested in finding out whether citizens have experienced any quantifiable time and money savings as a result of using government online services.

Cost savings

The Canadian government has not invested in e-government to reduce costs and spending on public services. However, they do envision that once services reach a critical mass, cost saving will be realized. The problem lies in reaching that critical mass. Although access is not a problem, Canadians have yet to embrace interacting with government online.

Usage

The Government of Canada's websites are being visited more regularly. For example, Neilsen Netratings in March 2002 has the Government of Canada and its' websites as one of the 10 most visited web properties in Canada - in the same space as well known sites such as Yahoo!, MSN and AOL. One example which illustrates the delivery of government services on-line is the Canadian Customs and Revenue Agency's (CCRA) NETFILE Project which provides Canadians with a convenient option for filing personal tax returns on-line. NETFILE often receives attention national and worldwide on its initial take-up rate.

Last year, for returns filed in 2001 for the 2000 taxation year, more than 1.4 million tax returns were received through the NETFILE service. This exceeded expectations of the initial take-up rate estimate of 1.2 million for the service. When the CCRA conducted an on-line survey, respondents indicated NETFILE was easy to use and said they would definitely recommend it to other Canadians. The service has proved to be very successful, and CCRA expects that, as electronic commerce grows in popularity, so will NETFILE, attracting more participants each year.

Obstacles

The Canadian government has found that the most difficult challenges are the following:

— Seizing transformation opportunities is difficult - it puts to the test partnerships and commitment to citizen-centered service; and

— That it must now move from information and services that are grouped together to those that fit together.

In summary, these are the critical elements to consider when strategizing e-government initiatives:

— Establishing E-Government national objective

— Building internal commitment and ownership

— Involving constituents and meeting their expectations

— Effecting change in the public sector environment

— Obtaining adequate funding

— Managing complexity, risk and costs

— Establishing an appropriate governance structure

Lessons From Developing Countries

The Canadian model sparked much debate about the experience and goals of Canada and how they relate to the needs and interests of the developing world. Unlike Canada, developing countries have different e-government objectives that are tied to economic development. India for example seeks to increase foreign direct investment, Yemen hopes to help the private sector develop and reduce the burdens placed on the private sector by the government, and other developing countries hope to increase government revenue through e-government.

Self service seems to be an important objective for Canada, while in the developing world, e-government has emerged an assisted model, where intermediaries help citizens interact with government online in public places rather than interacting online from home. In many developing countries, where there are limited channels available to interact with the government, sometimes e-government applications provide the only channel available to a citizen. While the Canadians invested first in reforming the back end processes, many developing countries start with the front-end first.

Since most back-end processes are manual and are difficult to change, the front is developed first to have quick impact and buy-in from officials to reform the back end process at a later stage. Transparency is often an important goal for developing countries, where corruption and lack of knowledge about the way government works has resulted in a poor image of the public sector. While it is not an explicitly stated goal, many e-government initiatives improve government transparency to citizens and enhance internal transparency. In some cases, corruption is reduced as well. E-government in the developing world, provides significant value added, even when only part of the process is automated. For example, publishing of information, such as a tender notice, creates transparency and build public confidence in the procurement process, which is often marred by secrecy and corruption in the developing world. The collaborative strategy, which has produced results for Canada, is comprised of 3 key areas: service improvement to citizens; modernization of the federal Public Service; and integrated service delivery across department and other levels of government. This required a governance model involving technology, service delivery and policy working committees to address cross-jurisdictional issues and identify workable solutions to ensure efficient and effective implementation of Canadian Government On-Line.

This implementation model may represent challenges for developing countries where due to political and infrastructure considerations, much of the initiative and interest for implementing e-government initiatives tends to reside at other levels of government, particularly at the state and municipal levels. While there is certainly a need for developing country governments to come up with a strategy at the central level, the strategy should encourage and not stifle innovation that comes from lower levels of government. In many cases, e-government processes are outsourced because governments do not have the human resource capacity and technical expertise to do everything in-house.

Many governments have outsourced training, data entry to change from manual to electronic processes, network design and maintenance. To ensure sustainability and internal buy-in, the change management and business process re-engineering are not outsourced.

The challenges that remain for the developing world are:

— *Comprehensive electronic reform:* do the developing world governments have the human and technical resources to re-engineer their process?

— *Raising awareness:* citizens need to be made aware and educated on how to interact with government through ICT networks

— Can enough change be accomplished in reforming the culture of public servants which is often tied to rent seeking for political offices and services?

— Pilot projects have successfully showcased the benefits that e-government can offer, but where do countries go from there, and how do they achieve sustainability?

Centralizing IT departments sometimes creates obstacles in terms of equipment procurement and standardization. In many cases, central IT departments are unaware of the infrastructure challenges and diversity across the different levels of government. Most e-government projects have succeeded because of buy in from the government at the highest level and constant engagement of senior government officials in the different stages of development and implementation.

Bibliography

Asian Communication Handbook. 1998. Asian Mass Communication Research Information Centre, Singapore.

Bangemann Group, 1994. High Level Group on the Infor-mation Society, Europe and the Global Information Society, Recommendations to the European Council. Brussels, May.

Carty, W. 1997. *Challenges to Academic Networks in Latin America,* Infolac, Vol. 8, No. 2, pp. 39–42.

Cerf, V.; Kahn, R. 1974. *A Protocol for Packet Network Interconnection.* IEEE Transactions on Communications, May.

Freedom of Expression on the Internet. Human Rights Watch Special Report, December 1998.

ITU. 1998. Telecommunication Development Bureau. Internet Diffusion Trends. Geneva

Mason, A. 1997. Public Interest Objectives and the Law of Copyright. In: B. Sherman and J. Thomas (eds.), Defining the Public Domain, Special Issue of Journal of Law and Information Science.

Melody, W. H. 1996. "Toward a Framework for Designing Information Policies". *Telecommunications Policy*, Vol. 20, No. 4.

Munk Ris, A. 1997. The Information Welfare Society: An Assessment of Danish Government Initiatives Preparing for the Information Age. In: Brian Kahin and Ernest Wilson (eds.), *National Information Infrastructure Initiatives: Vision and Policy Design.* MIT Press, Cambridge, Mass.

OECD. 1997. Summary of the Telecommunications Act of 1996. Communications Outlook 1997. Vo l . 2 , Regulatory Annex.

Ondobo, C. 1998. AMIC Annual Conference: Information Technologies Must Complement Traditional Educational Methods. AMCB, Vol. 28, No. 3, May-June.

Proceedings, 1997. Third EU/EEC Information Society Forum. European Parliament, European Commission, Brussels.

Sharma, M. 1997. Communications Technologies in Open and Distance Learning in Asia: The Experience of the Asian Development Bank. Educational Technology 2000: Global vision for Open and Distance Learning, pp. 19–30. Conference papers, Singapore, 15–17 August 1988, Commonwealth of Learning, Vancouver, B.C.

Sixty-Fourth IFLA Council and General Conference, 1998. *Conference Proceedings,* 16–24 August, Amsterdam, Netherlands.

Squire S Anders and Dempsey, 1998. Study on Adapting the EU Telecommunications Regulatory Framework to the Developing Multimedia Environment. A Study for the European Commission. January.

The Digital Age. European Audiovisual Policy. 1998. Report from the High Level Group on Audiovisual Policy. European Commission, Brussels.

Ure J. (ed.). *Telecommunications in Asia: Policy, Planning and Development.* pp. 1 4 7 – 91. Hong Kong University Press, Hong Kong.

Von Euler, M.; Berg, D. 1998. *The Use of Electronic Media in Open and Distance Education.* UNESCO, Paris.

Index